Tourism, Tourists and Society

— also by Richard Sharpley —

TOURISM & LEISURE IN THE COUNTRYSIDE
SECOND EDITION

Material for a full year's course with nine stand-alone chapters on
countryside recreation, management, planning and the law.
Level Higher National and above.

Book, 336pp, 185450 245 X, £12.95
Tutor's Manual – with one year's teachng materials
185450 440 1, £59.00

Tourism, Tourists and Society

second edition

Richard Sharpley

This second edition of **Tourism, Tourists and Society** is published October 1999 by ELM Publications, Seaton House, Kings Ripton, Huntingdon, Cambridgeshire PE17 2NJ.

Tel: 01487-773254 or 01487-772238
Fax: 01487 773359
email elm@ndirect.co.uk

Printed by St Edmundsbury Press, Bury St Edmunds, Suffolk, England.

Bound by Woolnough Bookbinding, Express Works, Church Street, Irthlingborough, Northants, England.

ISBN 1 85450 280 8

British Library Cataloguing-in-Publication Data. A catalogue record for this publication is available from The British Library.

Contents

List of Figures

Introduction

It is impossible to ignore tourism. During the twentieth century it has grown into what is widely described as the world's largest industry and, for many destinations, it represents a vital source of income, foreign exchange and employment. More importantly, however, tourism is about people. The annual number of international arrivals has exceeded 600 million and an estimated six times that number participate in domestic tourism each year, figures which represent an enormous, yet temporary, migration of people both across international borders and within their own countries. Thus, tourism is above all a social phenomenon, and an understanding of the social processes involved is of fundamental importance to the study of tourism.

This book approaches tourism from a sociological perspective, considering both tourists themselves and the societies which generate, sustain and receive tourism. Easy to read and to understand, it introduces basic sociological theories and their relevance to tourism before examining the major themes and issues concerning the social nature of tourism. In particular, it explores the relationship between tourism and society from two perspectives: the influence of society on tourism, and the influence of tourism on society. In both cases, reference is made where relevant to sociological theory to explain the various processes and phenomena introduced.

This second, revised edition also includes two new chapters, addressing the consumption of tourism (Chapter 6) and the links between tourism and development (Chapter 8), reflecting more recent research into sociological aspects of tourism. Extensive and up-to-date references are used throughout, and each chapter develops arguments which are of relevance to the practical planning and management of tourism.

Whilst every effort has been made to seek permission, if any unknowing use has been made of copyright material, could the owners please contact the author via the publishers.

Richard Sharpley
3rd September, 1999

About the Author

Richard Sharpley is a senior lecturer in Travel and Tourism at the University of Northumbria at Newcastle. His main research interests include tourism and development issues, the sociology of tourism and tourism consumption, and rural tourism. He has written a number of other books and articles, including *Tourism and Leisure in the Countryside*, second edition.

One

Tourism: A Sociological Approach

Introduction

Tourism is all things to all people. To the holiday-maker, for example, tourism may be the chance to relax and unwind, a temporary period of escape from the responsibilities of work and from the stress of everyday life. Conversely, for any one of the hundreds of thousands of tourism businesses, from large, multi-national organisations to small, independent operators, tourism is, simply, work. At the same time, governments may promote or positively encourage the development of tourism, considering it to be an essential ingredient of broader social and economic development policies (see Jenkins 1991: 61). Yet, to the local residents in popular destinations, the annual influx of hordes of tourists may be seen more negatively as something to be suffered or endured.

Equally, the *study* of tourism may be approached from a variety of academic backgrounds or disciplines, each providing a valid basis for explanation and argument. For example, economists treat tourism as a discrete form of economic activity, relating the demand, motivation, growth, scale and form of tourism to economic factors; even the impacts of tourism, or externalities, may be explained or justified in economic terms (Gray 1982). More generally, whilst much of the early research and academic study of tourism originated as a branch of geography, a multi-disciplinary approach has been increasingly adopted since the 1970s. There now exists a broad range of tourism literature based on academic specialisms, such as anthropology (Nash 1981; Graburn 1983; Smith 1989), psychology (Iso-Ahola 1982; Ross 1994), law (Grant and Mason 1998), political science (Richter 1983; Matthews and Richter 1991), history, (Towner 1996), cultural studies (Chambers 1997), marketing (Gold and Ward 1994; Witt and Mouthino 1989) and, of course, geography (Shaw and Williams 1994). At the same time, much

1

of the literature focuses upon particular types of tourism itself, such as heritage tourism (Boniface and Fowler 1993; (Herbert 1995), rural tourism (Sharpley 1996; Page and Getz 1997) and special interest tourism (Getz 1991), or on geographical or political classifications such as, for example, the UK (Yale 1992), Europe (Davidson 1998; Pompl and Lavery 1993), city tourism (Grabler *et al* 1997) or developing countries (Harrison 1992).

Despite this enormous variety of perspectives or academic approaches to tourism, there is one particular feature of tourism that cannot, or should not, be ignored. Unquestionably tourism is, or soon will be, one of the largest economic sectors in the world. Indeed, tourism is frequently described as the world's largest industry, though it is widely debated whether or not the myriad of businesses and organisations involved in tourism should be collectively described as a single, identifiable industry. For example, it has been suggested that *referring to tourism as an industry may be a major contributor to the misunderstanding, resistance and even hostility that often plague proponents of travel and tourism as worthy economic forces in a modern economy* (Davidson 1994: 20; see also Gilbert 1990).

There can be no doubting the scale and value of tourism. In 1997, international tourist arrivals totalled 613 million, whilst worldwide foreign exchange receipts from tourism reached US$444 billion (WTO 1998b). If the value of domestic tourism in all countries and the earnings of tourism related businesses, such as transport operators, are added to this then, globally, tourism is worth an estimated US$3.4 trillion. Moreover, no other economic sector can match the growth rate of international tourism. Between 1980 to 1990, international arrivals and receipts achieved annual growth rates of 4.2 and 9.3 per cent respectively and it is predicted that similar rates of growth will continue to be achieved into the twenty-first century. Thus, by 2020, it has been forecast that international tourist arrivals will have reached a staggering 1.6 billion, generating receipts of well over US$2 trillion (WTO 1998a: 3).

Most importantly, the sheer scale of tourism should not draw attention away from the simple fact that tourism is about *people*. It is about millions of individuals who comprise local, regional and national societies, travelling domestically or crossing international borders and experiencing and impacting upon different societies. It is about people who are influenced and motivated by the norms and changes in their own society, who carry with them perceptions, expectations and standards based on their own personal experience and background. Above all, tourism is about people, tourists, interacting with other places and other peoples, undergoing experiences that may influence their own or the host community's attitudes, expectations, opinions and, ultimately, lifestyles.

In short, then, the very basis of tourism is people and society. Thus, the study of tourism in general cannot, or should not, be divorced from an examination in particular of what may be termed the 'sociology of tourism'. A fundamental problem, however, is the extent to which tourism, as an essentially social but nevertheless diverse activity, lends itself to sociological study. Specifically, the question to be asked is, 'Is it possible to develop a sociological theory of tourism, or is it only possible to apply sociological theory to different aspects of tourism'? Moreover, other academic disciplines, such as psychology and anthropology, have equal claim as a basis for research into social aspects of tourism; one of the first major texts concerned with the tourist/host relationship and social impacts of tourism is sub-titled *The Anthropology of Tourism* (Smith 1977 and 1989) whilst, more recently, both disciplines have provided the foundation for a number of books (for example, Abram *et al* 1997).

The purpose of this introductory chapter is to define the context for a sociological approach to the study of tourism. The first step is to examine what is meant by a sociological approach or, more precisely, the meaning, purpose and extent of sociology as an academic activity. This may then be related to, and used as a basis for the consideration of, the human and social aspects of tourism throughout the rest of this book.

What is sociology?

It is probably true to assert that, although most people have some notion of what sociology is about, relatively few are able to define the term accurately. Unlike many other academic disciplines, such as history, geography and chemistry, both the scope and the purpose of sociology are either vague or, in the extreme, incomprehensible to the lay person (Browne 1992: 1). As a result, sociology is often regarded with uninterest or, at worst, with distrust by those who have little knowledge or understanding of the subject. Indeed, as Bilton *et al* (1987:1) point out, sociologists themselves may often feel tempted to say that they are historians or economists rather than sociologists in order to avoid the difficulty of having to explain what they really do!

This difficulty in defining sociology arises, in part, from the nature of the subject itself. For example, one explanation or description of sociology might be 'the study of the structure of human society and behaviour'. Although essentially accurate, this is somewhat simplistic. That is, sociology is certainly concerned with specific aspects of society, such as the family, class and gender divisions, work, religion or deviance (behaviour which does not conform to what is considered to be 'normal', crime being the most obvious example). Indeed, many introductory sociology texts are structured according to these social institutions (for example, see Browne 1992; Abercrombie *et al* 1988). This is, however, only half of the story. Of equal, if not greater, importance is the approach or perspective which determines how these particular aspects of society and the behaviour of individuals within society are studied. Sociology is, in effect, a *way* of looking at society. As Browne (1992: 2) suggests, *sociologists use a sociological imagination... they study the familiar routines of daily life... in unfamiliar ways*.

In other words, the basis of sociology is society. Society is made up of individuals who, with the exception of those who make a conscious decision to avoid contact with other people, perform or participate in a huge variety of actions every day. The great majority of these actions are socially acceptable (that is 'normal' behaviour); they are also, however, socially determined. That is, an individual's behaviour is generally constrained, or determined, by their society's rules, rules which may be set down by custom, by religion, or by laws. As a result, all the individual actions within a given society tend to occur in a co-ordinated fashion so that social life remains reasonably ordered and predictable. For example, in many Western societies it is considered 'normal' for a young person to take a year off in between school and university to go travelling whereas an individual who does so in, say, his or her forties, might be considered unusual, eccentric or even, perhaps, irresponsible (see Chapter Four for a discussion of the concept of independent travel).

The important point, therefore, is that sociology is concerned not only with the structure of society and the behaviour of its members but also with the rules, or wider social forces, that determine social structure and patterns of behaviour. It is this latter characteristic that differentiates sociology from other disciplines, such as anthropology, and that causes most confusion amongst non-sociologists.

Whereas many people attempt to explain or describe different forms of human behaviour as natural, instinctive or just plain common sense, all of which place the emphasis firmly on the ability of the individual to make his or her own decisions, sociology rejects notions of individuality and places human behaviour within the wider context of social forces which are beyond the control of the individual. Also, socially normal or acceptable behaviour is relative to different societies and reflects a society's rules or constraints that must be learned by the individual. Thus, *one person's 'common sense' is somebody else's nonsense* (Bilton *et al* 1987: 6). For example, in Western societies it is generally accepted as common sense or normal that it should be men, rather than women, who undertake heavy labouring work; in India, it is more often that such work is done by women, a role determined by the social forces of religion, male dominance and the caste system.

The basic tenet of sociology, then, is that human society and behaviour is structured, moulded and constrained by wider social forces and influences, and it is this approach that underlies sociological research and analysis. Yet, although sociologists share this common approach, there is a variety of theories about what society actually is, how it may be explained and, hence, how it determines individual behaviour. The following section briefly traces the development of sociology as an academic discipline and the evolution of the different theories of sociology (see Swingewood 1991 for the history of sociological thought). The relevance of these theories to the study of tourism is then discussed.

The development of sociology

Modern sociology, as a distinct discipline, has its roots in Europe in the mid-nineteenth century. The 'father' of sociology is generally held to be the Frenchman Auguste Comte (1798-1857). Not only did he coin the term 'sociology' but also he was the first to adopt a rigorous, scientific approach to the study and explanation of society. Prior to this time, many people had concerned themselves with the development and structure of society; early Greek philosophers, such as Plato and Aristotle, had developed theories about the nature of society, but even by the mid-eighteenth century the work of social theorists, such as Jean-Jacques Rousseau (1712-1778), was largely based on a philosophical, rather than a formal, scientific, approach to the study of society. As Bilton *et al* (1987: 2) point out, *philosophers and thinkers frequently constructed grand models and schemes about humans and their societies without looking at how societies actually worked.*

One exception was Robert Owen. Born in Newtown, Wales, in 1771, by the age of 28 he was a successful businessman and co-owner of a cotton mill at New Lanark in Scotland. As a social reformer, his business success allowed him to test his theory that individuals are formed by their environment and that the basis of a happy, harmonious society is education. In other words, Owen believed that people are not born with inherently good or bad traits but that they acquire them from their environment. Thus people, particularly children, can be taught *any language, sentiments, belief, or any bodily habits and manners, not contrary to human nature* (Owen 1991: 12). He therefore developed a model village around the cotton mill at New Lanark, the purpose of which was to provide a stable, healthy and happy environment for his employees and their families. He provided medical care funded by what was, in effect, an early and local form of National Insurance and the village shop was run as a co-operative. Moreover, various forms of unacceptable behaviour, such as excessive drinking, were discouraged, and all the children in the village received schooling at his 'Institute for the Formation of Character'. In short, Owen adopted and put into practice a sociological approach to providing for his workforce. His motives were treated with suspicion in many circles yet he made what was, arguably, the first practical attempt to test a sociological theory. Interestingly, New Lanark is, today, a major tourist destination in the Clyde Valley near Glasgow.

In contrast to Owen's practical work, Comte was the first academic to develop a sociological theory, or a basis for the study and explanation of society. His work evolved against a background of profound change in Europe; the Industrial Revolution and rapid scientific and technological developments were transforming traditional rural society whilst dramatic advances were being made in the scientific understanding of the world. As a result, Comte attempted to apply scientific method to the study of society, believing it to be the path to a full understanding of society and, thereby, the means for improving it. In other words, Comte asserted that true knowledge is scientific knowledge and, therefore, that social phenomena could be explained, understood and controlled scientifically in much the same way as natural phenomena. He called this a *positive* approach and, thus, he established Positivism as a distinct school of sociological thought.

Positivism falls under the broader heading of Structuralism, a wider sociological perspective that not only dominated much sociological research and thought up to the late 1950s, but which also is one of the two major competing theories about the way in which society is structured and develops. Structuralism refers to any form of sociological analysis that is concerned with society as a whole and how it is structured. Stucturalists adopt a macro-sociological approach, taking as their starting point the assumption that there exists a *central value system which, either by constraint or consensus, normatively prescribes and sanctions role attitudes and behaviour* (Dann and Cohen 1991). Thus, an individual's values, beliefs and behaviour are, according to structural theory, predominantly shaped, developed and constrained by the social world in which that individual lives. Conversely, structural theory tends to ignore or to play down the role of the individual, the 'human actor', in the formation and development of society; human individuality is, in effect, subordinated to the constraining influence of society. It is this latter characteristic of Structuralism that has attracted most criticism, as it *reifies* society. That is, Structuralism views society as being real or as a 'thing' rather than as an abstract concept. (Reification is a term used by

7

sociologists to describe the interpretation of a general concept, such as society, as something solid or real.)

Despite this and other criticisms, the structural perspective dominated much sociological analysis from the birth of modern sociology until the mid-twentieth century. Within Structuralism, however, there are two distinct and opposing camps. Both adopt the holistic approach to the study of society but, whilst one group concentrates on what is known as *consensus theory*, the other advocates *conflict theory* as the basis for sociological analysis.

(i)   Consensus Theory

A basic assumption of structural sociology in general is that the values, beliefs and behaviour of all the individuals who comprise a particular society are formulated and, most importantly, constrained by what may be described as the rules of that society. Some of these rules may be prescribed by a society's laws which constrain an individual's behaviour by the threat of punishment or sanctions. Not all of society's rules and constraints are backed up by laws; indeed, most social behaviour is, arguably, constrained by an individual's own beliefs and values. As a simple example, the British are well known for forming queues while waiting to be served in, say, a post office. Jumping the queue is normally considered to be bad manners, yet in many other countries queuing is unheard of and seen, perhaps, as a quaint British custom.

The important point is that, continuing with this example, queuing is not instinctive; people learn that, at least in Britain, it is normal social behaviour to form queues. More generally, individuals are not born with a concept of right and wrong, of what constitutes good or bad manners. These beliefs and values, which effectively constrain an individual's behaviour, are determined by society. To put it another way, at birth an individual is rather like a new computer; the hardware, with particular capabilities, exists but the software has to be installed to make the computer function effectively. Of course, a child inherits certain characteristics from its parents – hence, the 'nature *versus* nurture' debate – but, like a computer, 'software' (that is beliefs, rules, values) needs to be installed through a process called *socialisation*.

Socialisation continues throughout an individual's life and in all spheres of life. Society's rules and constraints are learned, or *internalised*, from a variety of sources. Initially it will be an individual's immediate family which has the most influence but school friends, peer groups, institutions such as schools, colleges and universities, the work environment, religion and even the media will constrain and shape an individual's beliefs and behaviour during his or her lifetime. Moreover, the rules that an individual learns are those rules which are generally accepted by a particular society to be appropriate or acceptable. That is, there is a *consensus* about how members of a society should behave, about what the central values and norms of that society are. It is this, according to consensus theory, that determines people's roles and behaviour and ensures the continuation of an integrated, regulated and stable society.

One of the first sociologists to develop a theory of society based on a structural-consensus approach was Emile Durkheim (1858-1917). Following on from and developing the ideas of Comte, Durkheim viewed modern, as compared with primitive, pre-industrial, society as being held together by what he termed *organic solidarity*. While society as a whole determines an individual's role and behaviour, organic solidarity develops from a new moral consensus which, Durkheim believed, could be disseminated through education. Indeed, one of his objectives was the creation of social harmony through the state's use of sociological knowledge.

A central assumption of organic solidarity as suggested by Durkheim is that society is differentiated into separate areas and institutions, such as education, religion or the family, each of which deals with a particular aspect of social life. Each part plays a necessary role or *function* in the harmonious continuation of society, the analogy being that society is like a living organism; each part, or organ, is essential to the well-being of the organism. Yet the character of the organism can only be viewed as a whole, rather than being reduced to its constituent parts. Thus, society should, likewise, be viewed as a whole, with societal institutions examined and explained on the basis of their function in society. This approach to sociology became dominant during the first half of the twentieth century and developed into what was seen at the time as *the* sociological theory, namely, *Functionalism*. The American sociologist Talcott Parsons (1902-1979) was, in particular, at the forefront of the functionalist approach to sociology.

Although functionalism has become less popular since the 1960s, it is nevertheless of direct relevance to a sociological approach to tourism. As discussed in Chapter Five, an analysis of tourist motivation cannot be divorced from the function of tourism as, say, an escape from the 'real' world. At a more socio-psychological level, functionalism provides a framework for examining the satisfaction of needs, such as adventure or curiosity, provided by tourism, whilst the functionalist perspective may also be applied to the classification and analysis of tourism as a social system (see Nash 1981).

(ii) Conflict Theory

Whereas Durkheimian sociology views human action and behaviour as resulting from wider social forces and influences developed by consensus, conflict theorists, although still adopting the macro, holistic approach, believe that sociological study should be concerned primarily with the influence of societal conflicts, such as domination and subordination. In other words, consensus theory favours the harmonious evolution of society and its rules, values and norms; conflict theory is based on the assumption that these rules, values and norms, which are then internalised through the socialisation process, are founded on the ability of a dominant group in society to impose their values and behaviour onto subordinate groups. Through the imposition of their values, dominant groups are able to sustain a social structure that favours their own position in society. Thus, according to conflict theorists, social change must result not from evolution but revolution.

Charles Darwin (1800-1882) attempted to show that evolution was based on conflict and a clash of interests but it was Karl Marx (1818-1883) who, although a philosopher and an economist rather than a sociologist, was to have a profound influence on this branch of sociology. In brief, Marx believed that the basis of society and social structure is the economy; in order to survive people need to produce economic necessities, such as clothing and food. The production of such economic necessities entails an individual's involvement in the system of production, whereby people enter into *relations of production*. It is these relations which influence and determine social structure and, hence, roles, values and behaviour, because relations of production become class relations. In particular, the working class, the *proletariat*, become subordinate to the capitalist class, the *bourgeoisie*.

Under the burgeoning European capitalist system of the nineteenth century, Marx saw the human condition becoming one of *alienation*. With the new methods of mass production and the division of labour, individuals became involved in relatively meaningless tasks which were only part of the wider production system. As a result, workers became alienated from their work, from the product of their labour, from their fellow human beings, from nature and, ultimately, from themselves. In effect, their labour became a commodity, bought by capitalists for the cheapest price. Thus, labour has a value. Marx labelled the difference between the value of labour (that is wages paid to a worker) and the value of the commodities produced as *surplus value*. This surplus is extracted from the subordinate class through the process of *exploitation*.

According to Marx, it is surplus value that is the very foundation of the capitalist system. The surplus created within the production system, the profit, enables capitalists to own and control the system of production, including labour, thereby becoming the dominant class. The economically dominant class is also able to dominate other spheres of life, from politics to religion, in the extreme creating an ideology that hides the true nature of social relationships from the subordinate class. Therefore, social progress can only be achieved, Marx argued, by removing exploitation, alienation, and economic domination, which in turn can only be achieved by abolishing, through revolution, the economic system (capitalism) which creates those conditions. The responsibility for such revolution lies with the subordinate, working class.

Conflict theory, especially the work of Marx, has attracted both widespread support and criticism. Within the context of this book, it provides a valid basis for what may be described as a neo-Marxist perspective on tourism. It may be argued, for example, that mass tourism, as a subset of leisure in general, is no more than a capitalistic domination or exploitation of working class leisure time. Since the beginning of the nineteenth century, the development of leisure, both as the social condition of time free from work and specific activities that leisure encompasses, may be seen as having been shaped and controlled by the needs of the dominant, capitalist classes (see, for example, Clarke and Critcher 1985; Rojek 1993). Tourism, and mass tourism in particular (in the narrow sense of the mass tourism product – the package holiday), is designed, produced, marketed and sold by the capitalists, the tour operators. The consumers (mass tourists) are, arguably, deceived by the lure of a holiday that promises escape from the capitalist system yet which is, in effect, an extension of it. Thus, the 'revolution' in tourism could be manifested in a widespread rejection of the mass, package tour in favour of more individually orientated forms of tourism. Conflict theory is, therefore, of relevance to the study of the social determinants of tourism, tourist motivation, the nature and political-economy of the tourism industry and the structuralist theory of tourism as a reflection of societal change.

The major criticism of both consensus and conflict theory is that they both, in different ways, over-emphasise the socialisation process, thereby denying the ability of individuals to influence and change society. In addition to the reification of society, an interpretation which attributes abilities and powers to society, such as thought and reason, only possessed by humans, consensus theory tends to view individuals as robots conforming to predictable patterns of behaviour. In the context of tourism, one form of such predictable behaviour that may be explained by consensus theory is the annual mass migration of tourists in search of summer sun, behaviour that has been described by one observer as irrational (Ryan 1997: 3) and likened by another to that of lemmings (Emery 1981)! In contrast, conflict theory is based on the premise that the majority of people within society are subordinate to the rules and values of the dominant class; conformity results, therefore, not from harmony and consensus but from power and dependence. However, both consensus and conflict theory adopt an ahistorical approach. They ignore the historical development of society and minimise human involvement in society's structural development. In contrast, the second major school of sociological theory, the micro approach, highlights the role of individuals and groups of individuals in the determination, explanation and understanding of social reality. This micro approach to sociology is known as Social Action Theory.

(iii) Social Action Theory

Social Action Theory, which essentially adopts a humanist perspective to sociology, is a broad heading under which a number of sociological approaches are found. These include the formal sociology of Georg Simmel (1858-1918), a German who was one of the first to reject the positivist, structural approach to sociology, the work of Max Weber (1864-1920), who introduced the concept of *Verstehen* (meaningful understanding) to sociological analysis and explanation, *symbolic interactionism*, which developed primarily as an American branch of sociology, and the more recent and radical *ethnomethodology* and *phenomenology* (see Jary and Jary 1991 for definitions and explanations of sociological terminology).

The basic perspective of social action theory is that society is not distinct from, but is formed by, the individuals who comprise it, and that social reality results from the social action between individuals. Such action, or behaviour, in turn results from the way in which one individual understands or interprets the behaviour of another individual, with one of the simplest forms of interpretation between individuals being the spoken word. Through this ability to interpret and understand, the individual thereby takes on a more active and creative role in the development of society.

Thus, for action theorists the development and continuation of society and culture is still dependent on socialisation, but the rules and values that are internalised are neither static, nor are they determined by society. Rather, individual members of society have the ability to adapt and change their behaviour within a process of negotiation, or meaningful encounters, with other members of that society. In short, the rules and values that influence an individual's behaviour are not determined and fixed by a reified society, as proposed by structural theorists, but are being continually being changed and adapted by the actions and decisions of individuals within society.

Simmel argued that the fundamental subject of study should be the individual or, more precisely, the ways in which individuals act socially. Society, therefore, results from an intricate amalgamation of the multitude of interactions and relations between individuals; that is, society is made up of individuals who are connected by social interaction. The type or nature of interaction determines different social institutions or groupings, such as the family, marriage or religion, and it was with the *form* rather than the content of these social groupings, or sociations, with which Simmel was concerned (hence, 'formal' sociology). Thus, Simmel defined the form of a social relationship between two individuals as a *dyad*; the content may vary (for example husband and wife, manager and subordinate, teacher and pupil) but the form of the relationship depends on the continued interaction and participation of the two individuals concerned. Should a third person join the group (a *triad*), then the form of the relationship changes from two-way interdependence into interaction based on mediation. Formalism, then, presents a way of looking at tourist groups, such as comparing the difference between individual and mass tourism or the role of a tourist guide as the mediator between tourists and local people.

Similarly, Weber defined society in terms of sociation, but he also sought to link the meaning attached to social action with a more positivist cause-and-effect approach. In other words, he introduced the concept of motivation into sociology, combining an understanding of the meaning of social action with the result of such action. The Weberian perspective is of direct relevance to the study of tourism in general and tourist motivation in particular, providing an alternative basis of analysis to, for example, the functionalist explanation of tourism (see Chapter Five). Of the more recent social action perspectives, symbolic interactionism is, arguably, of most relevance to tourism analysis and research.

(iv) Symbolic Interactionism

Symbolic interactionism concentrates on the way in which social rules and identities are established through social interaction emphasising, in particular, the importance of the response of other people to an individual's behaviour. Rather than simply internalising society's rules, individuals are able to analyse and adapt their own behaviour; social identity results from the interpretation of the responses of others to an individual's behaviour. To put it another way, social identity, knowing oneself, can only be achieved by interpreting how others respond to our actions, the response being communicated through symbols, such as language, in a social situation. Behaviour and values are developed, therefore, through social interaction.

The most immediate and general relevance of symbolic interactionism to tourism is its potential contribution to an understanding of the tourist-host relationship. Tourist-host encounters are, more often than not, characterised by inequality and a variety of differences between the participants and their expectations. Symbolic interactionism provides the foundation for the analysis of, and potential solutions to, the socio-cultural impacts of tourism that result from such unequal or unbalanced encounters. These issues are discussed in Chapter Nine.

Additionally, Dann and Cohen (1991) point to a number of other ways in which symbolic interactionism may be applied to tourism. They suggest, for example, that it provides a basis for researching issues of authenticity/inauthenticity in tourist experiences and, in terms of motivation, that it may lead towards an explanation of the desire to escape from the rules and morals of the home society whilst on holiday. That is, the *ludic* (play) qualities of tourist behaviour, such as excessive drinking and eating or casual sexual encounters, may be associated with an avoidance of normal social interaction that might discourage such behaviour (see, for example, Lett 1983).

These and other social action theories, including phenomenology and ethnomethodology, have been criticised for over-emphasising the role and influence of the individual in the development of society. It is certainly true that people possess the ability to act individually and creatively, to reason and to make individual decisions, and to make sense of their physical and social world. However, the great majority of people also live according to the rules, values, morals and constraints of their societies and, consequently, most societies maintain a sense of order and harmony. Thus, neither of the two primary sociological perspectives, the macro, structuralist, theories or the micro, social action, theories, can alone fully or adequately explain all social phenomena. Indeed, a kind of halfway house has been proposed by the British sociologist Anthony Giddens. His *structuration theory* develops the notion that social structure is both the medium and the outcome of social action. That is, both structuralism and social action play a role in the development of society, yet neither is afforded primacy.

Inevitably, perhaps, these conflicting perspectives on sociology continue to be a subject of debate amongst sociologists themselves. It is important to point out that they are just that; different approaches, but united by the objective of studying and explaining the development, structure and functioning of human societies. Indeed, most general texts on sociology utilise some, if not all, of the sociological theories in the analysis of different aspects of society. There is, therefore, no single, all-encompassing theory of sociology and, by implication, no single sociology of tourism. This brief review of the development of sociology and sociological thought has served simply to highlight the scope and breadth of sociology as a perspective on society, and it is now important to consider how such a perspective may be applied to the study of tourism as a distinct area of social activity.

Tourism and sociology

Tourism is about people and societies. It is a social activity generated by some societies and impacting physically, economically, socially and culturally on others. Some commentators, adopting a structuralist, neo-Durkheimian perspective, would argue that tourism is a reflection of the condition of modern society as a whole (see Krippendorf 1986; MacCannell 1989 and, more generally, Chapter Three). In other circles, tourism is viewed as a vehicle for the development of international peace and understanding, a social force for overcoming international barriers and conflict (D'Amore 1988). For example, the World Tourism Organisation (WTO) states that *tourism stands out as a positive and ever-present factor in promoting mutual knowledge and understanding and as a basis for reaching a greater level of respect and confidence among all the peoples of the world* (WTO 1980: 3). On the other hand tourism, and mass tourism in particular, is often accused of being a destructive influence on host societies and cultures. During the early 1970s, a number of books questioned the true value of tourism by highlighting the non-economic costs of tourism development (for example, Young 1973; Turner and Ash 1975; de Kadt 1979). More recently, this negative attitude towards mass tourism, perhaps epitomised by Croall's assertion that *a spectre is haunting our planet: the spectre of tourism... In its modern guise of [mass] tourism, it can contribute to the continuing degradation of life on our planet* (Croall 1995: 1), has underpinned the debate surrounding alternative, sustainable forms of tourism.

Whichever standpoint is taken, tourism is an increasingly widespread social activity and is, therefore, a valid and important subject for sociological analysis. Furthermore, as a perspective on tourism, sociology offers the potential for explanation and understanding of many factors and issues within tourism. Two approaches may be adopted. On the one hand, it is possible to study tourism within the encompassing discipline of sociology (that is, treating tourism as another social institution, along with the family, work, education and so on), permitting a broader approach to the subject than is often taken. On the other hand, as much, if not more is to be gained by taking tourism itself as the starting point. In other words, it is possible to study tourism, exploring its inherent concepts, structures, processes and characteristics, by referring to and applying different and relevant sociological theory as necessary. It is the latter perspective that provides a platform for much of the discussion throughout this book.

A number of issues immediately become apparent but two questions in particular arise. Firstly, which aspects of tourism can be usefully examined from a sociological viewpoint and, secondly, which sociological theories are most applicable to those aspects? In answering these questions another problem becomes evident, namely, which is the most appropriate 'ology' to use? This refers specifically to the study of the socio-cultural impacts of tourism which is not only one of the four main areas of research identified by Cohen (1984) in his review of the *sociology* of tourism, but also the prime concern of what has been called the *anthropology* of tourism. *Hosts and Guests: The Anthropology of Tourism* (Smith 1989) includes a number of case studies that could be legitimately claimed as sociological research. Conversely, issues of authenticity and the commoditisation of culture, topics frequently

17

examined in the literature by sociologists (see, for example, Cohen 1988a) are no less a valid subject for anthropologists.

A simple response to the first two questions might be that tourism is concerned primarily with the movement of people and, therefore, all areas of tourism should justifiably be included under the umbrella of sociological analysis. A clearer picture is obtained from a brief review of sociological approaches to tourism in the literature and a summary of the sociological theories outlined above and their relevance to the study of tourism.

(i)   Sociology and tourism in the literature

In addition to the socio-cultural impacts of tourism, a field of study to which socio-*economic* impacts may quite legitimately be attached, Cohen (1984) lists three other principle areas of analysis that have emerged in sociological treatments of tourism in the literature. These are, firstly, tourists themselves and their motivations, attitudes, perceptions and so on; secondly, the tourist-host relationship; and, finally, the structure of the tourism system. In fact, since the publication of his seminal paper *Toward a Sociology of International Tourism* (Cohen 1972) Cohen himself has been a leading figure in the development of the link between sociology and tourism, and his work is referred to extensively throughout this book.

Some of the earliest contributions to sociological research in tourism originated in Germany. Research was undertaken as early as 1930 but the first major work appeared in 1960 (Knebel 1960, referred to in Cohen 1984), around the time that mass tourism as we know it today was emerging as a major social force. Nuñez (1963) adopted a strictly empirical, as opposed to theoretical, approach in his study of the development of a tourism destination, as did Forster (1964) who documented changes in the structure of the work force in Pacific island societies resulting from tourism development. In contrast, Boorstin (1964) lamented what he called the *Lost Art of Travel* in his criticism of mass tourism in general and mass tourists, who he perceived as cultural dopes easily satisfied by inauthentic, pseudo experiences, in particular.

Boorstin's élitist sentiments were echoed to an extent by Mishan (1969), an economist who argued that the growth of mass tourism resulted from the cost of travel being too cheap. That is, the tourism industry, *in a competitive scramble to uncover all places of once quiet repose, of wonder, beauty and historic interest to the money-flushed multitudes* (Mishan 1969: 141), ignored the environmental and social costs of tourism development in calculating their prices. The danger was that the longer term survival of host destinations and communities was threatened by short term profit motives. The solution according to Mishan: to ban all international air travel!

Despite their élitism, the approach of both Boorstin and Mishan is of relevance to the present concern for the impacts of mass tourism (see Chapter Ten). Their critical stance with respect to mass tourism was also continued, albeit with a less generalised and more balanced and considered approach, by a number of authors, especially Young (1973) and Turner and Ash (1975). It was also during the 1970s that a more rigorous and theoretical sociological approach was applied to the study of tourism. For example, Cohen (1972) was the first to challenge the generalised notion of the 'tourist' with his model of tourist typologies (discussed in Chapter Four). He went on to develop a phenomenology of tourism (1979), arguing that not only is there a variety of tourist types, or roles, but also a variety of experiences by which tourists may be categorised.

Perhaps the most influential work to emerge at this time, however, was that of MacCannell (1973 and 1976). In firmly rejecting Boorstin's arguments, MacCannell proposed a new sociological theory of tourism based upon the notion that tourists actively seek the authentic in times and places away from their normal lives. What they actually experience, though, is a reality which is constructed for their benefit, a *staged authenticity* (MacCannell 1973). Similarly, Cohen and Taylor (1976) presented the case that tourism is an escape from the alienated condition of modern western society and a search for self identity, a theme explored more explicitly by Dann in an early discussion of tourist motivation (Dann 1977). The concept of authenticity and tourist experience/expectations, introduced to tourism research by MacCannell, has since been developed by other authors (see, for example, Pearce and

Moscardo 1986; Cohen 1988a; Hughes 1995) and is directly related to broader issues, such as the development of eco-tourism, the commoditisation of culture, heritage and the commercialisation of history, the marketing of 'authentic experiences', and so on.

The theoretical approaches of the 1970s were balanced by empirical studies which were also undertaken during the same period. These were primarily concerned with the different relationships and perceptions embodied within tourist-host encounters and the socio-cultural impacts of tourism development (see Smith 1977; de Kadt 1979), and signified the advancement of anthropology as a separate area of tourism research.

Since the early 1980s there has been nothing less than an explosion in the range and depth of research and literature concerned with tourism in general and the sociology of tourism in particular. Most general tourism texts include sections concerned with the social and cultural impacts of tourism, tourist demand and motivation, types or categories of tourists, definitions of tourism or resort life-cycles, all of which are topics that respond to sociological treatment, yet most tend to adopt an empirical, 'face-value' approach. At a more specialised level, a number of books and many papers and articles, too numerous to list here, have considered particular aspects of tourism which could be categorised under the heading of the sociology of tourism. Some of the most influential articles are conveniently published in an edited collection (Apostolopoulos *et al* 1996).

For the most part, the literature addresses specific topics or questions that may be considered 'sociological' rather than adopting a 'broad-brush' sociological approach to tourism, although Pearce's analysis of the social-psychology of tourism covers a range of issues (Pearce 1982). The topics are diverse. Many, for example, examine the meaning and motivation for tourism as a social activity, addressing topics such as tourism as a form of escape (see Rojek 1993), as a reaction to modern society (Krippendorf 1986; 1987), as a search for meaning, self-identity and authenticity, thereby drawing parallels with religious experience (Graburn 1989; Vukonic 1996), or even tourism as a return to a childlike stage of existence (Dann 1989; 1996).

Another well-researched area is that of tourist-host interaction whilst, more recently, attention has been focused on the influence of social and cultural change on tourism. For example, a number of authors have considered the influence of postmodern culture on the consumption of tourism (Munt 1994; Pretes 1995; Sharpley 1996), whilst the more general relationship between tourism and culture is also attracting increasing attention (Rojek and Urry 1998; Robinson and Boniface 1999).

However, in addition to this more specialised research, overall sociological treatments of tourism have also been published in recent years. Perhaps the most notable and certainly the most widely cited is the work of Urry, in which he has developed a sociological examination and explanation of tourism based upon the central theme of the tourist 'gaze' (Urry 1990a). Similarly, Dann (1996) explores tourism from a 'sociolinguistic' perspective, arguing that tourist behaviour is influenced or controlled through the language of tourism as presented in brochures, advertisements and other media. Other authors, including Voase (1995) and Ryan (1997) have also approached tourism from an essentially human or social perspective.

(ii) Tourism and sociological theory - a summary

Although this necessarily brief review of the literature demonstrates the evolution of the sociological and anthropological treatment of tourism, it does not indicate the extent to which sociological theory can be usefully applied to tourism. It is important, therefore, to consider not only the ways in which tourism and sociology have already been linked, but also to identify areas of potential research. This is best done by relating the major sociological perspectives outlined earlier in this chapter to relevant issues within tourism.

(a) Structural-Consensus Theory

The structural, macro sociological perspective firmly places tourism within the study of society as a whole whilst, at the same time, directing attention towards the wider tourism system than towards the individuals who participate in tourism. As a basis for studying tourism the structural approach may be criticised for reifying what is, in effect, the combined actions and behaviour of tourists and those who are employed in, benefit from, or whose lifestyles are affected by, tourism. Nevertheless, a general macro perspective and the more specific functionalist approach provide a foundation for tourism research in a number of areas.

Firstly, it is important to explain and describe the development of tourism within the context of the development of society as a whole and, in particular, how tourism has become institutionalised. The growth and democratisation of tourism from what was once an activity enjoyed by the privileged few to the mass social phenomenon that it is today is frequently explained by the three facilitators: increases in free time, more disposable income and advances in technology. Whilst these three factors have undoubtedly played a significant role in the emergence of tourism, it is nevertheless true a rather simplistic explanation. Tourism is directly related to the development of leisure which, in turn, is linked to societal change and forces. Thus, for example, factors such as industrialisation, urbanisation, mass production and consumption, environmentalism and broader cultural transformations have not only directly influenced the development of tourism and its transformation from luxury to perceived necessity, but also have brought about significant changes in the style or ways in which tourism is consumed and, by implication, produced.

Secondly, as Dann and Cohen (1991) point out, a macro perspective can be adopted when considering the evolution of the tourism system itself, either as a linear development from local, small-scale beginnings through to international business, or as a cyclical process such as that proposed by Butler (1980). A functionalist approach either places tourism in the context of its role in the functioning of society as a whole, such as its function in promoting international understanding, or views tourism itself as a social system. In the latter case, different parts of the tourism system may be categorised by function and linked to, for example, product development and marketing.

The greatest potential for tourism research within the holistic, macro approach is in adopting the basic assumption that tourism is a reflection of society. In particular, the positioning of tourism as a search for the authentic (MacCannell 1976) as a reaction to the contrived, inauthentic condition of modern life in tourism generating societies, or even as a sacred experience (Graburn 1989) compared with the ordinary, demands the consideration of factors such as the authenticity of the tourist experience, the commoditisation of culture and tourist motivation, and thematic issues such as the link between post-modernism, consumer culture and contemporary tourism.

(b) Structural-Conflict Theory

Conflict theory is a valid basis for research into a variety of tourism issues. Brief mention has already been made of the conflict-based relationship between the tourism industry and its customers, manifested in the domination and control of the mass tourism, package holiday market by the tour operators. This relationship is, arguably, founded on paradox and deceit. The product is sold as an escape from the mundane, the ordinary, the routine; it promises change, excitement and temporary freedom from day-to-day institutionalised life. Yet, despite the apparently huge choice available to the customer, the product is standardised and mass produced. Rooms may have more or fewer facilities, accommodation may be self-catering, bed and breakfast or half board, a hotel is near the beach or a bus ride away, or the overall product might be designed to appeal to the 'independent' traveller, as in the case of the tours sold by specialist adventure travel companies. However, the basic product is still the same: transport, accommodation, food and entertainment. Also, in cases where a tour operator also owns the travel agent, the airline and possibly the accommodation, the entire process is controlled by one organisation. Customer choice is, generally, constrained by price and, far from escaping from the capitalist system, the tourist is actually contributing to it.

Within the broader, international tourism system conflict theory brings issues of dependency and tourism-related neo-colonialism into clearer focus. The international tourism industry is becoming increasingly dominated by large multi-national corporations (MNCs) based in Western tourism generating countries (see, for example, Dunning and McQueen 1982). These organisations frequently support, finance, manage or own the tourism facilities in destination countries or regions, particularly in the developing world, which lack the necessary financial and human resources to develop tourism. The MNCs gain increasing control over tourism to and in the destination (Bull 1991: 181-197) which, in turn, becomes increasingly dependent on western finance, products and tourists.

Britton (1982) found that many previously colonised nations, such as Kenya, are particularly susceptible to overseas domination of their nascent tourism industries, a situation he describes as neo-colonialism whilst, more generally, Nash (1989: 39) comments that it is the *power over touristic and related developments abroad that makes a metropolitan center imperialistic and tourism a form of imperialism.* In short, conflict theory provides a theoretical basis for exploring both the political-economy of the tourism system and, more generally, the alleged positive contribution of tourism to social and economic development in destination areas.

The third area in which conflict theory is of relevance to tourism is the study of the tourist-host relationship and the concept of *commercialised hospitality* (Dann and Cohen 1991). What is, possibly, a unique experience for a tourist may be business as usual for the host whose 'hospitality', in reality, is motivated by profit. Conflict theory also highlights the unequal, transitory basis of tourist-host encounters and the growing incidence of what may be termed 'inverse-exploitation'. Increasingly, tourists may be invited to take a photograph or to visit a local home, only to be asked afterwards for a 'gift', usually money. Such behaviour may be seen as exploitation of both the tourist and a country's tradition of hospitality whilst, overall, conflict theory directly challenges the notion that the development of tourism can lead to greater knowledge and understanding between different peoples and nations.

(c) Social Action Theory

The micro-sociological approach directs research and analysis towards the tourist as an individual as opposed to the tourism process and system. Focusing as it does on the interaction between individuals, the most logical application of social action theory is to the explanation of the different expectations, perceptions, relationships and outcomes of tourist-host encounters. The success of such encounters is often undermined by

24

misunderstandings based on differences in race, gender, class. For example, potentially meaningful encounters between southern European males and northern European female tourists or between European visitors and Gambian beachboys (known locally as 'hustlers') may be limited by opposing expectations and cultural differences. The analysis of tourist-host encounters may then be related to the broader field of socio-cultural impacts of tourism and an exploration of the practical ways in which such impacts may be reduced.

Social Action Theory may also be applied to the study of tourist motivation, one of the primary themes in the sociological treatment of tourism. Examining and explaining tourist motivation or, in simple terms, determining the reason why people travel, is a complex process. Motivation is related to both *push* and *pull* factors (Dann 1981); push factors are those which directly influence motivation and may be socially, psychologically, economically or physically determined, whereas pull factors are the attractions of the destination. Thus, the various social action approaches are of direct relevance to an examination of both push and pull factors. These are discussed in greater detail in Chapter Five.

(iii) The sociology or anthropology of tourism?

Within the tourism literature there appears to be a degree of confusion as to what constitutes a sociological or an anthropological approach to the study of tourism. For example, Selwyn (1992: 354) describes Cohen as *one of the most prolific anthropological writers on tourism* and Dean MacCannell's *The Tourist* as *one of the most influential books in the anthropology of tourism*, whereas both Cohen and MacCannell are more generally considered to be sociologists. This blurring of the boundaries between the two disciplines arises, perhaps, because of the overlap in their subject matter. Anthropology is the study of humankind; *anthropologists are interested in everything human, whenever and wherever it occurs* (Nash and Smith 1991). Thus, sociology is, arguably, a discipline that falls within the broader concerns of anthropology. Furthermore, anthropology's claim on tourism cannot be disputed: *modern tourism accounts for the single largest peaceful movement of people across cultural boundaries in the history of the world. Given that, tourism is unavoidably an anthropological topic* (Lett 1989: 276). Little is to be gained here from a semantic discussion of the two disciplines but a brief consideration of anthropological concern with tourism will clarify the approach adopted in this book.

The application of anthropology to tourism was relatively late in comparison to other disciplines. This, according to Nuñez (1989), was because tourism was considered by anthropologists not to be a proper or serious subject worthy of their attention. Indeed, it was Nuñez himself who was responsible for one of the first anthropological works on tourism (Nuñez 1963), but it was the publication of *Hosts and Guests* (Smith 1977) that firmly established tourism as a valid target for anthropologists. Since that time, a sizeable body of literature has been produced concerned with tourism, literature which, according to Lett (1989 276) can be divided into two broad categories: (a) work which empirically assesses the impact of tourism on host societies and cultures and (b) the meanings of tourism to the tourist. The latter category includes such topics as motivation, tourist roles and the semiology of tourism, whilst the dichotomy between the two is embodied in the work of Graburn (1989), who views tourism as form of sacred journey, and that of Nash (1989) who describes tourism as a form of imperialism. Crick (1989) adds the political economy of tourism to the list of identifiable categories of the anthropological treatment of tourism.

It is immediately apparent that there is a large area of overlap between sociology and anthropology within the context of tourism research. Indeed, the only major difference is that anthropology is traditionally constrained by its holistic, comparative, cross-cultural approach, a fundamental basis of the discipline being that anthropological theories must be applicable to all peoples in all places. However, returning to the main points made throughout this chapter that tourism is, essentially, about people and societies and that tourism itself, rather than associated disciplines, should be the starting point for any analysis or research, then inter-disciplinary conflict becomes irrelevant. It is the perspective adopted that is important so that what we are concerned with, in effect, is the 'humanology' of tourism.

What is tourism?

Such has been the growth and spread of tourism during the latter half of the twentieth century that it is now, as Cohen (1974: 527) suggests, *so widespread and ubiquitous...that there are scarcely people left in the world who would not recognise a tourist immediately*. Tourism, however, cannot be viewed as *one monolithic, static sort of phenomenon* (Graburn 1983); it has already referred to it here as both a social and an economic phenomenon and there is a wide variety of other definitions and descriptions attached to the term tourism in the literature. This reflects in part the multidisciplinary nature of the topic (Gilbert 1990) and in part the *abstract nature of the concept of tourism* (Burns and Holden 1995: 5).

Ryan (1991: 6) demonstrates how tourism may be defined from a variety of viewpoints. For example, an economist might define tourism in terms of the supply of and demand for tourism products, a tourist board might adopt a technical, statistical definition based on purpose and length of stay, or an environmentalist might describe tourism in terms of the legitimised exploitation of natural resources. Despite these differences, however, it is important to establish a working definition of tourism as a foundation for the discussion in the following chapters. As a starting point, Chambers English Dictionary refers to tourism as *the activities of tourists and those who cater for them*, immediately reflecting the traditional dichotomy between tourism as a form of social activity (the focus of this book) and tourism as the industry which enables and facilitates participation in that activity. Similarly, Burkhart and Medlik (1981: 41-43) identify two main groups or classifications of tourism definitions. First, *technical* definitions attempt to identify different types of tourist and different tourism activities, normally for statistical or legislative purposes, and which, by implication, view tourism as an economic, as opposed to human, activity. Second, *conceptual* definitions are concerned with the nature and meaning, or essential characteristics, of tourism as an activity.

(a) Technical definitions of tourism

Many of the earlier attempts to define tourism, undoubtedly influenced by the need of tourism destinations for a set of criteria by which to identify and measure tourism, followed the technical, rather than conceptual, perspective (Gilbert 1990). The first international definition of tourism, proposed in 1937 by a group of statisticians at the League of Nations, defined a tourist simply as someone who travels for 24 hours or more outside their normal country of residence. This definition included those travelling for business in addition to pleasure, health or other purposes, and it also introduced the 'excursionist' as someone who stayed in a destination for less than 24 hours. However, the definition excluded domestic tourism and overlooked the fundamental meaning of tourism as a social activity.

A similar definition, though resorting to the more general description of 'visitor', was produced by the United Nations Conference on Travel and Tourism in 1963 and later adopted by the International Union of Official Travel Organisations (IUOTO), the precursor of the World Tourism Organisation (WTO). It states that a visitor is:

> *any person visiting a country other than that in which he has his usual place of residence, for any reason other than following an occupation remunerated from within the country visited,*

a visitor being either a tourist, who stays overnight, or an excursionist on a day visit. According to Murphy (1985: 5) this definition is the most widely recognised, yet its focus remains the measurement of tourist traffic and, again, the role of tourists themselves in the tourism process is overlooked. In an attempt to rectify this omission, the Tourism Society in the UK define tourism as

> *the temporary short-term movement of people to destinations outside the places where they normally live and work, and their activities during the stay at these destinations; it includes movement for all purposes as well as day visits or excursions*

The major drawback with this definition is that it implies that anyone who travels, for virtually any purpose, is a tourist. Indeed, by including business travel (as do most statistical data on tourism) it contradicts the generally held perception that tourism is a leisure activity whereas, interestingly, the word travel comes from the French *travail*, or work.

(b) Conceptual definitions of tourism

In contrast to technical, measurement-based definitions, attempts have also been made to conceptually define tourism from an essentially anthropological perspective. Nash, for example, considers that *at the heart of any definition of tourism is the person we conceive to be a tourist* (Nash 1981: 461). Approaching tourism from the perspective of motivation and touristic practices, he defines tourism as simply the activity undertaken by *a person at leisure who also travels* (Nash 1981: 462), thereby firmly identifying tourism as the antithesis to work activities. Smith develops this theme with a more explicit reference to motivation, a tourist being a *temporarily leisured person who voluntarily visits a place for the purpose of experiencing a change* (Smith 1989: 1). Similarly, Graburn emphasises tourism's functional role inasmuch as it *involves for the participants a separation from normal 'instrumental' life and the business of making a living, and offers entry into another kind of moral state in which mental, expressive, and cultural needs come to the fore* (Graburn 1983). Finally, in a broader, metasociological sense, MacCannell (1989: 1) describes the tourist as a model of 'modern-man-in-general' and tourism as a modern pilgrimage, a kind of refuge from modernity (Short 1991: 34). Such conceptual definitions place the emphasis firmly on the implicitly leisure role or meaning of tourism. Unfortunately, however, by creating the work/leisure dichotomy, certain categories of travel activity which are strictly neither leisure nor work, such as religious pilgrimages or long-term budget travel (see Chapter Four), are omitted, thereby creating a narrow set of parameters within which to place the activity of tourism.

(c) Holistic definitions of tourism

The conceptual approach, concentrating as it does on the tourist as an individual, misses out much about the tourism system (Crick 1989). In other words, the technological and conceptual categories of definitions represent two extremes of a definition continuum (Buck 1978) which are constrained by their disciplinary focus. It has been suggested that *as the tourist is part of the subject world, we should search for other definitions which balance out the need for both measurement and tourist identity*

29

(Gilbert 1990: 9). Therefore, a holistic definition which embraces both the factual and theoretical perspectives of tourism, is required. Jafari (1977) goes some way towards achieving this by epistemologically defining tourism as:

> *the study of man away from his usual habitat, of the industry which responds to his needs, and of the impacts that both he and the industry have on the host's socio-cultural, economic and physical environments.*

The essential point remains that, such is the variety of disciplinary treatments of tourism and, given the vast array of activities, motivations, organisations and so on that comprise tourism, to attempt a single, all-encompassing definition is a difficult, if not impossible task.

Tourism is, as stated earlier, primarily a social activity. In other words, if people had neither the ability nor the desire to travel from one place to another, tourism would not exist. Thus, tourism is an activity which involves individuals who travel within their own countries or internationally, and who experience and interact with other people and places. It is, in short, a social phenomenon which involves the movement of people to various destinations and their (temporary) stay there.

Tourism on its present international scale could not occur without the existence of a large and sophisticated 'industry' which enables people to be tourists. That is, without the provision of accommodation, transport, entertainment and other facilities, and the without the existence of businesses that organise, package and sell tourist experiences or provide essential support, such as insurance or financial services, the majority of people would be unable to participate in tourism. Therefore, as a widespread activity that is embedded in modern society, tourism also embraces the following characteristics:

1. It is normally considered a leisure activity, generally associated with short-term escape from the routine or ordinary. An implicit assumption is that tourism involves freedom from paid or domestic work, although some forms of non-leisure travel (for example pilgrimage, exploration/adventure travel) or work-related travel

(for example, conferences, incentive travel) are also accepted as forms of tourism

2. It is socially patterned. That is, the ability to participate in tourism and the nature of tourism consumption is influenced by tourists' socio-cultural background, with wealth, gender, age, class, education and other social factors all having an influence on the frequency, duration, destination and style of tourists' trips.

3. It is supported by a diverse, fragmented and multi-sectoral industry. Extensive vertical and horizontal diversification has resulted, however, in the domination of the industry by a relatively small number of multi-national corporations, mostly based in the industrialised, tourism generating countries. Thus, the structure and characteristics of this industry and its inherent power relationships are likely to be significant determinants of the nature of tourism-related development.

4. It is largely dependent on the physical, social and cultural attributes of the destination and the promise of excitement, authenticity and the extraordinary. It is also, therefore, an 'ecological' phenomenon inasmuch as tourism not only requires an attractive, different environment, but also interacts with and impacts upon that environment.

5. It is a commercial activity based on encounters between tourists and local people or communities. Tourism acts, therefore, as a catalyst in the development of commercialised hospitality, the potential commoditisation of culture, and as an agent of social change.

6. It is a sector of the broader leisure market and reflects trends and changes in tourism generating societies.

Many of these characteristics and issues are addressed throughout this book. Indeed, they constitute a form of agenda for the following chapters, an agenda which may be summarised by observing that a dialectical, or two-way relationship exists between tourism/tourists and society. On the one hand, tourism is itself influenced or impacted upon *by* society. As history shows (see Chapter Two), mass tourism has evolved as a result of transformations and developments in society; it is, in a sense, a social victory (Krippendorf 1986). More importantly, however, society has been, and continues to be, a powerful force in shaping the character of tourism. That is, a variety of social factors are instrumental in determining the motivation for and style of tourism, influencing how, when, where and why people participate in tourism. On the other hand, tourism itself impacts on societies. In other words, the development of tourism inevitably results in both positive and negative consequences for destination societies. Indeed, the rapid growth of mass, international tourism since the 1960s has been mirrored by ever increasing concern about the consequences of that growth on local people in tourism destinations.

This two-way relationship is reflected in the structure of this book. Chapters Three to Seven focus upon the ways in which society determines, shapes or otherwise influences tourists behaviour, motivation, consumption and attitudes. The subsequent chapters then explore the ways in which tourism impacts upon destination societies and cultures, with particular emphasis placed on the role of the tourist-host encounter. Firstly, however, it is important to trace the historical development of tourism as socially determined activity as a background to the rest of the book.

Two

The Evolution of Tourism

Introduction

It is widely accepted that the roots of modern tourism lie in the industrial, economic and social transformations that occurred during the nineteenth and early twentieth centuries. Technological innovation and increasing levels of income and free time provided the means for more widespread participation in travel and tourism, whilst changes in the social condition, resulting, in particular, from rapid urbanisation and the new, industrial work practices, provided the motivation. Thus, it would be logical to assume that tourism is a phenomenon of modern society, emerging as a kind of inevitable by-product of what may be described as the modernisation of society.

Two points must be emphasised here. Firstly, *like many other modern industries, tourism can trace its ancestry back to the Old Testament* (Young 1973: 9), the means of travel having been available, albeit to a privileged minority, for thousands of years. For example, sea-going ships were first designed and built around 3000 BC (Casson 1974: 21) and chariots were first introduced around 1600 BC. Similarly, people have been able to be tourists, in the sense of travelling for pleasure, education, spiritual fulfilment and interest rather than trade or warfare, for as long as they have been physically able to travel from one place to another. Indeed, some of the earliest indications of tourism are to be seen in Egypt, where ancient graffiti dating back to 1300 BC have been found scratched onto the great pyramids at Giza (Casson 1974: 32; Holloway 1998: 16). Therefore, although modern, mass tourism is a feature of the late twentieth century, tourism has existed in one form or another for almost as long as societies have existed. Secondly and, perhaps, more importantly, the enabling factors of time, money and transport technology, combined with the freedom and desire to travel, frequently

33

cited as the reasons for the growth of tourism. Although these factors have certainly given the majority of people (at least in the wealthier, developed countries) the ability and opportunity to participate in tourism, they do not adequately *explain* the evolution of tourism. Since the 1600s, an enormous variety of tastes in, and styles of, travel and tourism have become popular and have either remained fashionable or become less widespread. Such tastes and styles, however, have not been universal, nor have they occurred at the same time in different societies, even though the enabling factors of tourism have been present.

For example, as discussed later in this chapter, the spa towns in Britain became less fashionable as tourist resorts around the end of the eighteenth century, yet in a number of European countries spa tourism remains popular to this day. Similarly, although technological advances in transport made travel to and through wilder, less hospitable landscapes easier, safer and more comfortable, it does not explain why it became popular to visit or gaze upon such landscapes. Or, why is it that many people nowadays eschew modern transport and accommodation facilities to travel in a more 'traditional' style?

In short, different societies have favoured different types of tourism at different periods, and continue to do so. Therefore, the historical and continuing evolution of tourism cannot be explained simply and universally by describing those factors which enable people to participate in tourism. We should consider not only the *socio-economic, cultural, political and technological context* (Towner 1996: 6) of tourist generating areas but also those of destination areas. At the same time, broader cultural and ideological factors must also be taken into account, such as the emergence of 'consumer culture' (see Chapter Six) or the ideology of environmentalism.

This suggests, of course, that there are as many 'histories' of tourism as there are societies which participate in tourism and that a complete discussion of the evolution of tourism is beyond the scope of this chapter. But, it is important to trace briefly the historical development of tourism, identifying the major factors and influences that have underpinned the growth of tourism, as a socially determined activity, from an élite activity enjoyed by a privileged minority into the mass phenomenon that it is today. A number of broader cultural factors that pattern contemporary tourism are then discussed in subsequent chapters. (For a detailed discussion of the history of tourism in terms of both content and methodology, see Towner 1984; 1988; 1995; 1996).

Tourism in ancient times

For the earliest civilisations, the major factors which inhibited the development of tourism were the difficulty and danger of travelling any distance and, for most people, a lack of money. With the exception of the Minoan (2000-1500 BC) and the Mycenaean civilisations (1600-1200 BC), road building was virtually unknown and, even by the end of the fourth century BC in Greece, roads were poor and highwaymen frequently preyed on unsuspecting travellers. The most convenient and safe mode of transport was by ship, although even sea travel was not immune to danger from either the elements or piracy, and, as most travel was motivated by either trade or warfare, the opportunity to travel for pleasure was very limited.

Nevertheless, tourism of a sort existed within ancient Greece, although normally associated with attending religious or sporting festivals or consulting oracles. For example, the oracle at Delphi drew people from far and wide to seek advice on various matters whilst the Pythian Games, also at Delphi, were a popular event. Many sick people travelled to Epidaurus in the hope of being healed by the gods, similar to modern day pilgrimages to Lourdes in France, but Olympia, home of the Olympic Games, was probably one of the most popular tourist destinations in Ancient Greece. The first Games were held in 776 BC and thereafter attracted thousands of visitors from both Greece and abroad to witness the sporting contests and other events which gave the Games their deep religious significance. Thus, tourism in ancient Greece *was not so much a voyage of adventure as a trip in accordance with tradition and ritual. The man who travelled tightened his links rather than liberated himself from his social background* (Sigaux 1966:10). In other words, leisure was regarded by the Ancient Greeks not as a time to relax and unwind but more as a means of self-development through education, sport and music; leisure was seen, by the philosophers of the time, as the basis of civilised society. Visits to oracles or festivals were, therefore, part of Greek life and travel for pleasure was uncommon. As a result, tourism as a form of escape or relaxation, a common motivation for much present day tourism, did not become widespread until Roman times although holiday resorts were developed near major cities. The most famous of these was Canopus near Alexandria.

One notable exception was Herodotus, a Greek historian who lived during the fifth century BC and died around 425 BC. An educated man from a wealthy background, he spent much of his life travelling and recording what he experienced and is, therefore, often considered to be the first travel writer. Usually travelling by ship, a fact which accounts for his frequent descriptions of harbours and river towns, Herodotus travelled widely around Egypt, Syria, Persia, and Asia Minor, reaching as far as Sicily and Italy in the west and Babylon in the east. In his writings he describes what he encountered on his travels, sometimes relating his own experience and observations, sometimes relying on information from guides and other people he met. He wrote to both inform and to entertain and his work is a unique record of early tourism.

One of the major hurdles which limited the development of tourism in ancient times was overcome by the Romans. In order to administer their expanding empire and to maintain the *Pax Romana*, it was necessary for the Roman authorities to build a network of roads which not only allowed for the rapid movement of troops and administrative personnel but also increased the opportunity for ordinary citizens to travel. One of the first major highways to be built was the Via Appia, the Appian Way, the construction of which commenced in 312 BC. It eventually stretched across Italy from Rome to the port of Brindisi on the east coast and was one of literally thousands of major and minor roads which, by the first century AD, crossed the length and breadth of the Roman Empire. It was possible to travel along first-class, paved roads all the way from Hadrian's Wall in the north to the southern corners of the Empire in Ethiopia (Young 1973: 10), with travellers being able to break their journeys at staging-posts, or hotels, along the route. Indeed, travel and tourism during the Roman period was both relatively safe and convenient, yet long distance travel for purposes other than trade or military service was still uncommon. Even though general holidays and other festivities occupied about half the Roman year, most festivals and other events took place locally and there was no widespread touristic movement between provinces (Sigaux 1966: 11). Only the wealthier members of Roman society were able to indulge in foreign tourism. Athens and the Greek cities of what is now Turkey, such as Ephesus, were popular destinations and, as a forerunner of the Grand Tours of the sixteenth to eighteenth centuries, young Romans were sent to Athens or Rhodes to be educated. Many Romans also visited Egypt and were as anxious as previous visitors to scratch their names onto famous structures.

More generally, the Romans introduced the concept of tourism as a form of escape. Those in positions of authority, or who could afford to do so, built themselves villas or country houses beyond the confines of the cities, often in the hills to escape the summer heat. The Alban and Sabine hills around Rome offered cool relief from the heat of the city and, by the first century BC, were dotted with summer homes and villas. Nor was this practice restricted to Rome; villas and second homes were found around most cities throughout the Empire. The development of the road network also allowed easy access to coastal areas during the summer months and a string of resorts developed along the northern shore of the Bay of Naples, over one hundred miles from Rome. The wealthier members of Roman society owned villas both in the hills and in coastal resorts; of the latter, the most famous was Baiae, the first of Rome's summer resorts. Originally favoured as a winter resort because of its hot springs (taking the waters being an important ritual in Roman life), Baiae gradually expanded from a peaceful place to relax and to go fishing and boating into a major resort – a process that was to be repeated almost two thousand years later in places such as Spain! As it developed the town gained a reputation for moral laxity; loud parties, excessive drinking and nude bathing were commonplace and it soon attracted criticism from more straightlaced members of Roman society. For example, Seneca described the resort as *the home of vice... [where]... licence is triumphant*, a complaint which fell largely on deaf ears. Indeed, Baiae survived as long as the Roman Empire itself.

Despite the popularity of the coastal resorts around Naples, the establishment of a number of spa towns in various provinces, such as the

37

French towns of Vichy and Aix-les-Bains, which became popular entertainment centres, and the relative ease of travel with the extensive road network, tourism during Roman times was still limited and sporadic. The distances to be travelled were often great and travel during the winter months was often impossible. Nevertheless, the Romans added an important dimension to travel and tourism. Previously, tourism was motivated by trade, health and attendance at festivals or other religious events; the Romans introduced the summer holiday based, to a great extent, on the socially-sanctioned principle of pleasure and self-indulgence. It was a form of tourism that disappeared with the decline of the Roman Empire during the fifth century AD and that would not reappear until the twentieth century. Indeed, the fall of Rome signalled the virtual end of tourism as a leisure activity for almost a thousand years, although specific forms of travel and tourism emerged during the intervening period.

Tourism in the Middle Ages

With the end of Roman rule many roads fell into disrepair and, as a result, most people's mobility was severely impaired. But this was not the only reason for a decline in tourism. In addition to being extremely uncomfortable, travelling also became a much more dangerous activity, whilst the decline and widespread poverty of Europe during the Dark Ages meant that few people had the means, purpose or inclination to undertake journeys of any distance. Such tourism as existed at this time was limited to local fairs, festivals and religious holidays (literally, *holy days*); travelling was usually only undertaken for the purpose of trade or government business.

One form of voluntary tourism which was popular during this period was pilgrimage. *In its purest form pilgrimage was a voluntary journey to worship at some holy shrine, and the journey itself was expected to be hard and fraught with difficulties, a form of penance* (Jebb 1986: 3). Pilgrimages had been undertaken for some time. Indeed, Bethlehem was frequented by Christian visitors as early as the third century (Sigaux 1966: 18) but, from about the tenth century, when overland travel became more practicable and as more facilities for travellers became available,

38

greater numbers of people set out on such journeys. Most travelled on foot (although, by the time of Chaucer's Canterbury Pilgrims, horseback had become the favoured means of transport) and the three main destinations were Jerusalem, Rome, and Santiago de Compostella in north west Spain. All three attracted large numbers of pilgrims. For example, some three hundred thousand people visited Rome in 1300. However, shorter journeys within one country, such as English pilgrimages to Canterbury or Winchester, were also popular.

Thus, during the Middle Ages, tourism, as opposed to obligatory forms of travel, was largely associated with religion. The more adventurous also embarked on long distance journeys seeking fame and fortune, perhaps the most well-known being Marco Polo who travelled to China in the thirteenth century. The accounts of his journeys are one of the very few examples of travel writing remaining from this era and it was not until the sixteenth century that individuals not only began to travel for travel's sake, but also began to record and publish details of their travels and adventures for a public that was becoming increasingly interested in stories of faraway, exotic places. One of the better known of these early adventurers was Thomas Coryate who, in 1608, undertook a trip to Venice. His account of his travels, *Coryate's Crudities*, was to inspire others to follow in his footsteps and is an early example of the way in which travel writing, as one medium of the 'language of tourism' (Dann 1996), is a cultural influence on tourist behaviour. His writing was both vivid and humorous. For example, during a rough crossing of the English Channel he describes *varnishing the exterior parts of the ship with the excremental ebullitions of my tumultuous stomach*, an experience that has undoubtedly been frequently repeated over the centuries!

Coryate was typical of many tourists of that time in as much as his destination was Italy. Though a nation in decline, it was still the intellectual centre of Europe (Turner and Ash 1975: 31) and one example of the way in which the socio-cultural characteristics of destination areas are an important factor in the development of tourism. Academics, writers, artists and the aristocracy visited and were inspired by Italian art and culture. The artist Dürer, the philosopher Erasmus and the poet John Milton were among the many people who travelled there, whilst the Palladian style of architecture was introduced to Britain by Inigo Jones, following his own visit to Italy in the early 1600s. It was not only to Italy that tourists, in particular the English, travelled. It was one of a variety of destinations that made up what became known as the Grand Tour, a form of travel which was indicative of the re-emergence of tourism as a leisure activity for the first time since the decline of the Roman Empire.

Tourism 1600 to 1800

The seventeenth and eighteenth centuries are of particular importance in the historical development of tourism. Although they preceded the modernisation and industrialisation of society, the period most commonly associated with the birth of modern tourism, it was then that the pattern of tourism development through to the present time was set. In other words, it was this period which marked both the start of the social democratisation of tourism, a process which has culminated with the emergence of mass participation in tourism, and the beginning of the transformation of the fundamental meaning and purpose of tourism.

Two forms of tourism were prevalent during this period. The Grand Tour is *one of the most celebrated episodes in the history of tourism* (Towner 1996: 96). It was the main form of overseas travel from the sixteenth to early nineteenth century and is important as not only the first popular style of international tourism but also, as Towner (1996) observes, its legacy can be seen today in the cultural tours of Europe. Almost concurrently, spa tourism emerged in both Britain and Europe (and, to an extent, in colonial America) as the forerunner of modern resort-based tourism, although the patronage of spa towns in different countries varied enormously. Also important during this period were changes in the *style* of tourism which not only had an impact on the Grand Tour and spa tourism, but which also transformed the meaning of tourism.

(i) The Grand Tour

Like all tourist movements, the Grand Tour was the product of a particular social and cultural environment (Towner 1985). The religious conviction that had motivated overseas travel during the Middle Ages had, during the 1500s, been replaced by more secular desires and by the start of the seventeenth century it was customary for the English aristocracy to send their sons, once they had graduated from university, on a tour of Europe. Moreover, underlying the popularity of undertaking a Tour in Europe was the fact that the culture to which the British aristocracy aspired was to be found not in Britain but across the Channel, in France and, as referred to above, in Italy.

Usually accompanied by a tutor, the young aristocrat spent a period of anything up to three or four years abroad, the purpose of this extended trip being to complete a young man's education. In a sense, the cultural centres of Europe became a large finishing school for young Englishmen. They enrolled on courses at the universities in major cities and learnt not only academic subjects and languages but also social refinements, preparing themselves for careers as diplomats or in government. For example, amongst those who travelled in Europe in the early days of the Grand Tour (and by the mid-1700s, it is estimated that some 20,000 English were abroad at any one time) was Henry Wooton who, having gone on an extensive tour starting in 1589, was eventually to become the English Ambassador in Venice. The travels of these early Grand Tourists inevitably took them to Italy as part of what Towner (1985) describes as the *Classical Grand Tour*. The northern Italian cities of Turin, Verona and Venice were on the usual itinerary and the classical tastes of the tourists were also reflected in their routes along the Rhone valley in France. Switzerland, Austria, Germany and Holland were also included on longer tours.

The important point about the Grand Tour, in terms of the historical development of tourism, is that the characteristics of both the Tour and those who participated in it changed over time. In other words, during the two centuries or so that preceded the Napoleonic Wars, the Grand Tour underwent a fundamental transformation and, by the beginning of the 1800s, the purpose, destinations and length of trip of the tourists bore little relation to earlier tours. A greater number of tourists started to tour Europe, but their trips were shorter both in distance and duration; they came from increasingly older age groups; they tended to belong to the professional middle classes rather than the aristocracy; and their purpose was more for pleasure and sightseeing rather than education. In short, the

Grand Tour became popularised and the tourists themselves began to gain a reputation for showing little or no interest in the people, language or culture of the countries through which they passed, an accusation that may be directed towards certain forms of modern, mass tourism.

As the Grand Tour became *invaded by the bourgeoisie* (Turner and Ash 1975: 41), the aristocracy abandoned the traditional European tour in favour of more socially exclusive resorts or areas elsewhere in a pattern of behaviour that has been repeated throughout the development of tourism since the late eighteenth century. This transformation occurred for a number of reasons, primarily the emergence of a new middle class who could afford overseas travel. There was also a gradual shift away from education-motivated touring towards travel as a symbol of the leisured classes, a catalyst being the increasing popularity of travel literature during the eighteenth century which helped to *spread the culture of travel to the literate middle classes* (Towner 1996: 102). The notion of sightseeing also came to dominate travel culture. Whereas the early Grand Tourist travelled abroad for *discourse* (Adler 1989), to learn languages, to read and to meet and converse with eminent persons, later travellers relied more on visual observation. Initially, such sightseeing was impartial and objective, *the 'eye'... was deliberately disciplined to emotionally detached, objectively accurate vision* (Adler 1989). Soon, however, an element of subjectivity was injected. Nature, landscape and scenic beauty became the object of the tourists' gaze as the romantic movement emerged, influenced greatly by the writing of Rousseau. Mountain scenery, once feared or simply considered to be monstrous and ugly in comparison with more gentle, ordered landscapes, became the object of the tourists' attentions and their routes through Europe were adapted accordingly. Switzerland became popular and, towards the end of the eighteenth century, a number of visitors, including William Wordsworth, undertook walking tours there.

In England, too, the romantic movement came to dominate the ways in which people viewed the landscape, although more generally travel within Britain was not particularly popular or widespread until the late eighteenth century. Not only was transport slow and uncomfortable but, with the exception of the spa season, domestic travel simply did not constitute part of the culture of the leisured classes.

The change in landscape tastes in England is, perhaps, epitomised by the transformation of the Lake District from what Defoe described as *a country eminent only for being the wildest, most barren and frightful of any that I have passed over in England, or even Wales itself* into an area revered by writers, poets and artists alike. What had changed, of course, was not the landscape itself, but people's attitudes towards landscape and scenery. Certainly, improvements in transport made it easier to visit wilder, more isolated areas, yet the representation of the Lake District in art and literature was a powerful influence in the development of aesthetic tastes for landscape. At the same time, rapid social and economic change, in particular the urbanisation and industrialisation of Britain from the 1750s onwards, resulted in rural areas, such as the Lake District, being romantically held as the antithesis to urban life. In other words, tourism during the eighteenth century responded to socio-cultural and economic transformations which have continued to guide and influence the way in which mountainous and rural areas are viewed as tourist destinations (see Urry 1995: 193-210, and Chapter Three).

(ii) Tourism and the spa resorts

At the same time as the Grand Tour was becoming popular amongst the English aristocracy, the spa towns of England and Europe were once again becoming popular for the first time since the decline of the Roman Empire. Often described as the first step towards the development of resort-based tourism, renewed interest in the spas resulted from the belief amongst the medical profession at the time that mineral water could be beneficial to the health. Bath, in particular, became nationally and internationally famous, largely because of a book published by Dr William Turner in 1562, drawing attention to the alleged medicinal properties of its waters. Other spas were soon established in England, including Scarborough, Epsom and Tunbridge Wells, and the fashion soon spread across the English Channel as spas in France, Germany and Italy were re-developed to cater for the needs of an increasing clientele.

It was not long before the spa towns became social centres as well as health resorts. Indeed, health considerations rapidly took second place as

43

visiting spas became an annual event on the social calendars of the upper classes. By the beginning of the eighteenth century Bath was at the height of its popularity with Richard 'Beau' Nash, the Master of Ceremonies, organising the social life of the town and welcoming each visitor personally. Gradually, more and more facilities were provided to entertain visitors at the spas and they soon became, in effect, holiday resorts disguised as health centres, with only a minority of visitors being in anything but the best of health. A similar process was also occurring in Europe and some German spas, such as Baden-Baden, became little more than gambling resorts. Inevitably, perhaps, the spas began to attract increasing numbers of visitors from the expanding middle and professional classes and their social exclusivity began to suffer. Improvements in transport further increased their accessibility and, as shopkeepers, innkeepers and a variety of other trades moved in to take advantage of the increasing numbers of visitors, the resorts began to move down market. By the end of the 1700s, the spa towns were rapidly being transformed into residential and commercial centres as tourists turned their attention to the seaside resorts and new developments that were to emerge during the following century (for more detail, see Towner 1996).

Tourism in the nineteenth century

The nineteenth century is, without a doubt, the most important period in the history of tourism. Even by 1800, after two hundred years of the Grand Tour and the rise and decline of the spas, tourism was still an activity enjoyed by a relatively small, privileged proportion of the population. For example, it is estimated that about 40,000 English citizens were either living or travelling in Europe at that time (Sigaux 1966: 66) yet, by 1840, some 100,000 people were crossing the English Channel each year, a figure which rose to one million by the start of the twentieth century (Young 1973:18). The main factor which brought about this rapid growth in tourism was, of course, technological advance, especially the introduction of the railways, but society itself underwent a fundamental transformation that was to influence how and where people spent their leisure time in general, and the development of tourism in particular. In other words, the improvements in transport and communications during the nineteenth century, as well as increases in personal income and free time, enabled a far greater proportion of the population to participate in travel and tourism. Importantly, though, changes in the structure of society and social attitudes towards leisure and tourism also determined where, when and how different social groupings participated in tourism. Indeed, the development of tourism reflected broader social transformations. Thus, although the greatest growth in tourism has been experienced during the latter half of the twentieth century, the foundations for such growth were laid during the nineteenth, the emergence of seaside resorts in particular representing the first step towards mass participation in tourism.

(i) The development of the seaside resort

As the spas declined in popularity during the late 1700s, the attention of tourists turned towards coastal resorts. Once again, the initial impetus was provided by the medical profession which extolled the supposed recuperative powers of sea water. In 1753, Dr Richard Russell published a famous paper in which he described the benefits of bathing in, and even drinking, sea water and, to practice what he preached, he moved to Brighthelmstone (now Brighton) on the south coast. By the turn of the century Brighton had become a fashionable destination, its popularity having been given an important boost following a visit by the Prince of Wales in 1783, and the town expanded rapidly. Similarly, a number of northern coastal resorts, such as Blackpool, Southport and Scarborough, also grew in popularity. For example, in 1795, Blackpool was described in the *Blackburn Mail* as being *the first watering place in the Kingdom, whether we consider the salubrity of the air, the beauty of the scenery, the excellence of the accommodation or the agreeable company of which it is the general resort.*

The initial exclusivity of the seaside resorts was dependent on two factors. Firstly, sea bathing was considered to be a medicinal rather than a pleasurable activity and was, therefore, a structured ritual (see Urry 1990a) which, frequently, took place during winter. Secondly, travelling at the end of the eighteenth century was still slow and relatively expensive. For example, the trip from London to Brighton could take up

45

to two days and the cost of such a journey was beyond the means of most people, even if they had the time. Thus, up until the 1830s, the seaside resorts were still the preserve of the wealthier, leisured classes, although some resorts had become accessible to other social groups, largely as a result of new transport services. In particular, the resorts near the Thames estuary became increasingly popular following the introduction of steamboat services. The first service between London and Gravesend started in 1815 and to Margate in 1820 (Holloway 1998: 22). By 1830, paddle steamers were carrying Londoners in their thousands down the Thames to the Kent coastal resorts, where the famous piers were originally built for landing passengers rather than entertainment.

In 1829, Stephenson's *Rocket* travelled from Liverpool to Manchester at an average speed of sixteen miles per hour (twenty six kilometres per hour), signalling the advent of rail transport and the technological revolution which brought about the birth of mass tourism. The expansion of the railways was remarkable. In 1836, there were 700 miles (1126 km) of track in England, in 1843 there were some 2000 miles (3218 km) and, by 1848, the total length of the railways exceeded 5000 miles (8045 km). This expansion was matched by the rapid increase in the number of passengers travelling by rail and by 1847 the annual number of train passengers had risen to 51 million (Holloway 1994: 24). For the first time, cheap, safe and relatively fast transport was available to the majority of the population, although the railway companies were slow to recognise the potential opportunities of mass leisure travel, and the seaside resorts expanded rapidly. The growth and success of some individual resorts was almost entirely dependent on the railways. For example, Rhyl in north Wales developed entirely as a result of the construction of the Chester to Holyhead railway line and, furthermore, the social status of resorts also depended to some extent on the rail links, although other factors were also important (Urry 1990a: 22). Some destinations, such as Torquay and Bournemouth, remained relatively exclusive owing to their distance from major industrial cities and the later arrival of the railways, whereas Blackpool had moved down market by the 1850s. A number of authors have explored the history of the seaside resorts in some detail (see Walvin 1978; Walton 1983; Towner 1996: 167-216; or, more generally, Pimlott 1947). In particular, Shaw and

46

Williams (1997) provide an in-depth analysis of the factors that have led to the changing fortunes of coastal tourism resorts.

It was not only the development of the railways that led to the growth and democratisation of tourism at the seaside resorts. Of equal importance were the social changes that were occurring during the nineteenth century which created the time, the money and, perhaps most importantly, the desire to participate in tourism. At the beginning of the century, Britain remained, by and large, a pre-industrial, rural society. About eighty per cent of the population lived in rural areas rather than in towns and cities and social life, including leisure, was determined by traditional customs and the agricultural calendar. The Industrial Revolution, which led to the developments in transport technology, also brought about a variety of transformations and created the social and cultural conditions under which tourism could thrive.

From a positive point of view, there was a general increase in wealth amongst the industrial population as the average income per head quadrupled over the course of the nineteenth century (Urry 1990a: 18). Although poverty was widespread in the rapidly expanding industrial cities, some working people were able for the first time to accumulate savings to pay for holidays, holidays with pay not being made available until well into the twentieth century. Free time for leisure and tourism was initially limited. Most people worked a six day week, with Sundays reserved for rest and worship, until half-day holidays were introduced during the second half of the century, and bank holidays in 1871. Also, during this period the leisure time available to the working classes was often structured and organised by the dominant capitalist class as *part of the phalanx of nineteenth-century regulative mechanisms formed to create an obedient, able-bodied, law-abiding and docile class of working people* (Rojek 1993: 32). For example, it is no coincidence that both the Football League and Rugby League in Britain were formed in the northern industrial areas towards the end of the 1800s (Clarke and Critcher 1985: 62; see also Ryan 1997).

As life became industrialised and urbanised, work time and leisure time became differentiated and the different social classes emerged, often with their separate, class-defined residential areas within towns and cities.

The working classes, in particular, found their lives becoming increasingly structured, organised and dominated by the capitalist system. Long working hours, the Protestant work ethic, social reform campaigns and cramped urban areas which lacked space for leisure and recreation all combined to create the conditions under which people longed to escape from the towns and cities. Employers began to realise the benefits of offering regular, official holidays to workers and wakes weeks, when factories, mills or even entire towns closed for a week's holiday, became commonplace in the industrial north. Importantly, this meant that communities took holidays together and, for many towns, this was manifested in trips to the seaside, with particular resorts becoming associated with different industrial cities or regions. For example, Morecambe catered for tourists from Yorkshire whilst Blackpool was favoured by Lancashire workers; south coast resorts near London were mainly visited by day-trippers and others, such as Southport, managed to retain a more exclusive atmosphere.

Thus, mass tourism to the seaside resorts was a direct result of the Industrial Revolution (although, as some have observed, recreational enjoyment of the sea existed well before the discovery of the seaside by the wealthy) and tourism, generally, came to be seen as a formalised and regular form of escape from the stress and strain of modern, industrial life. The development cycle that had become evident through the popularisation of the Grand Tour and the spas once again meant that, as the nineteenth century progressed, the higher social classes had to look further afield to retain their exclusivity. International train travel was introduced with services, such as the Orient Express, offering luxurious travel across Europe. It is also interesting to note that proposals to build a Channel Tunnel were first mooted during the nineteenth century and, at a Select Committee meeting in 1883, the potential cost of building the tunnel was put at £3 million! The Mediterranean resorts along the French Côte d'Azur were popular amongst the European aristocracy and became the favourite haunt of Royal tourists. For example, Queen Victoria visited Cannes in the 1890s, as did the Russian Czar and, at the end of the century, the Riviera was about five times more expensive in real terms than it was during the 1950s and 1960s (Turner and Ash 1975: 69). However, another vital characteristic of the development of tourism during the nineteenth century was the institutionalisation of tourism and the beginnings of an identifiable tourism industry.

(ii) Thomas Cook

Although travel opportunities became available to increasing numbers of people with the rapid development of the rail network, greater wealth and a more formal approach to the provision of free time for those, other than the leisured classes, to whom work was a necessity, *there was no tradition of travel amongst the new Victorian middle classes* (Young 1973: 20). In other words, most people had little idea about how to overcome the potential problems of overseas travel, such as language barriers, exchanging money, knowing where to go and where to stay, and so on. What was needed to bring overseas travel within the reach of these potential tourists was an organisation that would provide all the necessary services and help, and that organisation was set up by Thomas Cook. Cook was not the first person to organise tours for the public; Sir Roland Hill is accredited with 'inventing' excursion trains and by 1840 such trips were not unusual. But, it was Thomas Cook who did more than anyone to revolutionise tourism, transforming it from the preserve of the privileged classes into an international industry and creating the package tour as one of the most popular forms of tourism (see Brendon 1991 for a complete history of Thomas Cook).

Thomas Cook's main business was printing but he was also a firm believer in temperance. It was as he was walking to a meeting in Leicester in 1841 that he first had the idea of organising a special train to take delegates to a temperance meeting in Loughborough and, on 5th July 1841, 570 travellers boarded a Midland Counties Railway Company train for the eleven mile journey from Leicester. Each had paid one shilling for the return journey but, more importantly, that short trip was the first step to Thomas Cook becoming a worldwide force in tourism. The success of the first trip soon led to other trips being organised, motivated more by Cook's altruism than a drive to be commercially successful (a characteristic that was to lead to a serious conflict with his son, John, who was more concerned with building a successful business). Soon he was running regular excursion trips. From 1848 tours were made in Scotland, with 5000 tourists each season using Cook's services and, in the same year, he took a group to Belvoir Castle. He first contemplated overseas tours in 1850 but the Great Exhibition of 1851, to which he conveyed a total of 165,000 visitors, delayed his ambitions. Indeed, it was not until 1855 that the first overseas Cook's tour occurred and, owing to resistance from the French railway authorities, the tour ended at Calais.

Throughout the 1850s most of Thomas Cook's business was in Britain. From 1862 onwards, following a successful excursion to Paris, his operations abroad began to expand. The first tour to America was undertaken in 1866 and John Cook joined his father as a partner in the business. Thereafter, the organisation's size and prestige expanded rapidly. In some parts of the world, the company began to wield much power and influence. For example, it had control of all passenger steamers on the Nile from 1880 onwards and a virtual monopoly of all tourism from India. The latter included pilgrim traffic to Mecca and the responsibility for the travel arrangements of Indian princes attending Queen Victoria's Jubilee celebrations. In 1872 the first Cook's Circular Notes were issued. These were similar to letters of credit used by travellers during the previous century but were much more flexible as they could be exchanged at any hotel or bank in the Cook's scheme. In effect, they were the ancestors of the modern traveller's cheque which was first developed in the 1890s by American Express. 1872 was also the year when Thomas Cook's first round-the-world tour was organised.

One hundred and fifty years on, Thomas Cook is still a major force in international tourism and the company continues the tradition of innovation started by its founder in the 1840s. For example, early in 1994 a revolutionary new information and booking system using a mobile travel kiosk was launched, reducing the need for customers to visit a travel agency and making information and booking services more widely available, thereby making it even easier to book a holiday. Indeed, the greatest contribution that Thomas Cook made to the development of tourism was just that; through his organisational skills, his eye for detail and his contacts he took the worry out of travelling and brought the opportunity of travel to millions. In other words, Thomas Cook was a major influence in the democratisation of travel and tourism, removing much of the mystique of overseas travel and undoubtedly influencing people's attitudes towards tourism. Not that he was without his critics. On the one hand, he set standards of comfort and convenience that brought tourism to the masses but, on the other hand, he could also be accused of diminishing the authentic travel experience (see Chapter Seven) and of creating, in the broader sense, the institutionalised mass tourist. However, whichever viewpoint is adopted, there is no doubting his contribution to what was, in effect, the socialisation of tourism.

Tourism in the twentieth century

In the early years of the twentieth century, the development of tourism continued along the course that had been set during the previous century. The English seaside resorts became increasingly popular and greater numbers of tourists travelled abroad. The upper classes spent their summers on the French Riviera but, for the majority, tourism was still very much based around the mass exodus to the seaside. Already there were signs of the internationalisation of tourism as large numbers of Americans crossed the Atlantic and it was estimated that, in the years preceding the First World War, up to 150,000 American tourists came to Europe each year. Travelling was becoming increasingly comfortable and easy. No passports were required in Europe and many countries were becoming increasingly reliant on tourism as a source of income.

New types of tourism were also becoming popular; skiing holidays in Switzerland had been introduced by Sir Henry Lunn in the 1880s (Holloway 1998: 26) and, domestically, the countryside was becoming a popular destination for walkers and cyclists. The first holiday camp, Cunningham's, on the Isle of Man, had already been established at the turn of the century (see Ward and Hardy 1986) and, generally, tourism expanded rapidly. The pattern of development also continued. Those with time and money went abroad, those with less of both went to the seaside resorts and, as more and more people were able to travel, once exclusive resorts became popularised.

(i) The inter-war years

Following the First World War the growth in tourism continued, although there were a number of important developments which had both a direct and indirect influence on the evolution of tourism. Passports were introduced but, in the Europe of the prosperous 1920s, this had little effect on the numbers of people participating in tourism. Trans-Atlantic travel, in particular, grew spectacularly as Americans visited Europe in their thousands, bringing with them styles and fashions that were to dominate the European social scene for a number of years. Tourism offered wealthier Americans the opportunity to escape from the restrictions of their own society, in particular Prohibition, and many spent their summers travelling in Europe or staying on the French Riviera.

It was on the Riviera during this period that sunbathing first became popular. Until the 1920s, most middle and upper class Europeans and Americans avoided exposing their skin to direct sunlight. Pale complexions were considered to be a symbol of higher social status, whereas darker, sun-tanned features were identified with lower, rural classes or black people. Thus, British women in colonial countries, such as India, maintained their strict dress code in order to avoid darkening their skin and, hence, being identified with local people. However, during the years immediately following the First World War, sunbathing became an increasingly popular leisure activity and the sun tan became highly fashionable. By the early 1920s, social life on the French Riviera centred on the beach and the sun tan became a symbol of wealth and of the leisure classes. A hot summer in 1928 finally made sunbathing more popular in England (see Turner and Ash 1975: 80) and with it emerged an entire new industry, supplying bathing costumes, sun tan lotion and so on. Achieving a sun tan soon became a major motivation for tourism. It was a visible sign of wealth and prestige in the major northern European urban centres, differentiating between those who could or could not afford a summer holiday by the Mediterranean, and, even with the onset of mass tourism in the 1950s and 1960s, the symbolic importance of the sun tan did not decline. Despite scares about skin cancer caused by excessive sunbathing, escaping for two weeks in the sun remains a primary motivation for many tourists.

During the 1920s and 1930s, travelling became much easier and more accessible for many people. Initially, the introduction of motorised public transport by road in the form of the charabanc, an early type of coach, improved accessibility and the ride on the charabanc became part of the attraction of a trip to the seaside. But, it was the motor car that did more than anything to improve personal mobility. International travel was still beyond the means of most people and the car provided a new found freedom for the middle classes who were no longer dependent on public transport services. Motoring became a popular leisure activity, new destinations, such as the countryside, became popular and, by the outbreak of the Second World War, there were some two million cars on the road in Britain. Inevitably, increasing car ownership and less reliance on public transport resulted in the beginning of the decline of the railways, a process that has continued throughout the twentieth century. By 1999 there were over 22 million cars on the roads in Britain and car travel is, without a doubt, the most popular mode of tourism transport, both domestically and abroad. (See Department of the Environment 1999). Indeed, the great majority of tourism within Europe is based upon the car and the opening of the Channel Tunnel in 1994 further increased opportunities for the British to travel independently by car on the Continent. Cycling also became more widespread in the early part of the twentieth century. The Cyclists' Touring Club was founded in 1878 and, coinciding with a trend towards healthy activities, the founding of organisations such as the Youth Hostels Association in 1930 and a growing interest in the outdoors, cycling became a popular form of tourism during the 1930s.

With regard to air travel, the First World War had stimulated research into aircraft design and, following improvements in safety, the first scheduled fare-paying passenger flight took place between London and Paris in August 1919 (Young 1973: 24). However, the service was not a success. Flights were relatively slow, noisy and usually very uncomfortable and the service was soon cancelled. Longer journeys required frequent stopovers for refuelling and aircraft tended to be unreliable. It was also, initially, a very expensive way of travelling compared with rail and sea transport and so it was not until after the Second World War (international conflict, once again, having provided the impetus for rapid advances in aircraft technology) that air travel became a viable and realistic mode of transport for large numbers of tourists. Nevertheless, by 1939 there were regular air services between all the major European cities and Pan Am was operating a regular trans-Atlantic service.

Another factor that stimulated the growth of tourism in the inter-war years was the increasing amount of free time that people were able to enjoy, in particular socially-sanctioned free time. Throughout the latter half of the nineteenth century, various pieces of legislation had improved working conditions and reduced the length of the working week. By the 1920s, most people worked a 48 hour week. A number of enlightened employers also gave their workers paid time off, but there was no legal requirement to do so. Throughout the early twentieth century there was increasing pressure for holidays with pay. By the mid-1920s up to seventeen per cent of the work force were receiving paid holidays, but it was not until 1938 that the Holidays With Pay Act was passed, giving all employees a legal right to enjoy paid holidays. With the onset of the Second World War it was to be some years before the legislation fully took effect but, since then, people's holiday entitlement has gradually increased. For example, in 1969, ninety-seven per cent of all full-time manual workers in Britain received two weeks paid holiday; by 1988, ninety-nine per cent received four weeks.

The introduction of holidays with pay firmly established the popularity of the British seaside resorts, confirming their virtual monopoly on British holidays; even by the late 1960s, three-quarters of all domestic holidays were spent at the seaside. Many resorts, such as Scarborough and Brighton, were at the height of their popularity and Blackpool at the end of the 1930s attracted some seven million visitors between June and September each year. Importantly, it was during this time that the family holiday became socially institutionalised.

(ii) The holiday camp

One of the major features of tourism in Britain during the inter-war years was the development of the holiday camp (for a history of the holiday camp, see Ward and Hardy 1986). Indeed, as a result of publicity and nostalgia embodied in television programmes such as *Hi-de-Hi!*, the holiday camp is probably the most widely recognised symbol of British tourism up until the late 1950s. The person normally accredited with the concept and development of holiday camps is Billy Butlin and, certainly, his vision, flair and entrepreneurial skill were significant factors in the growth and popularity of the camps. However, the idea of holiday camps dates back to the turn of the century. Cunningham's Young Men's Holiday Camp was established on the Isle of Man in 1897 and, by the time Butlin's first camp opened in 1936, about 60,000 visitors a year stayed at Cunningham's. The Caister Camp on the Norfolk coast was founded by John Fletcher Dodd in 1906 as a summer camp for socialists and, throughout the 1920s and early 1930s, a number of organisations set up camps around the coasts of Britain. Some, such as those run by the Holiday Fellowship, were run as non-profit schemes to provide the opportunity for healthy holidays and fresh air for young people. Others, such as camps organised by the Co-operative Holidays Association and the Workers Travel Association (by 1939, the second largest holiday organisation in Britain), provided holidays for workers and their families. A number of these early camps had rudimentary chalets for accommodation but in many others people slept in tents; indeed, *by 1939 it was estimated that a million and a half people spent their holidays under canvas and in camps of all kinds* (Ward and Hardy 1986: 42).

Butlin's first camp opened at Skegness on Easter Sunday 1936 and, compared with earlier holiday camps, it was relatively luxurious. It comprised 600 chalets, dining and recreation facilities, a swimming pool, a theatre, tennis courts, services such as child-minding and organised entertainment and, perhaps most important of all, modern sanitary arrangements, which had been noticeable by their absence at many other camps. Holidays, with full board and free entertainment, were offered at an all-in price, ranging from 35 shillings (£1.75) to £3 per week, depending on the season. The camp was an immediate success. His second camp opened in Clacton in 1938 and more followed after the Second World War, with other entrepreneurs such as Fred Pontin and Harry Warner building up their own holiday camps. By 1948, it was estimated that one in twenty holiday makers stayed at a Butlin's camp each year (Ward and Hardy 1986: 75) and throughout the 1950s and 1960s the camps remained popular. The Clacton camp was closed in 1983, along with those at Filey and Barry Island, and in recent years the remaining camps have been extensively modernised in order to compete with newer inland resorts, such as Center Parcs.

Holiday camps were successful for a number of reasons. They provided all-in holidays aimed at the middle, rather than working classes, they retained the atmosphere of a seaside holiday but with much better facilities than in the traditional hotel or boarding house, there was plenty to do, especially in poor weather, and they were bright, fantasy lands where 'campers' could forget about life outside and immerse themselves in a dream world. Their success also depended on people's willingness to be organised; holiday camps were developed when the great majority of the population first enjoyed paid holidays and, for many people, having free time was a novel experience. They were used to the routine of work and the culture of mass production and consumption and, thus, the regimented life of holiday camps reflected the broader social condition of the time. But, from the 1960s onwards, the popularity of holiday camps diminished. Their image as 'camps' became unfashionable and developments in tourism, in particular the growth in overseas holidays, provided competition with which the camps, in their original form, were unable to compete.

(iii) The development of mass tourism

The Second World War effectively put an end to the development of tourism for a number of years. However, the half century since the end of the war has been the most spectacular and, from a sociological point of view, the most significant in the history of tourism. Within the modern, Western world, international tourism has been transformed from a luxury enjoyed by a privileged minority into a leisure activity enjoyed by a large majority of the population and, as a social activity, tourism has become internalised. That is, it has become an accepted, or even expected, part of life, a necessity rather than a luxury, and a mass activity. For example, in 1950 there were approximately 25 million international arrivals, a figure which had risen to 616 million in 1997. (Recent estimates suggest that there will be 1.6 billion annual international arrivals by 2020!) If the number of people taking holidays in their own country is added to this (it is estimated that there are six times as many domestic tourists worldwide as international tourists), then the size and scale of tourism becomes apparent.

This remarkable and rapid growth in tourism since 1950 has resulted from the same three factors that have enabled the development of tourism from earliest times, namely, increases in time and money and technological advance, particularly in transport. Reference has already been made to the increasing amount of socially-sanctioned free time that most people in Britain enjoy, including holidays with pay and bank holidays. It is likely that the amount of time available for tourism will continue to increase as people retire earlier and live longer and as new forms of employment, such as job-sharing, become more widespread. It has also been forecast that, in the future, peoples' careers may be based on '35's'; thirty-five hours a week, thirty-five weeks a year and a thirty-five year working life.

Whether this is likely to occur is open to debate but there is no doubt that people will generally have greater amounts of free time in the future. Increasing wealth has also played a significant role in the growth of tourism. For example, real disposable income in Britain increased by 25 per cent between 1981 and 1988 and *it can be demonstrated that, historically, a growth of one per cent in incomes tends to be accompanied by a growth of rather over one per cent in travel* (Cleverdon 1982). Taken together, greater amounts of income and free time are most likely to result in an increase in the number of holidays that individuals take, rather than an increase in the number of people having holidays. Thus, although there has been an increase in the number of British tourists travelling abroad over the last decade, the volume of domestic tourism in Britain has remained level as a result of the increase in second and third holidays.

It is important to point out here that that the discussion so far has focused primarily on tourism development in Britain. Undoubtedly, the rapid growth in tourism and the factors that have facilitated that growth have been reflected in other countries, primarily in Europe and North America, but, as Shaw and Williams (1994: 23) point out, *this should not be taken to imply that global mass tourism has now arrived and that the populations of most countries are caught up in the whirl of international travel*. A closer examination of the international tourism data reveals, according to Shaw and Williams (1994: 23), three distinctive patterns of tourism flows (see also Vellas and Bécherel 1995: 13-23):

- *polarity*: international tourism is still largely dominated by the wealthy, industrialised world, with the major tourism flows being either between the more developed countries or from developed countries to developing countries. Interestingly, recent years have witnessed the emergence of newer destinations, such as Hungary, which are challenging this dominance, at least in terms of arrivals numbers. However, the economic benefits of international tourism are highly polarised, *with exchanges of money generated by tourism...[being]...predominantly North-North between a combination of industrialised and newly industrialised countries* (Vellas and Bécherel 1995: 21).

- *regionalisation*: not only is international tourism dominated by developed countries but it is also highly regionalised. The largest international movements of tourists occur within well defined regions, in particular within Europe. Other significant regions include north America, with major flows between Canada and the United States, the United States and the Caribbean, and the Japan and East Asia region.

- *European dominance*: the third major characteristic of international tourism is that it is largely concentrated within Europe and, indeed, has probably been so since the eighteenth century during the Grand Tour era. During the early 1960s Europe's share of world tourism peaked at over 70 per cent but, since then, it has gradually fallen and, by 1995, 59.68 per cent of world arrivals occurred within Europe (WTO 1997: 5). Nevertheless, it is Europe that, on a global scale, benefits most in terms of opportunities to participate in, and earnings from, tourism.

Together, these three characteristics of international tourist flows suggest that, whilst tourism may well have been a social victory (Krippendorf 1986) in wealthy, Western countries, the same cannot be said for many other parts of the world. This has significant implications for the potential contribution of tourism to social development in destination areas (see Chapter Eight).

To return to the evolution of tourism in the twentieth century, it is technological advance, the emergence of a sophisticated tourism industry and the development of the package tour that has done most to influence the rapid growth of international tourism. Following the end of the Second World War, the large number of surplus aircraft and, during the 1950s, the introduction of jet airliners, set the scene for the rapid expansion of the air transport industry in general and charter air travel in particular (see Holloway 1998: 32-35). As the large airlines bought new jets, smaller charter companies could buy cheap, second-hand aircraft to fly tourists to their holiday destinations and, working on the principle of economies of scale, the cost of international travel became almost as cheap as rail or road travel. The first person to operate a charter holiday flight was Vladimir Raitz who, in 1950, organised a trial trip to Corsica. He went on to build his business under the name of Horizon Holidays (now owned by Thomson's) and, following his success, a large number of other tour operators were established both in Britain and abroad.

Since that time, the package tourism industry has become increasingly sophisticated and diversified. Companies have integrated vertically and horizontally so that some tour operators own their own airline, their own chain of travel agents and, frequently, hotels in resorts. The scale of operations has increased enormously, with some twelve million passengers annually taking package holidays out of Britain, and the introduction of wide bodied jets and increasingly efficient aircraft has extended the package *pleasure periphery* (Turner and Ash 1975).

Whilst holidays to Spain, the Balearic Islands, Greece and other traditional package resorts continue to thrive, newer, more distant destinations now appear in the tour operators' brochures. For example, Mexico, the Seychelles, the West Indies, Thailand and Bali can all be visited on package tours, and at prices which would have been considered impossible a few years ago. The package product has also diversified. Cultural or sightseeing tours may be combined with more traditional beach holidays on 'two-centre' holidays, such as a week's sightseeing in Sri Lanka followed by a week on the Maldives, and some of the most remote areas of the world can now be visited on package tours.

A fuller examination of the development of tourism over the latter half of the twentieth century is beyond the scope of this chapter. Different destinations and countries around the world attract different types of tourists, offer different products and suffer different problems related to the growth of tourism. The important point, however, is that the development of tourism over the last fifty years or so has mirrored the pattern of development that has been evident throughout the historical evolution of tourism. In other words, since the earliest times when tourism emerged as an identifiable and distinct sphere of social activity, those destinations or types of travel which were once the exclusive preserve of the well-to-do or the higher social classes have, almost inevitably, become assimilated under the umbrella of mass tourism. The Grand Tour became popularised as the aristocracy were replaced by a middle class more intent on pleasure than learning, whilst both the spas and the seaside resorts soon lost their exclusivity. Similarly, the Mediterranean resorts which were once frequented by the royalty of Europe gradually became less exclusive, firstly with the influx of American tourists in the 1920s and 1930s and more recently as a popular summer destination for car-borne tourists from other European countries. Nowadays the more distant, exclusive destinations also attract the package tourists as international tourism has become geographically more democratic.

This process whereby exclusive destinations become caught in the popular, mass tourism net has been called the *aristocratic model* of tourism development (Thurot and Thurot 1983). Although some would argue that it is overly simplistic to explain the emergence and democratisation of tourism on the basis of *transport technology or the mechanistic process of successive class intrusion* (Towner 1996: 13), the process is, nevertheless, highly evident within the evolution of tourism. Moreover, it is a process which is also evident in many other forms of consumption, the desire to emulate being a powerful force in people's buying habits, and one which, certainly in the context of tourism, has accelerated in recent years. Up until the onset of modern, mass tourism, the exclusivity of a resort or a form of tourism was normally 'safe' for at least a generation but, *nowadays, the European upper middle class...has been caught up with by the lower classes within a period of ten years*

(Thurot and Thurot 1983). One example is the way in which mainstream package tour operators in Britain now offer cruise holidays. Once an exclusive form of tourism, the 'luxury' of cruising is now available to the masses at low prices.

The extent to which this model continues to influence the development of tourism in the future remains to be seen. The mass package holiday of the 1960s and 1970s is gradually being replaced by a more individual approach to tourism, with self-catering holidays, fly-drive packages and special interest holidays becoming more popular. This, in turn, can be seen as a response to changing customer demands and an emerging new tourism consumer culture (see Chapter Six). At the same time, a number of factors might influence the future of tourism. For example, if sunbathing became unfashionable owing to health concerns or, if technological progress brought electronic imagery, such as virtual reality, within the reach of most people, then the development of tourism may, in fact, go into reverse. Present trends indicate that, globally, tourism will become even more widespread, more democratised and viewed, increasingly, not as a luxury but as a right.

Three

Tourism, Modernity and

Postmodernity

Introduction

Tourism, in particular mass tourism, is frequently described as a phenomenon of modern society. It has been referred to as *the single largest peaceful movement of people across cultural* boundaries in history (Lett 1989: 276) and, certainly, tourism has expanded in both scale and scope throughout the twentieth century. Nowadays few, if any, parts of the world have not become tourist destinations – in 1997, some 15,000 tourists visited the Antarctic – and the overall number of people participating in tourism continues to grow.

In one sense tourism is a phenomenon of modern society because it is modern society that has provided both the means and the opportunity for people to participate in tourism. As described in the previous chapter, the rapid growth in participation in tourism and the ability to travel ever further to more remote or exotic destinations would simply not have occurred without the development of fast, efficient and economical forms of mass transportation, increasingly high levels of disposable income and the provision of socially-sanctioned free time, such as bank holidays and holidays-with-pay. At the same time, tourism is a product of modern society inasmuch as people now not only expect to take a holiday, but also frequently feel the need to do so. In other words, modern society motivates people to participate in tourism. Whether to simply escape from the pressures and stress of modern life or to seek authentic, satisfying and meaningful experiences elsewhere, people increasingly believe that the only way to survive in modern society is to regularly remove themselves from it, albeit on a temporary basis. Tourist motivation is considered in detail in Chapter Five but the point here is that, in short, tourism is both caused and sustained by modern society.

Yet, whilst there is much truth in this proposition, the relationship between the development of tourism and modern society is not so simple or clear cut as it may at first appear. That is, the link between technological advances in, for example, transport, information technology and financial services, increases in wealth and free time and the growth of tourism is universally accepted. But, these so-called enabling factors of tourism do not explain a whole host of other characteristics of modern tourism. For example, a variety of activities or forms of behaviour can, arguably, provide the same benefits as tourism, so why is it tourism, as opposed to other forms of leisure activity, that has become so widespread? Similarly, why has international tourism, over the space of less than half a century, been transformed from a luxury into a perceived 'necessity'? And, why have styles of tourism changed? For example, in 1986, beach hotel holidays accounted for 72 per cent of all early (that is, by December of the preceding year) holiday bookings out of the UK and beach self-catering holidays accounted for 17 per cent. By 1993, the proportion had changed to 38 per cent and 36 per cent respectively (McCarthy 1994). Other forms of tourism, such as heritage tourism, urban tourism and eco-tourism, are also becoming more popular, whilst some claim that, more generally, the traditional package holiday is being increasingly rejected in favour of more individualistic forms of tourism.

These questions in demand may be simply put down to changes in fashion, but changes in fashion may, in turn, be related, to changes in the nature of modern society itself. In other words, the developments and trends that have, and continue to, occur in tourism cannot be simply explained as resulting from the technological and other advances associated with the modernisation of society. It is surprising, therefore, that relatively little attention has been paid to the ways in which both the significance of tourism as a form of consumption and also styles of tourism may be influenced by *cultural* changes and developments in the tourist's home society and environment (Taylor 1994). Nevertheless, it is important to do so. Tourism, as a social activity, is central to the modern leisure experience and cannot, or should not, be considered in isolation from the wider cultural framework within which it occurs; as Urry (1990b: 23) confirms, *explaining the consumption of tourist services cannot be separated off from the social relations in which they are embedded.*

In particular, it is important to consider what is meant by the term 'modern society'. That is, a distinction must be drawn between modern society in a temporal or periodic sense (modern as opposed to old, pre-modern or traditional) and modern society in the cultural sense. When analysing and explaining the development of tourism as a modern phenomenon it is, generally, the former approach that is adopted. As we have already seen, the birth of tourism as we know it today occurred when society was undergoing a process of industrialisation. Rapid technological advances throughout the modern era, commencing with the development of the railways during the nineteenth century, followed by the introduction of the motor car and, latterly, developments in aircraft technology, have resulted in the opportunity to travel being more widely available. At the same time, the mass tourism industry has been able to spread its net ever wider around the world; more and more countries now lie within what has been called the *pleasure periphery* (Turner and Ash 1975) of modern, industrialised societies.

In order to understand fully the link between society and the development of tourism, in particular trends and changes in tourism practices rather tourism as an overall human activity, it is necessary to consider the nature or condition of modern societies. That is, modern, industrial societies are characterised by a combination of economic, political, social and cultural processes that together create a form of social life that sociologists call 'modernism'. These processes are constantly evolving and adapting according to the needs and demands of society so that, whereas modern in the temporal sense is a fixed state, modernity as a social condition is dynamic. It has been suggested that as modern societies become post-industrial, with their economies becoming increasingly dependent on the tertiary service sector, modernity is being replaced by the condition of postmodernity (see Harvey 1990).

The purpose of this chapter, therefore, is to introduce the concept of postmodernity and to examine the relationship between tourism and contemporary culture, in particular the way in which certain characteristics of postmodern society impact on tourism. Thus, it provides a broad picture or framework within which the more specific discussion of society's influence on the consumption of and motivation for tourism in the following chapters may be located. First, however, it is important to consider the *nature* of the relationship between tourism and culture, before examining the specific implications of contemporary culture for tourism.

Tourism and cultural change

It has long been recognised that a positive relationship exists between the consumption of tourism and the cultural characteristics of modern societies (Urry 1988; 1990a; 1994). In a simple sense, for example, for tourism as a social activity to occur on a widespread scale it must be socially or culturally sanctioned; there are many cases of societies where specific forms of tourism are encouraged or discouraged, or where different social groups are culturally permitted greater or less opportunity to participate in tourism. Indeed, as indicated in the preceding chapter, the evolution of leisure and tourism in most Western societies has, throughout history, been organised and managed as a means of sustaining preferred socio-cultural arrangements (Rojek 1993).

More specifically, an identifiable relationship has long existed between what may be described as the cultural condition of societies and the style or meaning of tourism, with transformations in the former almost invariably reflected in changes to the latter. For example, reference has already been made to the English Romanticism of the late eighteenth and early nineteenth centuries which not only changed people's attitudes towards rural environments, such as the Lake District undergoing a perceptual transformation from a region considered both unattractive and dangerous into one where *all is but peace, rusticity and happy poverty, in its neatest, most becoming attire* (Gray 1884: 226), but also set the tone for the touristic enjoyment of such areas. According to Harrison (1991: 21), for the Romantics *the only right and proper way to enjoy the countryside was to walk through these landscapes in solitude and contemplative mood and thereby to achieve a new sense of solace, consciousness and spiritual awareness.*

Arguably, this cultural shaping of attitudes towards rural areas, what Harrison describes as the *countryside aesthetic*, remains today a powerful influence on the style of rural tourism, particularly amongst middle-class urban visitors (see also Urry 1995: 211-229; Wilson 1992).

Similarly, other tourism practices reflect broader cultural change. The widespread practice of sunbathing, for example, originated from new fashions amongst the social élite on the French Riviera in the 1920s and the resultant desirability of a suntan (previously associated with lower social classes, such as outdoor manual labourers). So too has the changing role and style of the holiday camp mirrored broader cultural transformations, from the early, rudimentary camps such as Cunningham's, established on the Isle of Man in 1897, through the heyday of the collective entertainment of Butlin's, to the emergence of the more sophisticated holiday villages of the 1990s, such as Center Parcs and, most recently, Oasis Villages (see Ward and Hardy 1986).

Although there is widespread evidence of a relationship between tourism and culture, it has not always been the case that this relationship has taken the form of tourist practices directly reflecting culture and cultural change. Indeed, it has been suggested that, in addition to the reflective relationship exemplified above, there are three other possible forms of the tourism-culture relationship (Urry 1994). First, tourism and culture may be in opposition or develop in opposite directions; second, tourism may lead to or indicate future cultural change and, third, *that tourist practices simply are cultural, that is, they comprise signs, images, texts and discourse* (Urry 1994: 223). He goes on to argue that the relationship has changed over time. During the nineteenth century, tourism and culture were largely in opposition. Thus, contrasting with *the bourgeois culture with its concerts, museums, galleries, and so on* (Urry 1994: 234) tourism for the masses was centred on the rapid development of the seaside resorts. These places of *ritualised pleasure* (Shields 1991) were the embodiment of mass, low culture, set apart from the high culture of the bourgeoisie which included, in a touristic context, the romantic, 'serious' participation in rural tourism mentioned above.

During the twentieth century, up until the 1970s, the tourism-culture relationship gradually transformed to the extent that tourism practices came to reflect cultural change. That is, the emergence of a culture based upon mass production and mass consumption was reflected in the development of mass forms of tourism. Importantly, however, as a social activity tourism was still separate or differentiated from broader cultural change. In other words, although the Fordist production methods which were attached to tourism (see below), whether in the context of the holiday camp or the mass package, holiday business, mirrored the wider production/consumption system, tourism remained, at least for the masses, a separate, identifiable activity differentiated by time, location and behaviour from other activities and institutions.

Since the 1970s, it is argued, this differentiation between tourism and other practices has become less apparent. *Tourism is no longer a differentiated set of social practices with its and distinct rules, times and spaces* (Urry 1994: 234); rather, it has merged into other social activities such as shopping or watching television. Purchasing ethnic goods, such as South American wood-carvings or Indian clothing, from specialist shops, eating in Greek or Italian restaurants or simply watching one of the multitude of travel programmes on television are all examples of how tourism has diffused into everyday life. Many people are tourists most of the time and, in short, tourism has, simply, become cultural.

There are, then two broad stages in the relationship between tourism and the cultural condition of society. Throughout most of its development, tourism has been separated off from other social activities and institutions, reflecting the differentiation both within and between other social practices and institutions, such as social class, employment, or gender roles. Even tourism itself has been subject to differentiation; different resorts or types of holiday became associated with different social groups, whilst the emergence of mass tourism has been contrasted with the so-called 'lost art' of travel (Boorstin 1964). Thus, as we shall see shortly, until the latter part of the twentieth century, tourism reflected the modern period. However, as suggested above, tourism has now entered a second stage of development where it is less distinct from other social practices. It is has become de-differentiated (Lash 1990: 11) from other activities, reflecting the wider emergence of economic, political, social and cultural processes that have been collectively referred to as postmodernity.

It is this transformation of culture from a condition of modernity to postmodernity that, for two reasons, is of greatest relevance to the study of tourism. First, it is suggested by some that, as a result of the alleged transformation from a condition of modernity to postmodernity in many western societies, tourism practices have also become postmodern. In other words, the de-differentiation of tourism from other social activities, representing *the marriage of different, often intellectual, spheres of activity with tourism* (Munt 1994: 104), has brought about a variety of new, *postmodern tourisms* (Munt 1994: 104). These are discussed later in this chapter.

Second, the emergence of consumerism or consumer culture is considered by many to be a defining characteristic of postmodern cultures. That is, *consumption has been seen as epitomising this move into postmodernity* (Bocock 1993: 4). Tourism is, in a sense, consumed; tourists are *consumers, whose primary goal is the consumption of a tourism experience* (McKercher 1993). Therefore, it is also important here to consider the potential influence of postmodern consumer culture on the specific practice of the consumption of tourism. This issue is addressed in Chapter Six.

Before looking at the relationship between postmodern culture and tourism practices, it is first necessary to consider what is meant by the terms modernity and postmodernity and the evidence that suggests society is moving from the former condition to the latter.

From modernity to postmodernity

It is difficult to grasp the notion that society or, more specifically, the social and cultural character of life in modern society, is undergoing an identifiable process of transformation from one condition to another. Indeed, there is much debate amongst sociologists themselves as to whether modern society has moved beyond modernity and is now identified by a set of characteristics that may be amalgamated and described as the condition of postmodernity. As Urry (1990a: 83) states, *in some ways it is difficult to address the topic of postmodernism at all. It seems as though the signifier postmodern is free-floating, having few connections with anything real, no minimal shared meaning of any sort.*

Moreover, even if there exists agreement that society has undergone a cultural shift into a condition of postmodernity, there is a continuing debate as to what the term means. This debate, according to Hollinshead (1993), centres on a number of questions, including does postmodernity exist? Is it a cultural style, an historic period or an economic phase? Is it an on-going academic craze? Or is it a self-perpetuating, *self-validating discourse on the part of a whole host of individuals concerned about their own legitimate place in society*?

To answer these questions is beyond the scope of this chapter. However, what is certain is that many of the economic, political, social and cultural forms that characterise modernity have changed or are in a process of change. The extent to which these changes are inter-related and signify an identifiable and all-embracing development in the nature of contemporary society is arguable but, nevertheless, postmodernity is a term that can be usefully applied to the organisational and cultural condition of modern society in the late twentieth century.

The purpose here, then, is not to analyse the arguments for and against postmodernity (for example, see Harvey 1990; Lash 1990; Jameson 1984; Lyotard 1984; and, more generally, Hall *et al* 1992b). But, it is important to outline what is meant by postmodernity and to highlight common themes among its various definitions before considering the links between postmodern society and tourism. The problem remains that there is little agreement as to what postmodernity actually is. Generally postmodernity is seen to represent the end of the structured, organised and rational state of society. It signifies the replacement of *the dominance of an overarching belief in 'scientific' rationality and a unitary theory of progress* (Jary and Jary 1991: 487) by an emphasis on choice, a plurality of ideas and viewpoints, image and the ephemeral, and the *eclectic borrowing and mixing of images from other cultures* (Voase 1995).

In other words, postmodernity represents a departure from modernity or, as Bocock (1993: 78) puts it, *the term post-modern can be seen as an analytical category which serves to highlight certain features of socio-cultural life, features which contrast with those in the paired analytical category of the modern.* A logical starting point is to consider briefly modernity, or the modern condition, from which postmodernity has evolved.

(i)   Modernity

The emergence of modern societies in a temporal, periodic sense can be traced back to the Europe of the sixteenth and seventeenth centuries with successive agricultural, scientific and industrial revolutions. It was during this period that, rather than being dependent on and controlled by nature, societies were increasingly able to dominate their natural world to their own advantage. Thus, the advent of the modern era was dependent on technological advance and scientific knowledge and those increasingly few societies today which have yet to embrace or to come under the influence of modern technology are described as pre-modern, traditional or authentic (see Chapter Seven).

It was much later that modernity, *that distinct and unique form of social life which characterises modern societies* (Hall *et al.* 1992a: 2), became an identifiable social condition. Its origins lie in what is known as the Enlightenment Project, a period of intellectual thought dating back to the eighteenth century but the major tenets of which are reflected in modernist thought and culture. During an age when *the scientific domination of nature promised freedom from scarcity, want and the arbitrariness of natural calamity* (Harvey 1990:12), the Enlightenment thinkers envisaged a similar situation whereby society, through the accumulation and application of rational, scientifically-based knowledge, could be released from the constraints of irrational forms of thought, such as religion, superstition, myth, prejudice and ideology. Distancing

70

themselves from history and tradition, they foresaw the triumph of reason and objective, rational knowledge and, through scientific progress and social scientific knowledge, they sought *mental liberation and social betterment amongst humanity generally* (McLennan 1992: 330). In particular, the Enlightenment thinkers believed that all natural and social phenomena could be scientifically explained and, therefore, that there was only one solution to any problem, a position that was soon to be challenged. But, their support for scientific, technological and economic progress in pursuit of an improved human condition continued through to the height of modernity.

The real foundations of modernity were laid during the industrialisation and urbanisation of society during the nineteenth century, based upon the social and political institutions that evolved in the wake of rapid change. Five main processes, in particular, emerged to give modernity its identifying character:

(a) The development of political, secular systems and the concept of the nation-state, supported and sustained by large-scale bureaucratic systems which increasingly sought to organise, regulate and control social life.

(b) The growth and expansion of the capitalist economy based upon private ownership, leading to mass production and consumption and, internationally, the distinction between the industrialised, developed countries of the West and the rest of the world.

(c) The evolution of national and international society into a system determined by class, gender, race, occupation and wealth.

(d) The cultural transformation of societies from religious to secular and the emergence of popular forms of art, entertainment and music.

(e) The demise of individuality and development of the mass market with the public perceived as a homogeneous group with similar tastes and attitudes.

71

The major characteristic of modernity which emerged from the nineteenth century onwards was that virtually every aspect of society and social life became differentiated. Guided by the over-riding objective of human and technical progress, modernism eschewed history and tradition. The past, the present and the future became separated, the present providing the opportunity to work towards an assured, better future. Time itself became a resource and, whereas during the pre-modern, agricultural era leisure and work intermingled within social life, a distinction came to be made between work time and leisure time. As tourism developed as an identifiable, widespread leisure activity it became a differentiated, separate sphere of social life with its own distinct time. It was also differentiated by location; work and home life was in the towns, tourism took place at the seaside. Urbanisation led to the differentiation between the countryside and towns and cities and their associated social systems, so much so that modernism largely came to be associated with the structure and order of urban society. For example, the inner-city tower-block architecture of the post-war period is often considered to be the most visible physical representation of modernity. Employment and work practices in capitalist industry resulted in differentiation between classes and occupation, the family became differentiated by gender roles; even nature and society became differentiated. Internationally, distinctions emerged between nation-states, between East and West, between North and South. In short, modernity *involves 'structural differentiation', the separate development of a number of institutional and normative spheres, of the economy, the family, the state, science, morality, and an aesthetic realm* (Urry 1990a: 84).

This differentiation, according to Urry, is both horizontal, representing distinctions between different institutions, roles, activities, and so on, and vertical, as in differentiations within different spheres of social life. In other words, not only is there a distinction between, say, tourism and other forms of leisure activity but also, in modernist culture, a distinction between travel and (mass) tourism. Similarly, distinctions exist between classical and popular music and within other art forms, and between mass and élite production and consumption. In recent years, however, this horizontal and vertical differentiation has become less distinct; society has embarked on a process of *de-differentiation* (see Lash 1990: 11), the fundamental trait of postmodernity.

(ii) Postmodernity

Although much of the literature on postmodernity is concerned specifically with changes in cultural styles in literature, films, architecture and art, during the latter half of the twentieth century a number of changes in society, its institutions and its direction indicate that a much more fundamental and widespread social movement is underway. In other words, the postmodern style of, for example, architecture which incorporates classical or traditional styles is symptomatic of a much deeper rooted shift in both the structure of society as a whole and its values and culture. Whether this shift has been towards a new, distinctive social and cultural experience is open to debate, yet there is little doubt that many of the ideas, objectives and cultural representations of modernity have been rejected and replaced by a new set identifying characteristics. Thus, postmodernity is, in effect, *a very loose term used to describe the new aesthetic, cultural and intellectual forms and practices which are emerging in the 1980s and 1990s* (Thompson 1992: 226).

Postmodernity can be considered from a variety of viewpoints. For example, in terms of the development of society, the modernist project of progress and change which rejected history and tradition has been replaced by a new concern for conserving, representing or recreating the past. Whether as a particular style of interior decoration, a style of building or as a tourism product in the form of heritage attractions, the past is being merged into the postmodern present. In other words, the past and the present have become de-differentiated as society appears to be gaining a preference for stability rather than change. Similarly, the distinction between society and nature has become de-differentiated as it has become increasingly recognised, under the aegis of the environmental movement, that, in order to survive, society must co-exist with rather than dominate nature.

Other structural differentiations, both horizontal and vertical, have also been reversed or removed. For example, class distinctions and boundaries are becoming less clear cut and bear more relation to family background and tradition as opposed to wealth or occupation. The emergence of multinational corporations and the interdependence of economies and organisations across international borders has diminished the distinct status of the nation-state whilst the increasingly cosmopolitan character of many societies has led to a de-differentiation of race, religion and culture. Thus, it is claimed that in Sydney it is possible to eat out at a culturally different restaurant every night for a year! Paradoxically, the globalisation of society has also served to heighten the awareness of how various societies and peoples are culturally different, in some cases leading to a resurgence of nationalism and fundamentalism. *Postmodernism is...*[also]*...anti-hierarchical* (Urry 1990a: 85); distinctions between high and low culture are disappearing as classical music becomes popular (for example, the music played by the violinist Vanessa Mae or, in 1994, the Gregorian chants performed by the monks of the Benedictine monastery of Santo Domingo de Silos in Spain have both appeared in the Top 20 album charts), as art and commerce merge and, through techniques such as audience participation, contemplation of art becomes entertainment.

Further evidence of de-differentiation is to be found in the way in which reality is represented. That is, a major distinction between the cultures of modernity and postmodernity is that *modernism conceives of representation as being problematic whereas postmodernism problemises reality* (Lash 1990: 13). Modernity was concerned with reality and fact based upon logical and scientific explanation; representations of reality, through the arts, advertising and the news media, reflected the importance placed on reality. Under postmodernity, however, it is claimed that there is a diminishing distinction between reality and representations of reality. Such has been the growth in the production of images, representations and simulations, exacerbated by the explosion in electronic imaging, such as television, video, films and home computers, that image is merging into reality. In some instances, such as computer games, representations and simulations replace reality. Social life in general and social identity in particular have become dependent on image; for example, styles and fashions represented in the media are translated into reality by an increasingly image conscious consumer society. The result is that postmodern society is dominated by image, by pastiche and by reproductions that lack depth and substance. It has become a *world of sign and spectacle... in which there is no real originality... Everything is a copy, or a text upon a text, where what is fake seems more real than real* (Urry 1990a: 85).

There are number of identifying characteristics which indicate that, socially and culturally, modern society is evolving from a condition of modernity into a new state that may be described as postmodernity. Not all modern societies are becoming, or have become, postmodern and some may be more or less postmodern than others. For example, America may be described as more postmodern than the majority of, if not all, European countries. Furthermore, different areas or regions within societies may possess cultural attributes which, to a greater or lesser extent, resemble those proposed by postmodernists, whilst not all aspects of culture within society need to be postmodern. Nevertheless, modern societies are increasingly adopting the characteristics of postmodernity, these being:

(a) a plurality of viewpoints and ideas, replacing the modernist concept of a uniform, mass society, and a corresponding rejection of all-embracing sociological theories. *The idea that all groups have a right to speak for themselves, in their own voice, and have that voice accepted as authentic and legitimate is essential to the pluralistic stance of postmodernity* (Harvey 1990: 48).

(b) the fusion or de-differentiation of distinct areas of social and cultural activity and structure and the unification of popular, mass consumer culture with 'high' culture, particularly in the commercial appropriation of culture (Zukin 1990).

(c) lifestyles which are increasingly dominated by spectacle, image, visual media and what has been called the 'three minute culture', resulting in ephemerality and a concentration on surface appearance rather than cultural depth.

75

(d) the merging of the past into the present and a preference for stability, implying a condition of discontinuity and a lack of historical progression (even though, paradoxically, postmodernity is considered to be the next stage in society's development after pre-modern and modern). *Postmodernity abandons all sense of historical continuity and memory, while simultaneously developing an incredible ability to plunder history and absorb whatever it finds there as some aspect of the present* (Harvey 1990: 54).

(e) the breaking down of traditional social structures and the emergence of new groupings and movements, such as conservation groups, political groups, New Age travellers, women's associations, special interest groups and so on which cross over ethnic, class, occupational and religious boundaries.

(f) identity formation through consumption. *Under modern conditions, work roles in production processes were defined as being central for identity, which is in contrast with consumption patterns of action being posited as central to post-modern identity construction* (Bocock 1993: 79).

There are many other elements and characteristics of contemporary society that theorists claim to be indicative of a move into postmodernity. At the same time, there are others who completely reject the notion of postmodernity, either as a cultural paradigm or as a new social and cultural epoch, writing it off simply as a term used to describe developments in society and culture that depart from the sense of order, rationality, cohesion and uniformity that typified modernity. Whichever viewpoint is adopted, a number of fundamental changes are occurring in society which may have a corresponding effect on tourism.

Postmodernity and tourism

Tourism, according to Urry (1990a: 87), is *prefiguratively postmodern because of its particular combination of the visual, the aesthetic, and the popular*. In other words, certain characteristics of postmodernity have always been identifiable in tourism, in particular the emphasis on spectacle and entertainment. For example, the English seaside resorts of the late nineteenth and early twentieth centuries, through to the heyday of holiday camps in the 1950s (see Ward and Hardy 1986), vied for business by offering the best entertainment, the longest pier, the brightest lights or the most exciting funfair. Blackpool, with its tower, ballrooms, piers, promenade, zoo, illuminations, gardens and Pleasure Beach was, perhaps, the most postmodern resort of all, offering a world of image, illusion and fantasy in contrast to the reality of social life in the northern industrial towns and cities. Importantly, the social life of the tourists in the seaside resorts, thriving on spectacle and mass entertainment, made little or no distinction between art, culture and society; the holiday experience was characterised by the de-differentiation that has come to identify postmodernity.

It is upon this concept of tourism as the consumption of fantasy, images or representations of reality, rather than reality itself, that much of the relevant literature remains focused. For example, as a result of the illusory, contrived and image-based nature of contemporary society, tourists seek out and, according to Boorstin (1964), are satisfied with 'pseudo-events' and contrived spectacles. They have become the *army of semioticians* (Culler 1981), looking for signs or images of cultural practices and attractions rather than seeking to understand their true meaning. The local tourism industry is obliged to satisfy this demand and, as tourist experiences become increasingly removed from reality, tourism develops into a *closed, self-perpetuating system of illusions* (Cohen 1988). In the extreme, these illusions or representations may be simulacra, or copies for which no original exists, and tourists become travellers in 'hyper-reality' (Eco 1995). One example of this is the successful promotion of Santa Claus as a tourist attraction in Lapland (Pretes 1995), whilst the Disney theme parks are frequently cited as the epitome of the postmodern tourism experience (Munt 1994).

Similarly, MacCannell (1989) argues that tourists do, in fact, seek authenticity, yet are frustrated by representations of authenticity being staged for their benefit. Thus, reality is constructed and tourists consume images of reality (Harkin 1995; Hughes 1995), although it has been suggested that the search for authentic experiences need not necessarily end in frustration or failure. Different tourists have different motivations and expectations and the experience of reality results from a form of negotiation between the tourist and the tourism setting (Pearce and Moscardo 1986). Much may also depend on the way in which images of reality are presented to tourists through advertising (Silver 1993).

Many of these issues are addressed in greater detail in subsequent chapters. Of concern here, however, is the way in which postmodern culture has influenced tourism as a particular sphere of social activity. That is, even though tourism has long displayed some of the characteristics of postmodernity, that postmodernity has, until recent times, been contextualised by tourism. In other words, whilst on holiday the social condition of tourists was essentially postmodern, yet tourism remained a distinct social activity, separate and differentiated from normal, modern, day-to-day social life. Specific periods of time were set aside for tourism, such as bank holidays and the annual week or fortnight's holiday, and tourism occurred in distinct places, such as the seaside or the countryside. Thus, tourism, both temporally and spatially, provided a contrast to normal life; indeed, it was, and still is, that contrast which is the major attraction of tourism.

To a large extent the contrast or differentiation between tourism as a separate and identifiable sphere of social activity has diminished. Tourism has become de-differentiated from, or merged with, other cultural and social activities to the extent that it may be suggested that most people are tourists most of the time. This can be better explained by considering a number of different types of tourism which can be related to the cultural transformation of contemporary society. These 'postmodern tourisms' result primarily from the de-differentiation of tourism place and tourism time, and from the merging of past and present manifested in the nostalgic yearning to experience heritage and authenticity (in the historic or pre-modern sense).

(i)   Tourism Place

Traditionally, people have travelled away from their place of residence and work in order to participate in tourism, a process still typical of much contemporary tourism. This relocation is not purely in the simple sense of moving from one place to another, from the city to the seaside or from one country to another. It also involves a change of social and cultural environment from, for example, the urban environment (signifying work, constraint, normality) to the holiday environment (signifying fun, escape, relaxation and so on). Throughout the modern era, the popularity of the traditional seaside resorts may have waned in favour of an ever increasing choice of different and more distant overseas destinations, but the basic formula has remained the same. More recently, new tourism destinations and attractions have emerged which indicate that the tourism place, where people participate in tourism, has become increasingly de-differentiated from the normal, day-to-day social place and, implicitly, the need for a change of environment has diminished.

A primary example of this 'postmodernisation' of tourist place is the development of urban tourism. If the residents of Bradford in the early 1900s had been able somehow to see into the future, they would have no doubt been amazed to discover that, in the 1990s, about six million people each year choose to visit their city as tourists! Virtually every major town and city in the UK now promotes itself as a tourist destination, frequently basing their tourism product on heritage which is a major manifestation of postmodern tourism. The important point is that there no longer needs to be a contrast between tourism place and normal work/residence place. People can be tourists in their own town as the social activity of tourism itself becomes entwined with other social and cultural activities. Factories and other workplaces, both historical and modern, have become tourist attractions, whilst the development of new complexes which permit a variety of social activities literally under one roof has further spread the location and diversity of tourist place into the urban area. Shopping malls, in particular, have served to de-differentiate between activities such as shopping, eating, going to the cinema and other forms of entertainment; Urry (1990a: 147) cites the West Edmonton Mall in Canada which, in 1987, attracted over nine million visitors, making it the third most popular tourist attraction in North America after Disneyland and Disney World.

The best British example of the shopping centre as a tourist attraction is the Metrocentre in Gateshead. Along with some three miles of shopping malls, a multi-screen cinema, restaurants and an indoor fairground, it includes a number of themed areas, such as the Mediterranean village where restaurants and cafés are designed in Greek and Italian styles. Thus, an attempt has been made to represent overseas cultures and styles in an artificially created tourist place; image and fantasy have replaced reality, a situation that has been taken to its extreme by the development of inland resorts, such as the Center Parc complexes. Here, simulation has been superimposed on reality in the ultimate manifestation of the de-differentiated, postmodern tourist place, an artificially created 'tropical' environment built in the normal, traditionally non-tourism place. Thus, inland villages represent the quintessential postmodern tourism place.

(ii) Tourism Time

As tourism has increasingly merged with other social and cultural activities, so too has the time spent being a tourist become less distinct from other time, such as work time and shopping time. Indeed, shopping, eating out, going to the theatre and participating in sports or hobbies have, in many instances, become tourist activities. For example, a weekend city-break may include the traditional activities of sightseeing and staying in a hotel, but shopping and visiting the theatre or cinema are also likely. Also, the time made available for tourism has also increased, as has the definition of what tourism time is. Thus, tourism is no longer restricted to the annual holiday; weekend breaks, additional short holidays, day and even half-day trips are now considered to be tourism time.

Nor does an individual have to leave home to be a tourist. As discussed in Chapter Five, the tourism experience does not start and end with the physical departure from and return to the home environment. Anticipation and daydreaming in the planning process and remembering or reminiscing after the holiday are equally part of the tourism experience but, in the context of postmodern culture, such is the bombardment of images of other cultures, peoples and places presented by the media, whether incidentally or in specialist television programmes and newspaper and magazine articles, that armchair tourism has become a reality. The future development of electronic imaging technology, particularly in the field of virtual reality, will ensure that people can become tourists whenever they desire and without ever having to leave there own homes.

Additionally, the plurality and multi-ethnicity of many modern societies, evidenced by the cultural diversity of restaurants, shops and entertainment in many towns and cities, means that, consciously or subconsciously, people are tourists for much of the time.

(iii)   Time compression and tourism

One of the main characteristics of postmodernity is the merging of different time periods. Postmodernists look to the past as a sign of stability, and symbols of the past are reconstructed or represented in the present. Styles of architecture, interior design and clothing fashions are the most common examples where the past is visually represented in the present, but tourism is also a sphere of social activity where the past, and the future, become compressed into the present. Moreover, postmodernity's fondness for pastiche and image is particularly evident within the context of tourism.

There are two areas where the past, or representations of the past, influence tourism. Firstly, the enormous growth in the heritage industry (see Chapter Seven) and the ways in which the past is represented are indicative the attraction of nostalgia as a tourist attraction. *Postmodernism and the heritage industry are linked, in that they both conspire to create a shallow screen that intervenes between our present lives, and our history* (Hewison 1987: 135). The past is brought into the present and is put on display through a variety of modern interpretative techniques, such as videos, the re-creation of noises and smells and live re-enactments, which represent the past, not as it was but as we wish to see it. History thus becomes a commodity, a tourist attraction based upon visual spectacle that is devoid of any true analysis of the past, a representation that bears little, if any, resemblance to reality. *The postmodern past is one where anything is possible, where fantasy is potentially as real as history because history as heritage dulls our ability to appreciate the development of people and places through time* (Walsh 1992: 113). In short, tourism based upon heritage is fundamentally postmodern (see Herbert 1995 for a more complete analysis of tourism and heritage).

The second way in which a relationship exists between the postmodern compression of the past into the present and tourism is linked to the issue of tourist experiences and the search for authenticity. If true authenticity is seen to lie in other times and places (that is, in destinations or countries that have yet to adopt the characteristics of modern, Western societies), then tourism that is motivated by the desire to experience cultures that are essentially pre-modern is an attempt to merge the past into the present. Tourists who travel to developing countries superimpose different, past cultures onto their own, modern experience; in effect, they compress the past into their own present. It is, however, an unreal past. Just as heritage presents a rose-tinted version of history, so too do tourists in many destinations experience a sanitised experience of local, historical culture. They experience visual representations, a romanticised version that is confirmed by the images reproduced in the media, that in many cases bears little resemblance to the reality of life in the countries being visited. It is famous sights, colourful festivals, exotic food and the promise of adventure that sells tourism, not images of poverty, starvation, illness and other problems that beset many developing countries. This has important implications for the future development of tourism, particularly with respect to the way in which many destinations are permitted to represent themselves (to become modern), in a world that, some would argue, is transforming into a global village.

Tourism and the global village

It is frequently stated that the world is getting smaller, that the world is becoming a global village and that, internationally, society is undergoing a process of globalisation. *'Globalisation' has become a widely used term within media, business, financial and intellectual circles, reflecting a fairly widespread perception that modern communications technology has shrunk the globe* (McGrew 1992: 65). Information technology that allows us to see history in the making and to communicate with people on the other side of the world at the touch of a button, transport technology that has brought distant countries ever closer in terms of travel time and opened up the whole world to international tourism, twenty-four hour dealings on the world's financial markets and a whole host of other factors have led to the impression that, in a physical sense, the world is, indeed, becoming smaller.

But globalisation is concerned with rather more than the increasing speed and ease of international travel and communication. It is about a world where there is greater inter-dependence between nation-states; where the activities and influence of political, economic, industrial, religious and environmental organisations transcend national boundaries; where the events in one country can have serious and immediate effects on another country far away; where there has been a significant migration of people; above all, where there is increasing recognition that 'spaceship earth' is one world shared by a huge diversity of peoples with the potential to develop into the first global civilisation (see Perlmutter 1991).

There is little doubt that globalisation is an identifiable process. For example, the demands made upon the United Nations as a peace keeping force, the expansion of multinational corporations, the attention paid to international problems, such as drug production and smuggling, pollution and international aid, the inter-dependency of the world's financial markets, the world-wide impact of political instability, terrorist atrocities or conflicts, such as the Gulf War in 1991, on international tourism, and the internationalisation of communities based upon religious, ethnic and cultural factors all point to the dissolving of national boundaries. Tourism itself has undoubtedly contributed to, and is affected by, the process of globalisation. Increasing knowledge and understanding of different nationalities and cultures has broadened people's horizons whilst the internationalisation of many countries' populations has undoubtedly led to a significant increase in tourism.

As to the cause of globalisation, there is less agreement. It is variously attributed to technological advance, the development of a world economy, political factors, or a combination of all three (see McGrew 1992). Equally, there is disagreement as to the longer term consequences of globalisation, although it is generally accepted that it will not be a smooth, harmonious process. In particular, the greater uniformity, integration and homogeneity of society that some envisage in the global village of the future is likely to be countered by efforts to retain national or local control and identity. For example, the move towards European union has served to highlight national differences, whilst pluralistic societies emphasise cultural and religious differences. Also, as discussed in Chapter Ten, tourism can both increase and decrease the gulf between different nation-states. But, a number of links can be identified between globalisation and tourism.

(a) One of the major characteristics (and causes) of globalisation has been the rapid advance in information technology. Tourists now have access to information and images of virtually every destination in the world, which may be combined with visual images on the television (for example, 'reality' images, such as news programmes, specialist travel programmes and nature programmes, or representational images, such as the Australia of *Neighbours* or the California of *Baywatch*) and in other media. As a result, tourists demand greater choice and variety and are able to make better informed decisions. At the same time, the tourist industry is more rapidly susceptible to localised problems reported on the world stage. For example, the activities of terrorist groups or threats of muggings and other crimes can lead to rapid cancellations of holiday bookings.

(b) The continuing globalisation of the international economy has a number of characteristics, in particular the greater inter-dependency of nation-states and the ability of one country's financial policies to have an impact on the economies of other nation-states. Indeed, such is the extent of international financial dependency that some people question whether the concept of the nation-state as a separate, identifiable form of society is still applicable at the beginning of the new millennium. Of equal importance has been the collapse of the centrally planned economies and the emergence of the free market in the former Eastern Bloc countries, which has signalled the advent of a truly worldwide capitalist economy and the gradual post-industrialisation of the advanced, Western economies. The latter has been matched by the industrialisation of a number of developing countries, in particular in the Far East, which means that, in a sense, the capitalist system which was once limited to individual nation-states has emerged as a worldwide economic phenomenon. This is part of what has been described as the age of *disorganised capitalism* (Lash and Urry 1987). The implication for tourism is that international tourism will continue to increase but with much of the growth accounted for by tourism from newly industrialised nations and also from those countries whose economies have been released from central control. For example, the Cyprus Tourist Organisation signed an agreement with its Russian counterpart in March 1994 as the first step towards the development of charter package tourism to the island. By 1997, some seven per cent of arrivals to the island were from Russia.

(c) It is generally accepted that globalisation is leading towards greater cultural homogeneity amongst nation states. For example, it is not unusual to see younger local people in many developing countries adopting the Western dress code of jeans, T-shirts and baseball caps, whilst the spread and popularity of symbols of American culture, such as McDonald's, is testament to the increasing uniformity of the world. This homogeneity, referred to by one commentator as the *McDonaldisation of Society* (Ritzer 1996) is exacerbated to an extent by tourism, although the activities of multinational corporations and worldwide communication have done more to spread Western culture around the globe. Cultural homogenisation may be linked to tourism in contrasting ways. On the one hand, it may lead to an increase in tourism as countries which have become Westernised appear 'safer' to potential tourists whilst, on the other hand, increasing cultural homogeneity may reduce the attraction of some destinations. In the latter case, it will be necessary for resorts and destinations to improve the quality of their tourism product in order to compete against other, similar destinations. Such a situation already exists around the Mediterranean coastal resorts where, for example, in the late 1980s, Turkey capitalised on the poor image of the Spanish resorts. Efforts by the Spanish to improve the quality of their destinations have now succeeded in returning Spain to its position as the most popular European tourist destination.

(d) The international tourism industry is becoming increasingly dominated by large, multinational corporations (MNCs). Both vertical and horizontal integration (see Holloway 1994:73-77) within the industry has resulted in the creation of large organisations with operations in many countries and which own or control, through management agreements and franchises, many, if not all, elements of a tourism 'package'. Thus, it is not unusual to book a holiday, travel to the destination, stay in accommodation and go on organised tours with different companies that are all owned by one parent company. Deregulation of the airlines and a number of other factors will continue to lead to the domination of the industry by a few major 'players', with the result that tourists, smaller businesses and even some entire tourist destinations will be increasingly at the mercy of the large MNCs. For example, Thomson's controls some forty per cent of all tourism into The Gambia, a situation that seriously weakens the country's ability to determine the future of its own tourism industry.

Tourism, post-Fordism and post-industrialism

Modern society and the more general characteristics of modernity are inextricably linked to the industrialisation of society. The nineteenth century modernist project of progress and economic growth, based upon the control and domination of nature and the resulting transformation of natural, raw materials into tangible and saleable commodities, was firmly rooted in the development of industrial processes and systems. These processes, in turn, led to the rapid urbanisation of Western societies and the corresponding evolution of social structures and institutions which came to represent the differentiated condition of modern society.

During the first half of the twentieth century modern industrial methods of mass production dominated Western economies but, more recently, there has been a recognisable shift towards new forms of production and consumption which reflect certain characteristics of postmodern society. This shift is marked by a growth in the tertiary service sector rather than in manufacturing industries, and a reorganisation of economic processes based upon flexible production. However, the new, post-industrial age has signalled, in particular, the end of the organised, rigid socio-economic structures of modernity and the advent of what has been termed post-Fordism.

Following the pioneering work of Henry Ford in developing mass production techniques for the manufacture of motor cars, the term Fordism has been used to describe both the system of mass production and the resultant mass consumption of the modern industrial era. Fordism was based on four main principles which became applicable to the production of most mass-produced goods (see Murray 1989). Firstly, all products were standardised, which meant that, in turn, each part and task involved in production could also be standardised. Following from this, certain, standardised tasks could be undertaken by machines. Thirdly, those tasks which could not be relegated to machines were performed by workers who concentrated on one particular task. Finally, the assembly line system introduced greater efficiency by bringing the task to the worker rather than *vice versa*. The main characteristic of mass production was high set-up costs but low unit costs and, overall, its success depended on, amongst other things, economies of scale, long runs of standardised products, a willing workforce and, most importantly, a mass market that would accept mass produced, standardised products.

A similar, but more simple, process is identifiable in the development of mass tourism and, in particular, the package holiday. The product, the holiday, is 'manufactured' by tour operators using the standard components of transport, accommodation and attractions. Each component part is further standardised by, for example, providing one-class, charter air travel and a minimum choice of basic meals in hotels. Unit costs (that is the cost of the holiday) are minimised by high levels of 'production' and are ensured by techniques such as the block booking of hotel rooms and fitting a greater number of seats into aeroplanes used for charter flights than would normally be found on scheduled flights (see Yale 1995). Equally, as with all forms of mass production, the continued success of the mass, package holiday is dependent on the acceptance of the product by the consumer. In other words, tour operators are only able to sell cheap, mass produced package holidays to a large number of tourists if the tourists themselves are willing to accept the lack of choice, the impersonal service, basic standards of food and accommodation, and cramped transport. (Indeed, a common criticism of package holiday tourism is that the tourist is frequently treated more like a unit of production than as a customer!). Once an element of choice or a demand for non-standard products enters the system, then the basis of mass production is undermined; the principles of Fordism no longer apply.

Since the late 1960s Fordist methods of mass production in general have been challenged by both workers and consumers alike and some have suggested that modern societies have entered the era of post-Fordism, an age where the consumer has begun to dictate, rather than accept, what is produced. In other words, the relationship between production and consumption has undergone a fundamental transformation (see Featherstone 1990, 1991). In the Fordist era, the role of production was dominant and, in the context of tourism, the producers of tourism were largely able to control the development and style of the mass consumption of tourism. More recently, however, consumers have adopted the dominant position; production methods have become more flexible as manufacturers, aided by advanced production technology and improved information systems, have had to become responsive to more rapid changes in consumer demand. Consumers themselves have become more quality conscious and demand a greater variety of products and styles, whilst products have a shorter 'life' as fashions change according to the image portrayed in the media. Many changes in demand are related to surface appearance; the basic product remains the same but the demand for colour, style or accessories changes. For example, the success of the clothes manufacturer Benetton is largely based on the company's ability to react quickly to changes in fashion colours, producing the same basic garments but in each year's new colours. Additionally, manufacturers have had to become more aware of different specialised and niche markets; the mass market approach has been replaced by market segmentation and the need for a variety of market research techniques.

Overall, the increasingly dominant role of the consumer and the growing demand for individualistic, niche products is indicative of the emergence of postmodern culture, a significant characteristic of which is, as we have seen, the growth of consumer culture. Chapter Six considers this topic in more detail but it is interesting to point out here that, within the context of tourism, the transformation from a Fordist to a post-Fordist system of production and consumption is, arguably, less marked than in other areas. It is frequently forecast that tourists are becoming more quality conscious and are demanding more specialised, tailor-made forms of holiday and travel experience (for example, see Lickorish 1990; Poon 1993) and, certainly, there is an ever-increasing variety of tourism products on offer. Newer, more distant destinations are being added to the range of package holidays offered by tour operators and different types of holidays, from adventure trips in the more exotic or remote regions of the world to winter-sun holidays for the older generations, are being supplied by specialist operators. At the same time, new products and attractions have been developed to satisfy the demands of an increasingly tourism and leisure oriented public whilst many popular overseas destinations, such as Spain and Cyprus, have recognised the importance of improving standards and quality to maintain market share. Nevertheless, recent experience, at least in Britain, demonstrates that the original Fordist-type basis of the package holiday remains as popular as ever. Early in 1994 a discounting campaign mounted by major tour operators and travel agents resulted in a level of bookings which was some forty per cent up on the same period in 1993, the implication being that price is still the dominant factor in mass market holiday purchasing. Similarly, it was reported in April 1994 that Britannia, Thomson's charter airline, was to increase the number of seats on its long-haul Boeing 767 flights, sacrificing passenger comfort for cheaper holidays (Atkins 1994). Moreover, recent evidence suggests little has changed. Although late discounting has been replaced by early-booking discounts, the major selling 'tool' remains price. Similarly, charter airlines continue to maximise the number of seas on their aeroplanes, even on long-haul flights, applying mass-production techniques to make exotic destinations, such as the Dominican Republic, more affordable to the mass, package tourist. Therefore, mass tour operators in Britain appear to be resisting the trend towards a consumer-oriented industry, although this is, perhaps, evidence of the effects of post-industrialisation.

Rather than looking at changes in the manufacturing and consumption process in particular, the concept of post-industrialisation is concerned with the transformation of modern economies in general, the main proposition being that modern, industrial societies are becoming increasingly dominated by service economies. Within service economies, both the kinds of work that people do and traditional social structures based upon occupation have fundamentally altered. Manual jobs have been replaced by machines and some would argue that the expansion of the service sector has led to jobs which involve creativity, social interaction and the delivery of a service rather than the production of an inanimate object, jobs which are, therefore, more satisfying and worthwhile. Others would argue that, although the nature of work has changed, resulting in a less clear distinction between the traditional working class and an expanding middle class, new social distinctions are appearing. In a postmodern society that is increasingly dominated by information technology and communication, power resides with those who have access to and use of information; in conflict theory, the capitalists (the owners of the production process) have been replaced by the bureaucrats, but the relative position of the workers remains unaltered.

Whichever viewpoint is adopted, the evidence suggests that, in the case of tourism, there is a move towards the provision of specialist, niche market products and an expansion in both the range and quality of holidays on offer yet, despite the generally accepted post-Fordist attitudes towards production and consumption, mass market package tourism remains firmly embedded in the industrial era.

Tourism and the environment

One of the principal areas in which postmodernity differs from modernity is within the context of the environment or, more precisely, *concern* for the environment. Continuing the basic tenet of the Enlightenment project, modernity sought human and economic progress through the domination and exploitation of nature; an objective which modern, Western societies appear, by and large, to have achieved. Most Western societies are able to live beyond the constraints of nature; natural resources are exploited to provide fuel, shelter and food, there are cures for most common illnesses, and people are generally able to travel where and when they want without having to wait for favourable weather conditions. In short, most people, at least in the developed world, are able to live in societies that have overcome their subordination to most of nature's constraints, although natural disasters, such as earthquakes, hurricanes and floods, do not respect national or developmental boundaries.

In recent years, in particular since the early 1980s, modern society has become increasingly concerned with the conservation, rather than the exploitation, of the environment. Governments, societies and individuals alike have become more aware that, in the long run, the survival of the human race depends not on the domination of nature and the environment but the harmonious, sustainable co-existence with our natural surroundings. Issues such as the destruction of the rain forests, the greenhouse effect and global warming resulting from the burning of fossil fuels, acid rain, and the depletion of the ozone layer have all become of international concern. Similarly, specific cases of resource depletion, such as excessive and indiscriminate whaling, have been publicised by the activities of conservation organisations, whilst green political parties have challenged the policy of economic growth which is the driving force behind capitalist economies. The history, political and social development of environmentalism and the green movement is beyond the scope of this chapter (for example, see Porritt 1984; Adams 1990; Yearley 1991) yet concern for the environment is not only evidence of the reflexive nature of postmodern culture (the interest in preserving the past being another example) but also, arguably, one of the greatest challenges facing the future of the international tourism industry.

Concern about the negative impacts of tourism has been expressed for almost as long as tourism itself has existed as an identifiable, modern leisure activity. For example, in 1848 Thomas Cook wrote in his handbook for visitors to Belvoir Castle that *to the shame of some rude folk from Lincolnshire, there have been just causes of complaint at Belvoir Castle: some large parties have behaved indecorously... conduct of this sort is abominable, and cannot be too strongly reprobated* (cited in Ousby 1990). In Britain the national park movement, culminating in the 1949 National Parks and Access to the Countryside Act, was the first attempt to reconcile the demands of tourists with the need to protect the environment, but it was not until the late 1960s and early 1970s that concern about the effects of tourism became more widespread. A number of authors (Mishan 1969; Young 1973; Turner and Ash 1975; Rosenow and Pulsipher 1979) expressed alarm at the rapid spread of mass, package tourism, predicting that the economic benefits of tourism could soon be outweighed by the costs associated with tourism's negative impacts: *the time has now come...to take the Goddess of Tourism off her pedestal and to place her in the garden with other statues* (Young 1973:168).

Since the 1980s new, alternative forms of tourism have been suggested to counter the impacts of mass tourism; variously termed as responsible tourism, green tourism, appropriate tourism, good tourism or eco-tourism, they all share the viewpoint that tourism should be sustainable. At the same time, an enormous volume of literature produced by academics, researchers and tourism organisations has been published, all suggesting that tourism should be developed in harmony with the environment, maintaining a balance between the needs of local communities, visitors, the tourism industry and the physical, social and cultural environment. Various organisations, such as Tourism Concern, Green Flag International, the Centre for the Advancement of Responsive Travel (see *Millman, R.* 1989) and the Ecumenical Coalition On Third World Tourism, strive to increase awareness of the impacts of tourism and to promote forms of tourism (other than mass tourism) that respect the local environment and the needs of local communities. Others stress that the responsibility for sustainable tourism lies with tourists themselves, seeing the way forward as the development of 'good' tourism (Wood and House 1991).

The impacts of tourism on the environment, the mechanisms and principles of alternative, sustainable tourism development and the arguments surrounding the viability of alternative forms of tourism to mass tourism are widely discussed and described in the literature. Indeed, since the early 1990s no other single issue has attracted as much attention, the concept of sustainable tourism development spawning innumerable books and articles, providing the focus of many conferences, and even enjoying its own dedicated journal. The purpose here, however, is to consider the extent to which the growth in tourism environmentalism is linked to the reflexive nature of postmodern culture.

Concern for the environment as a general and widespread social transformation is undoubtedly a major characteristic of postmodernity, representing the de-differentiation of society and its natural environment. As Munt (1994) observes, concern for the environment and sustainability are the *highest order discourse of postmodernisation*. It is also evidence of a significant departure from the Enlightenment / modernist project of progress through the control and exploitation of natural resources. The relationship between environmental concern, tourism development and postmodernity is not, however, quite so clear cut. Three points, in particular, cast doubt on the underlying motivation for the promotion of environmentally friendly, sustainable tourism.

(a) Much of the research into tourism is concerned with ways in which it may be more sustainable. In other words, it suggests methods of optimising the economic benefits of tourism to host countries whilst, at the same time, minimising the impacts of tourism on the environment. Rarely, however, is the question about the sustainability of tourism, in particular international tourism, as an overall social and economic development activity ever raised, although more recent research has addressed this issue (Wall 1997; Mowforth and Munt 1998; Sharpley 1998). *There is no example of tourist use that is completely without impact. If the primary goal is one of protection and preservation of the environment in an untouched form then, in all truth, there cannot be tourism development at all* (Cater 1993). Unlike other forms of economic activity that impact upon and deplete the world's natural resources, the continuing existence of tourism is generally accepted, no doubt because it is an activity that is enjoyed by a large number of people. It is also frequently motivated by the desire to escape from modern society, which includes escaping from the concerns, such as environmentalism, of modern life. Thus, it may be argued that much of the environmental concern surrounding tourism is motivated not by the need to protect the environment *per se*, but to sustain it as the resource upon which tourism depends. In short, the ultimate purpose is to sustain tourism itself (see Jenner and Smith 1992).

(b) Tourism is a global activity and, increasingly, new tourism generating countries are emerging. But, the great majority of tourists originate in the developed, industrialised countries which, to a greater or lesser extent, are becoming postmodern and, not surprisingly, most of the multinational corporations involved in tourism are also based in the main tourism generating countries. Conversely, many tourism-receiving nations have yet to achieve modern status in an economic and technological sense and are, in effect, culturally pre-modern. Also, many developing countries cannot afford to be environmentally aware; caring for the environment is a luxury to be indulged in once basic needs have been catered for. In other words, they require far greater amounts of foreign exchange than can be earned realistically from the small-scale, sustainable approach advocated by the (Western) promoters of sustainable tourism. Unlike those countries which have established and profitable tourism industries and diverse economies and can afford conservation programmes, developing nations depend on larger scale tourism development as a vital source of income. Much of the concern for the impact of tourism is an attempt to impose postmodern social values on nations which are unwilling, or in no position, to accept those values.

(c) It is important not to confuse genuine environmental concern with the postmodernist de-differentiation of the past and present. To a great extent, the concept of sustainable tourism proposes the conservation or protection of both the physical and the socio-cultural environment of destination areas. Whilst the protection of the natural environment from excessive or inappropriate tourism development and use falls entirely within the parameters of environmentalism, the desire to preserve social and cultural traditions and practices is linked to the issues of authenticity (see Chapter Seven) and time compression. In other words, the preservation of the socio-cultural environment in tourist destinations, as proposed by the tourism industry, is the preservation of *signs* of past cultures (in comparison to postmodern culture). Such 'environmentalism', therefore, is based upon the need to maintain the appeal of the environment to potential tourists and is, again, an effort to impose postmodern cultural values upon other societies.

Overall, then, the issues of postmodern environmental concern about the impacts of tourism should be considered from a global perspective. Whilst many tourism generating countries reflect the broader, international concern for the environment as a whole, it must be remembered that many countries, particularly in the developing world, are either unwilling or unable, for financial reasons, to embrace the concept of environmentalism and sustainable development. For them, the development of tourism is seen as a valuable tool to aid economic growth and diversification; only when a certain level of economic, technological and social development has been achieved can such countries begin to consider environmental issues.

At the same time, distinctions need to be drawn between the conservation of scarce natural resources, including those upon which tourism depends, and the preservation of societies and cultures which, to tourists from modern societies, symbolise different, past ages. The challenge for the tourism industry is to question its own motives in promoting sustainable or alternative forms of tourism; the challenge for postmodern, environmentally sensitive societies is to allow other societies to develop and modernise.

Tourism and postmodernity: a summary

As a basis for exploring the relationship between tourism and postmodernity, this chapter has suggested that developments and transformations in tourism as a social activity cannot be explained by making reference only to the enabling factors of tourism. Although important, inasmuch as tourists require the time and the means to be able to participate in tourism, of equal if not greater importance is the tourist's home cultural environment which, in a sense, provides the framework within which tourism is consumed. This implies that changes in the cultural condition of the tourist's society are likely to bring about changes in the style and significance of tourism.

There is little doubt that modern, Western societies have experienced a cutural shift from the condition of modernity to a less rigid, structured state that may be described as postmodernity. There is also little doubt that transformations in styles of tourism reflect this shift towards postmodernity, whilst tourism itself has, arguably, become de-differentiated from other spheres of social activity. New tourism 'places' and 'times' have emerged, challenging the traditional position and role of tourism and suggesting there is much truth in the proposition that people are tourists most of the time (Urry 1995). Equally, new styles of tourism, such as heritage tourism or eco-tourism, have become increasingly popular, although the extent to which a causal relationship exists between these and specific characteristics of postmodernity remains debatable. So, recognising and accepting the influence of cultural change in tourism generating areas is not only essential for a fuller understanding of tourism consumption patterns. It also provides a broader theoretical basis for assessing tourism typologies, demand and motivation, topics which the following chapters address.

Four

Tourists: Roles and Typologies

Introduction

It is generally accepted that the word 'tourist' first appeared in the English language around the end of the eighteenth century, although there is some debate as to when the word was first actually used (Theobald 1994). Some for example, attribute the origin of the term to Stendhal in the early 1800s (Feifer 1985), whilst others claim that its first known usage was in a 1780 guide book to the Lake District. Certainly, William Wordsworth used the word in his 1799 poem *The Brothers,* whilst in 1800 Samuel Pegge wrote in a book on new English usages that *a Traveller is now-a-days called a Tour-ist* (cited in Buzard 1993: 1). This indicates that, originally, 'tourist' and 'traveller' were inter-changeable terms describing, in a neutral sense, a person who was touring. More recently, the words 'traveller' and 'tourist' have acquired different connotations. The former, in a touristic sense (as opposed to gypsy, new age traveller and so on), is usually applied to someone who is travelling/touring for an extended period of time, probably back-packing on a limited budget. It connotes a spirit of freedom, adventure and individuality. The word tourist, on the other hand, is frequently used in a rather derogatory sense to describe those who participate in mass produced, package tourism.

The traveller/tourist dichotomy has, as Buzard (1993: 5) argues, *more to do with the society and culture that produce the tourist than it does with the encounter any given tourist or 'traveller' may have with a foreign society and culture*. In other words, the words 'traveller' and 'tourist' have acquired a socially constructed meaning that goes beyond a basic description of travelling and touring. As a result, it is probably true to say that, at some time or another, most people have tried to distance or disassociate themselves from other tourists, convincing themselves that they are somehow better or enjoying a more meaningful experience. That is, they suffer what Dann (1999) refers to as 'tourist angst', *that feeling which many tourists are reckoned to display towards fellow vacationers whenever they come into contact with, and seek to distance themselves from, them* (Dann 1999: 160).

This issue is discussed shortly. But, the important point is that the word tourist is nowadays applied to such a huge number and variety of people undertaking such vastly different types of travel that, as a way of collectively describing the individuals who made 613 million international trips in 1997, as well as the billions who participate in domestic tourism, it is a virtually meaningless term. Even if, as Witt *et al* (1991: 38) point out, about 70 per cent of international tourist arrivals are for holiday purposes, describing all the individuals concerned simply as tourists conceals a whole host of different factors, such as length and type of holiday, a person's demographic, social and psychological characteristics, the purpose of the trip, and so on.

For example, strictly speaking a young person embarking on a year's back-packing tour of Asia, a family having a two-week package holiday in Benidorm and an American of Irish descent visiting Ireland to discover his ancestry are all tourists, but there the similarity ends.

If we are to be able to better understand, explain and predict tourist behaviour, it is necessary to look beneath the all-encompassing label of 'tourist'. We have to ask, who is a tourist and what are the different types of tourist? We have to consider how tourists may be categorised by their behaviour (the roles they play), by their expectations and, adopting a structural approach, the extent to which tourist types and roles are determined by their social environment. This chapter discusses the different attempts which have been made to create typologies of tourists and examines newer, socially determined categories of tourist, such as the 'good' tourist (see Wood and House 1991), the 'new' tourist (Poon 1993) and the 'post-tourist' (see Feifer 1985; Urry 1988 and 1990a). It also suggests that a practical, useful typology of tourists should be based upon a broader approach than has been adopted to date.

Tourist or traveller?

When the word tourist was first used it was synonymous with traveller. That is, it was used in a totally neutral sense to describe a person who was touring for, normally, the purpose of pleasure or leisure. During the first half of the nineteenth century, distinctions came to be made between tourist and traveller, or tourism and travel, distinctions which implied as much, if not more, about the character of the individuals concerned as about the actual means of travel. The tourist, as opposed to the traveller, not only became associated with mass forms of travel but also with a particular mentality or approach to the travel experience. In effect, *high culture, the culture of the traveller, saw itself as the polar opposite of low culture, the culture attributed to the tourist* (Rojek 1993: 174), a distinction immortalised, perhaps, by Henry James' description of tourists as *vulgar, vulgar, vulgar*.

Writing in 1869, James was referring specifically to American tourists in Europe. However, not only do his sentiments reflect the continuing dichotomy in the way that people view tourists and travellers, but they are also evidence of a debate that continues unabated to this day (see Dann 1999). Moreover, it is a debate that underpins many issues within the sociological treatment of tourism, including tourist motivation, the social significance of tourism and the search for authentic tourist experiences. These issues are addressed in subsequent chapters but it is important here to explore the traveller-tourist dichotomy in more detail.

The distinctions between the two terms are, arguably, most evident in the literature on travel. Again, it was in nineteenth century writing that the distinction first emerged (see Buzard 1993) but the trend continues in the late twentieth century. Nowadays, much travel literature tends to emphasise and, perhaps, glorify in the unusual, the different or the unique way of travelling from one place to another. Authors' accounts of cycling, walking, running, or sailing particular journeys predominate; if it has been achieved against a background of political turmoil or civil war, under harsh weather conditions or without the approval of the authorities, then so much the better! To put it another way, modern travel literature 'writes out' the tourist (Dann 1999). That is, it concentrates on the feelings which the authors *experience and communicate, along with the questions of self-identity they rhetorically pose in their descriptions of far-flung places, sentiments which have the cumulative effect of physically and psychologically distancing themselves and their readers from the more familiar voyage of today: the tourist* (Dann 1999: 160).

As a result, such writing not only glorifies 'travel' in opposition to the more mundane, unexciting 'tourism', but also undoubtedly encourages many others to seek out similar places and experiences. Similarly, more recent series of guide books, in particular the Lonely Planet *Travel Survival Kits*, also emphasise the individualistic, adventurous approach in contrast to the easy, comfortable, package tour; not only do they mould the visitor's perceptions of the destination (Bhattacharyya 1997), but also they verify the self-image of those who wish to distinguish themselves from the tourist. Thus, as the number of places around the world yet to become tourist destinations continues to diminish, for travellers it is not *where* but *how* that has become important.

As important as travel literature has been in forging distinctions between the tourist and the traveller, the underlying cause was, and remains, technological advances in transport. During the latter half of the eighteenth century the train was seen as the prime culprit of the demise of 'real' travel; for example, John Ruskin wrote that the train *transmutes a man from a traveller into a living parcel* (cited in Buzard 1993: 33). A century later it is ironic that, in an age of supersonic air travel, international train journeys (preferably hauled by a steam engine) are now promoted as a return to the days of real, authentic travel. In short, it is not the actual form of transport but its degree or stage of technological advance that determines its acceptability and authenticity to travellers. No doubt a trip on Concorde will one day be sold as an authentic experience of real travel!

Of more importance are the social distinctions inherent in the traveller/tourist argument. All tourists, in general, are looked down upon by other tourists who, arguably, consider themselves to be undeserving of the tourist label. Also, it is a process or reaction that is found across the entire spectrum of touristic activity and one which does not always respect traditional social groupings or distinctions. For example, back-packers, particularly those on longer-term trips, are at pains to call themselves travellers rather than tourists (see Riley 1988); travel is associated with adventure, authentic experience, taste, individuality and self-discovery, whereas tourism is pre-packaged, pre-paid, comfortable and predictable. Travellers make their own choices; tourists have their decisions made for them. Travel is seen to be somehow 'better' than tourism, travellers 'better' than tourists, irrespective of class, wealth, education, age, nationality and other social distinctions.

At the same time, distinctions are made *within* similar forms of tourism, such as package beach holidays. Some people believe that certain destinations are not suitable or are too 'touristy' and so a fortnight's holiday in, say, the Seychelles may be perceived to be better than two weeks on Majorca; the two products are, in effect, the same, the primary difference being the cost. Even independent travel, or back-packing, is not immune to this process. Different countries are hierarchically listed according to degrees of difficulty, danger or hassle for visitors, whilst as Riley (1988) observes, a 'road culture' exists whereby individuals seek to enhance their status by claiming to have travelled for longer, visiting more places yet 'surviving' on less money, than other travellers.

Comparisons may also be made between different nationalities of tourists. For many years the American, 'if it's Tuesday it must be Belgium' style of touring Europe bore the brunt of the anti-tourists' criticism. Attention nowadays has shifted towards coach loads of camera-toting Japanese and the allegedly German habit of getting up early to claim the best places around the swimming pool. Tourist differentiation is even apparent within the context of a single mode of transport. As the opportunity for travel became more widespread during the 1800s, *status distinctions came to be drawn less between those who could and those who could not travel but between different classes of traveller* (Urry 1990b). For example, charter flights are more 'touristy' than scheduled flights and even in China rail travel is segregated into two classes of travel – 'soft seat' (first class) and 'hard seat' (second class).

Simply put, all tourists (and travellers), as Culler (1981) argues, *can always find someone more touristy than themselves to sneer at.* Disliking and trying to avoid other tourists at the same time as trying to convince oneself that one is not a tourist is, in fact, all part of being a tourist. The basis of the conflict is a kind of social arrogance which can be linked directly to the aristocratic model of tourism development described in Chapter Two. Throughout the nineteenth century criticism was directed at ordinary people who, taking advantage of the new forms of transport, were able to travel both at home and abroad in ever increasing numbers, thereby threatening once exclusive destinations. The implication was that not only would the new mass tourists impinge on the enjoyment of the previously privileged minority who had the time and money to travel but also that they were, somehow, unable to appreciate the travel experience.

For example, Wordsworth fought vigorously against the extension of the railway line to Windermere in the Lake District, fearing it would bring large numbers of people more intent on simple pleasures than admiring the sublime beauty of the region. Thus, as travel became increasingly democratised, the moral and cultural benefits of travel were seen to be becoming correspondingly diluted. As the growth of mass tourism has continued throughout the twentieth century, this perceived gulf between the traveller and the tourist has intensified; as more and more people become tourists, the less and less do they wish to be labelled as such.

One of the fiercest critics of mass tourists, highlighting the traveller/tourist dichotomy, is Daniel Boorstin. In lamenting what he terms *The Lost Art of Travel* (Boorstin 1964), he describes the onset of mass tourism as *the decline of the traveller and the rise of the tourist*. The difference, he continues, is that:

> *The traveller, then, was working at something; the tourist was a pleasure seeker. The traveller was active; he went strenuously in search of people, of adventure, of experience. The tourist is passive; he expects interesting things to happen to him... he expects everything to be done to him and for him.* (Boorstin 1964: 85)

The modern tourist, according to Boorstin, has become a passive onlooker who travels in organised groups, enjoys contrived, pseudo-events, rarely experiences, or seeks, the real or authentic and, as Cohen (1988) puts it, *seeks to enjoy the extravagantly strange from the security of the familiar*. It is important to point out that Boorstin is, in fact, concerned with the overall state of modern society and simply uses mass tourism as an illustration for his arguments. But, his opinions reflect the continuing and widely held belief that travellers are different and in some way superior to tourists, a belief that is based upon a number of misconceptions and generalisations.

1.   The art of travel imagined and, perhaps, romanticised by the protagonists of the traveller/tourist dichotomy has not been lost; it has been overtaken by modern technology. In particular, advances in information technology have rendered the recreation of 'traditional' travel impossible. It matters little what mode of transport is used for what distinguishes early from modern travel is not the speed, comfort or type of transport but the expectations and knowledge of what will be encountered either *en route* or at the destination. Television, radio, magazines, education, guide books and even the experiences of family and friends have irrevocably altered the fundamental experience of travel to the extent that the traveller/tourist knows what to expect and what will be found.

2.   Rather than leading to greater harmony and understanding, tourism serves to highlight social distinction and conflict. Different modes and standards of travel, different classes of accommodation, different destinations and even the difference between those who are able or unable to participate in travel and tourism are no more than a reflection of wider social differentiation and stratification.

3.   Travel cannot be separated from tourism. Not all travellers are necessarily tourists but all tourists are, by definition, travellers. There is, therefore, little point in attempting to distinguish between the two in a collective sense except, perhaps, as a marketing exercise. That is, the perceived difference between travel and tourism may be used as means of distinguishing between different types of holiday and for appealing to different market segments. For example, a month-long overland trip in a truck through South America may be sold as authentic travel but, from the tour operator's point of view, it is no less a package holiday than a two week beach holiday (see Chapter Seven).

4. The experience of independence associated with travel, as opposed to tourism, for the most part does not strictly exist. Bookings are made through travel agents, itineraries and accommodation are arranged with the help of specialist guidebooks, and most travellers follow recognised routes. It is ironic that events such as 'Independent Travellers' Fairs' are supported by a sophisticated sector of the travel industry.

5. By attempting to differentiate between the traveller and the tourist, generalised characterisations of each emerge. The word tourist, in particular, has come to be associated in a derogatory sense with mass tourism (which is also an overused and misunderstood term), yet those who continue to denounce mass tourism disregard the enormous variation in the motivation, experience and behaviour of different tourists. Similarly, there is no single type of traveller. For example, as discussed shortly, independent travel (or the generic term 'traveller') is widely associated with the younger, explorer type, yet it is a form of tourism which appeals to many socio-economic groupings. Some of the most influential modern travel writers do not fall into this category!

In short, then, there is no such thing as *the* tourist or *the* traveller. Such distinctions are normally self-imposed labels and, therefore, within the context of the modern tourism system, it may be concluded that a traveller is simply one type of tourist.

Tourists: types, categories and roles

An understanding of tourist categories and roles is essential, along with other factors, to the explanation and prediction of consumer behaviour within tourism. One of the earliest attempts to distinguish between different types of tourism was made by Gray (1970) who coined the terms *sunlust* and *wanderlust* tourism. Sunlust tourism is essentially tourism that is resort based and motivated by the desire for rest, relaxation and the three S's – Sun, Sea and Sand, whereas wanderlust tourism is based on a desire to travel and to experience different peoples and cultures. Implicit in each term are the characteristics of each form of travel; for example, climate and comfortable and familiar accommodation and cuisine will be more important to the sunlust tourist whereas the wanderlust tourist will be more interested in different cultures and the potential for experience and learning. As the two terms imply, sunlust and wanderlust are essentially categorisations based upon the purpose of the trip. They are a useful, though basic, form of market segmentation, describing rather than explaining or predicting the demand for tourism.

Since then a number of typologies, concentrating on the tourists themselves, have been developed. Some of these concentrate on tourists' behaviour whilst others adopt a more socio-psychological approach.

(i)   Cohen's typology of tourists

Erik Cohen was the first to propose a typology of tourists based upon sociological theory. That is, unlike previous attempts to categorise tourists, such as Gray's sunlust-wanderlust concept which focused upon tourists in isolation, Cohen developed his typology of tourists *on the basis of their relationship to both the tourist business establishment and the host country* (Cohen 1972). In other words, his starting point was to relate tourist behaviour to the tourism destination environment.

His work is also based on the fundamental assumption that all tourists, even those with a thirst for adventure and excitement, are unable to escape totally from the influence of their home environment. In other words, all tourists can be located along a 'familiarity-strangerhood continuum'. According to Cohen, all tourists carry with them their values and behaviour patterns when they travel and, as a result, need something to remind them of home, such as a newspaper, familiar food or a friend. At the same time, the way in which they view, and react to, new places and cultures is also determined, to a greater or lesser extent, by their home environment and culture. In short, tourists travel in an *environmental bubble*. Importantly, however, not all tourists are equally constrained by this bubble. On the one hand, some tourists, those at the familiarity end of the continuum, are unable to escape at all; they seek out the normal or the familiar and are unwilling to try or risk something new or different. On the other hand, others are able to break free from the bubble; they seek out the novel and unusual, and are found at the strangerhood end of the continuum.

Cohen's starting point is, therefore, similar to Boorstin's view of the mass tourist inasmuch as he suggests that tourist behaviour is structurally determined by the tourist's home social environment. But, unlike Boorstin's single and somewhat derogatory generalisation, he suggests that different tourists are more or less able to adapt to and experience the unfamiliar. Thus, progressing from the familiarity to the strangerhood position, four different types of tourist are identified:

(a) The organised mass tourist

The organised mass tourist is probably the type that conforms most closely to the stereotypical image of the tourist. On a package tour, the organised mass tourist travels around in air-conditioned coaches on a pre-arranged, inflexible itinerary, stays in hotels which recreate the home environment, makes virtually no decisions and at all stages of the trip is shielded from any possible contact with the host country's culture. If on a beach holiday, the organised mass tourist remains within the hotel complex, with the exception of an occasional organised tour, and at no time does he or she venture outside the environmental bubble. Domestic tourists on package trips, such as a week in Blackpool, also fall into this category.

(b) The individual mass tourist

Individual mass tourists are similar to the organised mass tourists in as much as their holiday or trip is arranged and booked through an operator. Less constrained by desired safety of the familiar, they are able to exercise a degree of personal choice and control. For example, a fly/drive holiday, where tourists choose their itinerary but still stay on the beaten track combines familiarity with a certain amount of novelty and is likely to appeal to individual mass tourists. In other words, they rely on the established tourism system, but are able occasionally to escape from their environmental bubble.

(c) The explorer

The characteristics of the explorer approximate to the behaviour of the independent traveller. The explorer makes his/her own travel arrangements, tries to avoid the tourist trail as far as possible by getting off the beaten track and attempts to associate with local people and culture by learning the language, eating in local restaurants and so on. In short, the explorer seeks novel experiences and largely rejects the familiar. But, a reasonable level of comfort and security is sought and although the explorer, for the most part, is able to escape the environmental bubble, some of the values and routines of home life are retained. For example, accommodation used by fellow travellers may be preferred and many explorers travel secure in the knowledge that they have their return ticket home.

(d) The drifter

At the opposite extreme from the organised mass tourist, the drifter attempts to merge into local communities, living and working with local people. The desire for strangerhood is maximised; the drifter has no fixed itinerary and becomes immersed in local culture and customs. Tourism and tourists are considered to be phoney and so all contact with the tourism system is avoided. Escape from the environmental bubble is almost complete, contact with the familiar is minimal and the sense of novelty is at its highest.

Cohen categorises the first two types of tourist, the organised and the individual mass tourist, as *institutionalised* tourists. That is, their tourism experience is planned, controlled and provided by the mass tourism industry. In order to serve their large number of customers as rapidly and efficiently as possible, each part of the tour or holiday is planned, packaged and predictable; novelty for the customer is, in many instances, a mass produced and inauthentic version of local culture (see Chapter Seven). The inherent safety or familiarity of the package holiday is a significant attraction to the institutionalised tourist. Conversely, drifters and explorers are *noninstitutionalised* tourists, requiring little contact with the tourism establishment. As Cohen argues, drifters and explorers often act as pathfinders for the mass tourism industry; destinations 'discovered' by or popular amongst explorers and drifters often become commercialised and open up to the mass tourism market. For example, Goa and Kovalam were once well-known haunts of travellers in India; both are now directly served by charter flights from Europe and are popular winter-sun package destinations.

One problem with Cohen's typology is that the institutionalised/ noninstitutionalised forms of tourism are not entirely distinct; whilst the traditional package-type institutionalised holiday remains as popular as ever, the concept of noninstitutionalised travel has become ever more tenuous. For example, the increasingly large number of people who travel 'independently' – backpackers, explorers, overland travellers – tend to rely on the tourism industry (albeit, not the mass package sector) as much as any other tourist. They use specialist guide books, such as Lonely Planet or Rough Guide books, which refer them to destinations, accommodation, restaurants, transport routes, budget flight agencies and so on that are frequented by other travellers. They often follow popular trails and, in many countries, a local tourism industry has emerged to serve the particular needs of independent travellers. In the extreme, their needs are provided for by specialist operators running overland trips for anything up to six months duration – adventure travel, certainly, but as institutionalised as the two week summer package. In short, although it can be argued that explorers' *approach to and preferences for travel do differ from traditional mainstream tourism* (Loker-Murphy and Pearce 1995), independent travel has, in the context of the tourist's relationship with the tourism industry, become as institutionalised as mass tourism.

It is also debatable whether or not the drifter is a feasible categorisation at all. As the world gets smaller and more homogeneous it becomes less likely that any individual can fully escape the home environment; as the 'global village' emerges so too does a global environmental bubble.

Another criticism is that this categorisation is based on observable tourist behaviour but gives no indication of the reason for that behaviour. Thus, an individual might prefer to be an explorer but, constrained perhaps by financial, work or family commitments, a form of organised mass tourism may be chosen in order to optimise the benefits at a given time.

Nor does this typology allow for variable tourist behaviour over time; the implication is 'once a mass tourist, always a mass tourist', whereas tourists frequently take different types of holiday from one year to the next or even within a year

To return to the example of the independent traveller/explorer, a number of researchers have addressed the roles, attitudes and behaviour of backpackers (Cohen 1973; Vogt 1978; Riley 1988; Loker-Murphy and Pearce 1995). Almost invariably, backpackers are considered to be youth tourists; young people, often at a particular juncture in their lives, undertaking a trip as a rite of passage. But, backpack tourism is popular amongst adults of all ages and to assign particular typologies to particular social groups is to overlook the role of the individual in making choices.

(ii) Tourist types, tourist numbers

A similar typology to Cohen's is suggested by Smith (1989). It is again based upon the behaviour of tourists, but Smith also links types of tourists to their numbers with implications about their impacts on the host environment.

(a) Explorers

There is a very limited number of explorers, constrained by the ever diminishing supply of areas to be explored. They are more akin to anthropologists than tourists and fully accept local lifestyles and culture.

(b) Elite Tourists

Elite tourists, rarely seen, *usually include individuals who have been 'almost everywhere'* (Smith 1989:12).   They participate in unusual activities and adapt fully to local ways but are, nevertheless, on a pre-arranged and, most likely, expensive tour.

(c) Off-beat Tourists

Equivalent to Cohen's explorer, off-beat tourists are uncommon but seen. They try to avoid other tourists and adapt well to local norms, staying in local accommodation and using local services.

(d) Unusual Tourists

Tourists who occasionally break away from an organised tour in order to experience some local culture are relatively few in number. They will adapt to local norms for a time but are happier within their own environmental bubble.

(e) Incipient Mass Tourists

Incipient mass tourists represent a steady flow of visitors to a destination that has a reasonably established, but not dominant, tourism industry. The incipient mass tourist will tend to seek out Western style amenities.

(f) Mass Tourists

There is a continuous influx of large numbers of mass tourists to a destination or resort and they expect Western amenities.

(g) Charter Tourists

Charter tourists arrive by the planeload in massive numbers. They demand Western style food and accommodation and, in the extreme, the actual destination may be of little importance to them as long as they enjoy their holiday.

Based as it is on tourist behaviour, similar problems emerge with this typology of tourists as with Cohen's. There is also little distinction sometimes between the different categories of tourists; the difference between a mass tourist and a charter tourist is not always clear. Other proposed typologies of tourists also suffer from the same limitations. Cohen (1974) suggests that different types of tourist are distinguishable by what he terms the *dimensions of the tourist role*. Factors such as permanency, voluntariness, distance and purpose of trip, and recurrence determine whether or not an individual is a tourist and, if so, what type of tourist. Pearce (1982) reviews a number of attempts to formulate tourist typologies and proposes fifteen different types of tourist based upon five role-related behaviour patterns. For example, a jet-setter is identifiable by a luxury life style, a concern with social status, a search for sensual pleasures, interaction with similar people, and frequenting famous places.

Typologies of tourists which rely upon observations of the behaviour and roles of tourists indicate the enormous diversity of activities that are included under the broad heading of tourism. They frequently reveal more about the researcher and the research methods used than about the tourists themselves (Lowyck *et al* 1992: 13). They also tend to be static, not allowing for variations in an individual tourist's behaviour, and view tourists in isolation from broader sociological factors which may determine and explain variations in tourist roles. However, attempts to link tourist categories with the tourism experience go some way towards overcoming these limitations of tourist typologies.

(iii) Tourists' experiences

Building upon his earlier work in distinguishing between different types of tourist, Cohen addressed some of the inherent weaknesses of his typology in his 'phenomenology of tourist experiences' (Cohen 1979). The primary criticism of his initial attempt it that is overly simplistic to assume that tourists can be categorised along a continuum ranging from, at one end, tourists as mass consumers accepting the superficial, inauthentic product of tour operators (as proposed by Boorstin 1964) to, at the other end, tourists as modern pilgrims on a voyage of exploration and self-discovery (MacCannell 1989). This continuum adopts a structural approach in as much as each category reflects, or results from, the influence of the tourism generating society. Recognising that tourism is a multi-dimensional phenomenon, Cohen proposes that a micro approach is equally valid in developing an understanding of different

111

tourist types and roles, concentrating not on observed behaviour but on different desired tourist experiences.

Again, the theoretical foundation of this typology is the familiarity-strangerhood continuum, although Cohen is now concerned with the extent to which the tourist enjoys a sense of belonging or, conversely, feels like a stranger in the home environment. Thus, the starting point is to ascertain where the 'spiritual centre' of the individual tourist is located, for different individuals identify with and accept to a greater or lesser extent their home culture and society. At one extreme, the 'centre' is located entirely within the home society and the individual finds no meaning in any other societies and cultures. Implicitly, all aspects of the tourist's home environment and life is satisfying and fulfilling and, therefore, as a tourist, the individual is not concerned with experiencing and learning about other peoples and cultures. At the other extreme lies the modern (in the sociological sense) individual who, alienated from the meaning and values of home society, locates his or her 'centre' elsewhere. In other words, the individual suffers 'placelessness' and believes that a sense of belonging can only be found by travelling elsewhere, to what sociologists term 'The Other'. Thus, in this case, the tourist seeks reality and meaning, or authentic experiences, through tourism (the notion of authenticity in tourism experiences is considered in detail in Chapter Seven). Between and including these two points Cohen identifies five categories of tourist experience:

(a) Recreational

The tourist whose centre is located in the home society seeks recreational experiences and has little or no interest in learning about or experiencing the society and culture in which the recreational experience is taking place.

(b) Diversionary

The diversionary tourist is an intermediate category. Although alienated to an extent from his or her own society, the individual does not seek authentic experiences elsewhere. In a sense, the purpose of a holiday or trip is to temporarily forget about home.

112

(c) Experiential

The experiential tourist is the modern, alienated individual who seeks authentic experiences elsewhere. Although seeking to experience alternative cultures and societies, the experiential tourist neither identifies with them nor rejects his or her own society. The trip thus compensates for the inauthenticity of home life to which the tourist inevitably returns.

(d) Experimental

The experimental tourist is seeking to relocate his or her 'centre', but lies midway between the 'centre' at home and an identified 'centre' elsewhere. Authenticity of experience is essential, but the experimental tourist does not become totally immersed in any one culture.

(e) Existential

The existential tourist is the opposite extreme to the recreational tourist. Alienated from the home society, the 'centre' is firmly located elsewhere. The tourist becomes fully immersed in the local, foreign culture and society, finding meaning and belonging in the new chosen 'centre'.

Actual types of tourist may be identified with any one of these five categories. For example, the mass tourist on a two week beach holiday or a skiing trip closely resembles the recreational tourist whilst a cultural tourist on a tour of, say, the Far East, may be categorised as an experiential tourist. Whilst adding an extra dimension to the behavioural typologies, this typology still does not allow for the different needs or requirements of an individual tourist. Nor is it based on any empirical research. It is a theoretical categorisation within which different tourists may be located but, as with other typologies, it considers tourists *per se* rather than in their broader social context.

(iv) Psychocentrics and allocentrics

One of the better known and widely cited attempts to link personality traits to tourist types and roles is Plog's tourist typology (Plog 1973).

Researching the reasons why people who, even though they could well afford it, did not fly, Plog identified two opposing character types at each end of a continuum. Psychocentrics are those who are inward looking, who concentrate on small problems and tend to be less adventurous. The corollary in tourism is the mass tourist looking for the familiar. The psychocentric tourist frequents popular, mass tourist resorts either at home or abroad and feels more comfortable surrounded by other tourists. Allocentrics, on the other hand, are adventurous and are prepared to take risks, as with Cohen's explorer and drifter. The allocentric tourist, therefore, prefers unusual, exotic destinations and enjoys the freedom of relatively autonomous travel. In between the two extremes lie the categories of near-psychocentric, mid-centric and near-allocentric.

Unlike other tourist typologies, Plog goes on to link different types of tourist with different destinations which they are most likely to visit. He suggests that (American) psychocentrics go to resorts such as Coney Island, near New York, whereas allocentrics are to be found travelling in Africa. Mid-centrics, the most numerous category, take their holidays in places such as Europe or Hawaii, destinations which offer the experience of a new, yet sufficiently similar, culture. Similarly, the destination choices of tourists of other nationalities could also be predicted according to this model.

One problem with attempting to link tourist type with destination in this way is that it is a static model. On the one hand, destinations change and develop over time; as a resort is discovered and attracts growing numbers of visitors it will evolve from an allocentric to a psychocentric destination. On the other hand, the parameters of each category of tourist may also change or become vague. For example, as long haul charter flights become more available and more exotic destinations are publicised and packaged, psychocentrics might be found travelling to destinations which, according to Plog's model, would normally attract allocentrics. Thus, although many authors refer to Plog's typology, there is some debate as to its applicability in practice. Indeed, Smith (1990) tested the model against a number of different countries and found that the results did not support Plog's contention that destination choice could be predicted according to personality types.

A number of other attempts have been made to create typologies of tourists (see Lowyck *et al* 1992: 13-32). Little is to be gained from a consideration of them all but, generally, they may be sub-divided into two distinct groups. Firstly, there are those typologies which concentrate on the tourists themselves, their behaviour and their experience (for example, mass tourists, independent travellers, vacationers, cultural tourists, and so on). The great majority of typologies fall within this category. Secondly, there are typologies which are based upon the life style of tourists, such as Dalen's (1989, cited in Lowyck *et al* 1992). Dalen applies a four segment categorisation of life style to tourism and suggests that, for example, the *traditional materialist* looks for low prices and safe products and, therefore, purchases the mass, package tourism product.

Neither approach is entirely satisfactory in explaining and predicting tourist behaviour. Typologies that concentrate on the tourist *per se* are, generally, descriptive, static and theoretical whilst life style categorisations are often developed in isolation from the tourism system. Some combination might be desirable but, as Lowyck *et al* (1992: 26) point out, *studies in which tourism consumer behaviour is linked to general life style variables are generally lacking.* From a sociological point of view, a typology of tourists should be based upon both a micro analysis of tourists themselves and a macro, structural approach which locates actual tourist behaviour and experience within a broader social context. This issue is discussed shortly but, firstly, it necessary to consider what may be described as socially determined tourist typologies.

Socially determined typologies

When a structural perspective is applied to the analysis of tourist typologies it becomes evident that types, or categories, of tourist have emerged which have more to do with the values of society as a whole than with the behaviour or life style of individual tourists. In other words, certain types of tourist have been given labels that reflect broader, societal attitudes towards tourism and tourists rather than being based on any empirical research of individual tourists. In particular, the term 'mass tourist' is a general, over-used and somewhat derogatory categorisation of tourists that bears as much relation to the widespread and growing concern for the impacts of mass tourism on host societies and environments as it does to the traditional, Boorstin-type attitude towards the tourists themselves. Mass tourism is not a single, specific activity but a phenomenon that encompasses a huge variety of products, demands, destinations, tourists and so on. Clarification is required of what is meant or understood by mass tourism and, hence, the mass tourist label.

(i)   What is mass tourism?

Since the 1960s the criticism surrounding mass tourism has increasingly shifted away from the tourists themselves onto the perceived negative impacts of mass tourism around the world. A number of well-known books published during the 1970s (Young 1973; Turner and Ash 1975; de Kadt 1979; Rosenow and Pulsipher 1979) all point to mass tourism's potentially destructive impact on societies, cultures and environments whilst, during the 1980s, the adverse publicity surrounding some Mediterranean destinations added to the negative attitudes towards mass tourism (and, by association, mass tourists).

Thus, mass tourism has evolved from what Crick (1989) describes as the *degenerate offspring* of early travel into what some see as an internationally destructive force:

> *The tourism industry is in crisis...a crisis of mass tourism; for it is mass tourism that has brought social, cultural, economic and environmental havoc in its wake, and it is mass tourism practices that must be radically changed to bring in the new.*
> (Poon 1993: 3).

This criticism is indicative of a widespread condemnation of mass tourism which is founded upon a subjective, socially constructed view of mass tourism. Just as mass tourists have come to be seen collectively as what may be described as the lowest common denominator of tourism, so too has the phenomenon of mass tourism itself achieved a notoriety based on generalisations and misconceptions rather than a balanced consideration of the situation. There are a number of different ways of defining mass tourism which provide a more objective basis for analysis.

(a) Mass tourism

Mass tourism is a social, economic, political and geographic phenomenon, commonly used as a means of describing the movement of large numbers of people, usually on standardised, inclusive tours, for the purpose of holiday taking. his movement of people is the manifestation of the fundamental nature of mass tourism, namely, the mass purchasing and consumption of a product. In turn, the product has evolved through technological advance, economies of scale and the combination of a variety of services into a single package.

It is both a tangible and intangible product; the purchase of transport, accommodation and so on is combined with the anticipated benefits of the holiday but, nevertheless, mass tourism is a distinctive type of tourism product that is 'manufactured', marketed and sold. Moreover, according to Shaw and Williams (1994: 181), the consumption of mass tourism is highly spatially polarised, with large numbers of tourists, frequently segmented by nationality, concentrated in a relatively small number of areas. The tourism products in these destination areas are themselves little differentiated, implying a high degree of substitutability between destinations. As a result, *their main point of competition is usually price* (Shaw and Williams 1994: 183).

Following this argument, the mass tourist is simply an individual who purchases the mass tourism product, a product supplied by the mass tourism industry. To categorise tourists as mass tourists, or even to sub-categorise them as organised, individual, incipient or charter mass tourists, simply identifies them as individuals who, to a greater or lesser extent, consume a mass tourism product. Assumptions about the character, limitations or needs of the mass tourist thus become irrelevant unless the decision making process leading up to the purchase of the product is also taken into consideration.

(b) Mass tourism: a social construct

As discussed earlier in this chapter, although the word tourist was originally synonymous with the word traveller, distinctions soon came to be made between the two. By the mid-nineteenth century, with the advent of mass forms of transport, the tourist, as opposed to the traveller, became associated not only with mass travel but also with a particular approach to the travel experience. Thus, the term tourist and, in its twentieth century manifestation, mass tourist, has become a socially constructed label attached to particular types of tourism, forms of tourist behaviour, and primarily tourists who are satisfied with inauthentic, 'pseudo' events experienced from the safety of their environmental bubbles. This derogatory connotation has been compounded in recent years by the publicised inappropriate behaviour of a minority of tourists, such as 'lager louts', to the extent that the problem of mass tourism is seen by some to be not the number of tourists, nor the type of tourism, but the tourists themselves. The socially defined mass tourist has become, in effect, an individual who is neither able to appreciate the tourism experience nor knows how to behave in an appropriate manner whilst on holiday. In this sense, the term mass tourist is a social construct referring to those who seek out and are satisfied by what is considered by some to be the lowest common denominator of tourism.

(c) Mass tourism: tourism for the masses?

A third way of defining or interpreting mass tourism is that it is tourism that is enjoyed by the masses as opposed to the privileged few, at least in the developed, industrialised nations of the West. As described in Chapter Two, technological advance and increased levels of leisure time and disposable income have gradually brought travel, and international travel in particular, within reach of the great majority of the population. If the increasingly rapid process whereby once exclusive destinations are becoming assimilated under the umbrella of mass tourism is also taken into consideration, then it becomes evident that tourism is becoming increasingly democratised. Simply put, all tourists are part of the mass democratisation of tourism and, hence, are mass tourists. The distinction must then be made not between mass tourists and other tourists, but

118

between tourists and non-tourists, demanding a sociological explanation of why individuals choose, or are able or unable, to be tourists.

Although it is logical and justifiable to consider all tourism as mass tourism, it is, sadly, in the second sense that the term mass tourism remains most widely used, whether generally or in the more specific context of being the alleged antithesis to more appropriate, sustainable forms of tourism. This is, of course, an extreme and inaccurate view. Being a mass tourist is easy, it is safe and, perhaps most importantly, relatively cheap, a combination that continues to ensure the popularity of mass, package tourism. At the same time, *people seem to enjoy being mass tourists* (Butler 1992) and they choose to be so. Categorisations that link mass tourists with recreational experiences, with an inability to escape the environmental bubble and with an implied lack of cultural awareness deny the mass tourist any individuality and any ability to choose and to make informed decisions.

Thus, typologies which include the mass tourist as a separate category say more about the researcher than the researched. Lumping together all mass tourists as a single, socially defined category is adopting what Emery (1981) calls the *lemming hypothesis. We do not know why [mass tourists] move, but we know that, at certain times of the year, they all start moving - and we have a fair idea of the destination.* The inevitable conclusion is, again, that a practical and realistic tourist typology should be based in the broader, social context.

(ii) The good tourist

A second, socially determined type of tourist that has emerged from the present concern for the negative impacts of mass tourism is the so-called 'good tourist' (Wood and House 1991), the implication being that mass tourism is 'bad' tourism. The way forward to more appropriate, less damaging forms of tourism, originally known as alternative tourism (see Smith and Eadington 1991), but nowadays more generally referred to as sustainable tourism, is seen to be the responsibility of not only the tourism industry as a whole but also of the individual tourist. In other words, it has become increasingly recognised that the solution to the undoubted problems caused by tourism lies not only in new approaches to the development, planning and management of tourism, but also in the adoption of more appropriate behaviour on the part of tourists themselves. As Ludwig *et al* (1993) succinctly argue, *resource problems are not really environmental problems: they are human problems.*

In a sociological sense, therefore, the emphasis must shift from the structural, mass tourism perspective towards the individual, social action approach. The individual tourist responds to the reactions of others (in this case environmentalists, pressure groups and the impacts of other tourists on host environments and cultures) and demands new forms of tourism. The new, responsible tourist seeks quality rather than value, is more adventurous, more flexible, more sensitive to the environment and searches for greater authenticity than the traditional, mass tourist (see Poon 1993).

In particular, the good tourist is exhorted to adopt a new code of travel although, interestingly, is not asked to question whether tourism in any form is appropriate in certain destinations (some would argue that the only good tourist is a non-tourist!). For example, the good tourist prepares for the trip by learning in advance about the destination, ensures that he or she uses a tour operator which is aware of and supports environmental programmes in the host country, behaves in an appropriate manner and recognises local customs whilst abroad and, wherever possible, tries to benefit the local economy rather than international tourism businesses. Thus, the good tourist is a category of tourist that could, potentially, embrace all other types of tourist. However, it does overlook some fundamental features of tourism, tourist motivation, and the consumption of tourism (see Chapters Five and Six and McKercher 1993). In a broad sense, tourism is associated with holidays which, in turn, conjure up visions of rest, relaxation, fun, escape from the regular and the mundane, freedom from work and so on. The good tourist, conversely, is being asked to work at tourism, to adopt a fundamentally different approach and interpretation of the tourism experience. Additionally, the concept of the good tourist frequently attracts criticism that it is no more than an attempt to attach an explorer/drifter image to certain tourism products and to develop a niche market for 'aware' tourists. This has led to accusations that the overall idea of alternative tourism is no more than a marketing ploy, a *green mantle* (Wheeler 1991; 1992a; 1992b) behind which the tourism industry is hiding.

More specifically, the concept of the good or new tourist relies heavily on the assumption that increasing environmental awareness, and the alleged emergence of green consumerism in general, will inevitably result in more appropriate styles of tourism consumption in particular. This is not necessarily the case. Certainly, since the late 1960s, environmental concern has become one of the most widespread social and political issues. Surveys also indicate, as Macnaghten and Urry (1998) point out, that public concern in both the US and UK over environmental issues has continued to increase in the 1990s, although it appears to have become relatively less important compared with other issues. Also, this concern appears to have been translated into people's buying habits; it has been found that, between 1990 and 1994, the numbers of people who in general considered themselves to be either 'dark green' (that is 'always or as far as possible buy environmentally friendly products') or 'pale green' (that is 'buy if I see them') consumers both increased slightly, together representing 63 per cent of those questioned (Mintel 1994).

Similarly, in the specific context of tourism, the growth in demand for activities or types of holidays collectively referred to as eco-tourism would also appear to support the argument that greater numbers of people embrace principles of green consumerism; indeed, eco-tourism is considered to be the fastest growing sector of international tourism. Cater (1993), for example, reports that the number of arrivals to certain destinations has virtually doubled over a ten year period, whilst others suggest that participation in eco-tourism has increased annually by between 20 to 50 per cent since the early 1980s and now accounts for up to 10 per cent of all international tourism arrivals (Hvengaard 1994; see also Steele 1995). Importantly, there is no evidence to suggest that the increase in popularity of eco-tourism is directly related to the emergence of green consumerism or wider environmental awareness. In fact, a number of researchers refer to consumer ambivalence in the context of environmentalism. For example, despite the apparently large number of green consumers revealed by various surveys, it has been observed that up to one half of those who claim to embrace green values never transfer these beliefs into their consumer behaviour (Witherspoon 1994). *Despite the earlier evidence of high levels of environmental concern...the proportion of adults who behave in a consistently environmentally friendly consumerist fashion is very low. Fewer than one per cent of consumers behave in a consistently environmentally-friendly way* (Witherspoon 1994: 125). Thus, care must be taken in assuming that greater numbers of people are becoming or have the potential to be new, good tourists.

(iii)   The Post-Tourist

One feature that unites all the typologies of tourists is that they propose separate and identifiable tourist roles but without making an allowance for tourists adopting either a combination of roles at any one time or a variety of roles over time. For example, an individual may be categorised as a mass tourist, an explorer or a special-interest tourist. Equally, a tourist may be concerned with a safe, recreational experience within the constraints of the environmental bubble or, at the opposite extreme, seeking an 'existential' experience. There is no room in the typologies for an individual to adopt different tourist characteristics or to seek different experiences according to specific needs and constraints and in reality, the distinctions between different categories are likely to be much more blurred. A tourist might be on a pre-paid, packaged tour but, as Rojek (1993: 177) explains, *there is always room for tourist bypassings and deviations from the tourist script.*

In short, most tourist typologies are static in both time and breadth. Most typologies are also limited by the proposed links between tourist behaviour and the assumed character of tourists. The explorer-wanderlust-allocentric tourist is typecast as being bold, adventurous, independent and empathetic to new cultures and societies, whereas the mass, institutionalised tourist is unadventurous, indecisive, easily pleased by staged, inauthentic events and has little or no interest in expanding his or her cultural horizons beyond the limits of the environmental bubble. Such categorisations, as has already been pointed out, have been developed without taking the broader social context into account but, especially in the case of the mass tourist, they also deny tourists the ability to make choices.

In direct contrast, it may be argued that tourism and tourists have come of age. In other words, the distinction between the traveller and the tourist is, in fact, no more than a manifestation of the first two stages in the evolution of travel and we have now reached the third stage, the era of the *post tourist* (Feifer 1985; Urry 1988; 1990a: 100). The post-tourist lives in an age of mass communication and rapid advances in information technology; most tourist sights and destinations can be seen, if not actually experienced, on video and television in the comfort of the tourist's own living room. The post-tourist is able, therefore, to make informed decisions and delights in the choice available.

More importantly, the post-tourist recognises and understands the fundamental change that has occurred in the nature of tourism. Armed with a mass of information and images, the post-tourist knows that it is no longer possible to experience authenticity because nothing is new. The pseudo-event or the cheap souvenir is accepted for what it is. Tourism has become a kind of game, *or rather a whole series of games with multiple texts and no single, authentic tourist experience* (Urry 1990a: 100) and the post-tourist understands the role he or she plays in that game. The post-tourist chooses sometimes to be a mass tourist, sometimes an independent traveller and sometimes not to be a tourist at all and accepts the conditions and constraints of each role. For example, the organised, packaged tour is purchased for what it offers - not an authentic cultural experience but the opportunity to collect a set of pre-determined images and sights, saved for all time, perhaps, as photographs. Above all, the post-tourist is aware of being a tourist, of being an outsider, *not a time traveller when he goes somewhere historic; not an instant noble savage when he stays on a tropical beach; not an invisible observer when he visits a native compound* (Feifer 1985: 271).

For the post-tourist, then, the traveller/tourist dichotomy is irrelevant. The traveller has matured and evolved into an individual who experiences and enjoys all kinds of tourism, who takes each at face value and who is in control at all times. In effect, the post-tourist renders tourist typologies meaningless.

Tourist typologies: a broader approach

Throughout this chapter it has been emphasised that a realistic typology of tourists is essential to the explanation, understanding and prediction of tourist behaviour. If this is combined with other factors, such as a consideration of tourist motivation (Chapter Five), a broader foundation for understanding and predicting the demand for tourism is then provided. A number of issues have emerged that point to limitations both in existing tourist typologies and the more general, all-embracing categorisations, such as the 'mass tourist' and the 'good tourist'.

1. Most typologies are static and do not take into account variations in tourist behaviour or experience over time. It is perfectly feasible for an individual to knowingly choose different types of holiday or trip at different times subject to broader constraints or needs. Also, people may mature as tourists as they become more experienced, giving credence to the concept of the post-tourist. They may, in fact, progress through a tourism career (Pearce 1992), adapting their behaviour in response to changing needs and greater awareness and experience. As Lowyck *et al* (1992: 28) argue, it must be questioned *whether it makes sense at all to divide people into different types without taking into account their full life spans.*

2. Most typologies are isolated from the wider social context of the tourist. As a simple example, the most convenient and affordable holiday for a young family might well be of the package variety, yet the parents may have travelled extensively as explorers or independent travellers before being constrained by financial, job or family restraints. Thus, being a mass tourist does not necessarily imply an inability to escape the environmental bubble or, in terms of Cohen's experiential typology, having one's 'spiritual centre' firmly embedded in one's home culture and society.

3. Each typology, in particular those concerned with tourist roles or behaviour, employs a variety of names to describe a lesser or greater number of categories, from Gray's two-category to Pearce's fifteen-category typology. The important point is that, in the absence of universally accepted parameters and names for tourist categories,

researchers create descriptions of different types of tourists according to their own sphere of interest. Thus, some typologies, though looking different, say the same thing.

4. Typologies of tourists tend to be *etic*, a word used by sociologists to describe a study that is undertaken from the researcher's point of view rather than centring on the object of the research (*emic*). In other words, the typologies depend more on what the researcher puts into it rather than on unbiased, empirical findings. For example, longer-term independent travellers may be described as adventurous, individual and culturally aware on the one hand, or as lazy, irresponsible 'drop-outs' on the other hand, depending on the experience and opinion of the researcher.

Overall, typologies of tourists tend to be descriptive and, although of interest in terms of highlighting the variety of tourist types and experience, fail to be of direct relevance to a better understanding of the demand for tourism. By concentrating on the tourists *per se* rather than locating tourist categories within the broader social context of the tourists' home environment, many important, if not dominant, factors which determine different types of tourists are excluded from the equation. A tourist typology should not be based upon a one dimensional, linear progression of observed (or imagined) behaviour or experience, such as the mass tourist to individual drifter continuum, but upon a multi-dimensional matrix which incorporates tourist roles with other factors which influence tourist types. These other factors fall under two broad headings:

(i)   Demographic and socio-economic factors

Tourism is not a single product. It encompasses a whole host of different products which are designed, packaged and marketed by the tourism industry to appeal to different potential tourists or, in marketing terms, different market segments (see Middleton 1988: 65-76). Simply put, the tourism industry recognises that different types of tourism suit different people according to a variety of demographic and socio-economic factors. Logically, each of these factors should be taken into account in the formulation of a tourist typology. There are four principal variables to be considered:

(a) Age

An individual's age will determine, to a great extent, the type of tourism that he or she participates in. A younger person is more likely to be attracted to independent travel or, perhaps, to the '18-30' style of beach package holiday, whereas older tourists may be less inclined to subject themselves to the relative uncertainty or possible discomfort of independent travel. Equally, an older person may, in a touristic sense, be more experienced and demand more specialised forms of tourism.

(b) Life cycle

Life cycle characteristics play a dominant role in the determination of tourist types. For example, a young, single person has greater freedom to choose different types of holidays (within the constraints of availability of free time, financial resources and psychographic considerations) than, say, a family with young children. At the other end of the scale, 'empty nesters' or people who have retired early have fewer family responsibilities and are able to be more flexible in the timing and duration of trips. They are also likely to have more disposable income.

(c) Gender

The gender of tourists may well influence their holiday decisions, irrespective of other factors. For example, some women may decide to not travel independently or to avoid certain countries for safety reasons. Gender is also of importance within the context of the family because although *the rigid roles which normally provide the base of family life become blurred* (Clarke and Critcher 1985: 172), under certain conditions those roles may become amplified. With the growing trend towards self catering holidays, women may simply find that their domestic work has been transferred to a new location and decide that other forms of tourism are more suitable.

(d) Income/employment

Income and occupation or, more generally, socio-economic grouping, are, perhaps, the most influential factors in determining tourist types. Generally, research has shown tourism to be highly price elastic (for example, see Gerakis 1965 or Edwards 1987); that is, small increases in the cost of a holiday are very likely to result in tourists choosing cheaper destinations. More specifically, those employed in professional or managerial positions (social groups A and B) benefit from higher levels of income and longer holidays than, say, skilled manual workers (C2) and have a much wider choice of what type of holiday to take. The latter group may also be more restricted with respect to the timing of holidays. Thus, it is not surprising that, of the 41 per cent of the British population who did not take a holiday in 1992, 45 per cent belong to the D and E (unskilled manual workers, unemployed and pensioners) social group (ETB 1993). At the same time, the D and E groups (32 per cent of the British adult population) account for just 13 per cent of all holidays taken overseas whilst social groups A and B (17 per cent of the population) account for 30 per cent.

Some of these factors are inter-related and also point to other determinants of tourist behaviour. For example, there is an obvious link between age and life cycle characteristics whilst socio-economic grouping may be related to other variables, such as the level and type of education, which in turn can influence the type of tourism that an individual participates in. Essentially, a clearer and more practical tourist typology may be created by combining the more traditional, role based approach with the techniques of market segmentation. For example, in the case of independent travellers, the characteristics of a spirit of adventure, an interest in new cultures and so on certainly apply, but they are also more likely to be younger, single, and of student status (that is with more time but less disposable income).

(ii) Structural social factors

Most tourist typologies adopt a micro perspective. They concentrate on the tourist as an individual and, even when demographic and socio-economic factors are taken into account, the emphasis is placed firmly on the ability of individuals to decide what type of tourist they wish to be. In other words, different types of tourist are taken, in most cases, to be self-determined. The one exception is the 'mass tourist', the implication of most typologies being that people become mass tourists more by default than by design.

It is true that most people are able to choose, within the constraints of time, money, family commitments and so on, what type of tourists they wish to be. An equally valid approach is to consider the extent to which tourist types are structurally determined. The manner in which certain tourist labels, such as the 'mass tourist' and the 'good tourist', are socially constructed has already been considered but a holistic approach reveals that, in some situations, society plays the dominant role in the determination of tourist types.

(a) Non-tourists

Non-tourists, or people who, for whatever reason, do not participate in tourism, are a valid and identifiable category of tourist but not one that is normally included in tourist typologies. They also comprise a category of 'tourist' that remains significantly under-researched, particularly those who make a positive decision not to be tourists, even though they are able to do so. In Britain, the proportion of people who do not take a holiday (a holiday being defined as a stay of four or more nights away from home) has remained at around 40 per cent of the population for a number of years, despite increasing levels of disposable income and paid holidays. Some of these will be people who have made conscious decisions not to be tourists, whilst others may be restricted by factors such as illness or family constraints. For many people, however, their status as non-tourists has been determined by society in as much as their labour has been deemed as excess to requirements.

In other words, for the unemployed the decision to be or not to be a tourist is beyond the control of the individual. The loss of paid employment and an income other than state benefits effectively removes an individual's access to most forms of tourism, especially overseas tourism. The unemployed, non-tourist is, therefore, a manifestation of the conflict theory of society.

(b) Capitalist tourism

As discussed in Chapter One, a structural-conflict perspective on tourism reveals that the tourism industry is, in effect, a microcosm of capitalist society. The tourism industry, though diverse, fragmented and comprising a large number of private operators, is dominated by a few powerful, multinational corporations (MNCs). These organisations have concentrated the ownership of different sectors of the tourism system, such as transport, accommodation, entertainment, travel agencies, to the extent that it is possible for one company to own and control all the components of a package holiday. The latter half of the 1990s witnessed a significant degree of vertical and horizontal integration within the British tourism industry, a pattern that is likely to continue on the global stage. As a result, tour operators in particular enjoy a dominant position within the tourism production system, possessing the ability to control tourist flows through marketing and the range of products they produce and promote (see Britton 1991). Therefore, the extent to which tourists as consumers of tourism products are able to influence the kinds of products that are on offer and, hence, the types of tourist they can choose to be, is in the hands of the larger tourism organisations.

In other words, the pluralist approach (power being shared by a multiplicity of groups or organisations), which implies that tourism suppliers follow market trends and consumer demand, *greatly underestimates the power of business to persuade consumers, through advertising in particular, to make the right choices* (Clarke and Critcher 1985:103 and generally for a neo-marxist perspective on leisure). Tourists can choose to purchase or not to purchase different tourism products, but they have little control over what is on offer. On the other hand, the tourism industry and, in particular, MNCs produce a range of products to appeal to a variety of tourists, products which recognise and, perhaps, reinforce social characteristics and divisions such as age, gender and class. Thus, despite the emergence of post-Fordist production methods in response to more diverse consumer demands, economies of scale have been replaced by economies of scope which allow new products to be introduced, not to satisfy customer needs but to increase diversity, market share and, ultimately, profit. For example, a number of tour operators now offer trips or holidays that are designed to attract the 'good' tourist, more likely to be a younger, relatively affluent, better educated and well travelled person looking for authentic yet environmentally friendly holidays. Arguably, such trips play on the environmental conscience of the individual and, whilst developing an image of 'good' tourism, are little more than a niche within the mass tourism market; ironically, the 'good' tourist becomes a mass tourist.

To develop a tourist typology that incorporates a multi-dimensional approach is, perhaps, an impossible task. But, given the limitations of existing typologies, a broader foundation that locates tourists in a social context provides a clearer picture and explanation of tourist categories and roles, contributing to a better understanding of the demand for tourism. It also provides the foundation for a more detailed analysis of tourist behaviour, particularly within the tourism demand process, in the following chapters.

Five

Tourism and Tourist Motivation

Introduction

The study of tourist motivation is concerned with the question, *why do people travel?* Many attempts have been made to answer this question, ranging from theories based in psychological research to more speculative or apocryphal explanations. For example, the desire to travel is still widely seen as resulting from the 'the travel bug' or 'having itchy feet', a supposed medical condition which John Steinbeck described in *Travels with Charley* as a *disease [that] is incurable* (cited in Pearce 1982: 48). The actual meaning of the motivation to travel is also open to wide interpretation. For some, tourist motivation results from deep, psychological needs often unrecognised by tourists themselves, whereas others equate motivation with the purpose of a trip or the choice of holiday.

Whichever viewpoint is adopted, motivation represents the how, why, when and where of tourism. In other words, *the importance of motivation in tourism is quite obvious. It acts as a trigger that sets off all the events in travel* (Parrinello 1993). It is not surprising that many authors and researchers in tourism have concerned themselves with motivation, recognising it as *one of the most basic and indispensable subjects in tourism studies* (Wahab 1975: 44). It is also one of the most complex areas of tourism research. In contrast to early travellers who were motivated by basic needs for survival, present day tourists are motivated by an enormous variety of factors, many of which are rooted in modern society. Equally, there have been a number of different approaches, some based on a variety of disciplines, to the analysis of tourist motivation. This chapter examines tourism motivation from a sociological perspective considering, in particular, the link between the motivation for tourism and modern society.

Motivation and the demand for tourism

Before looking at the different approaches to tourist motivation, two general points deserve consideration. Firstly, it is important to understand the role of motivation within the overall consumer decision making process. Although, as already noted, it is motivation that 'kick starts' the entire tourism demand process, it is only the first stage in that process. As Pearce (1992: 113) has observed, *the term tourism demand should not be equated with tourism motivation. Tourism demand is the outcome of tourists' motivation.* In other words, tourists pass through a number of decision-making stages, or what has been described as a *vacation sequence* (van Raaij and Francken 1984), the first of which is the motivational stage. This tourism demand process is discussed shortly but, secondly, we must emphasise that the demand for tourism, the vacation sequence, cannot be viewed in isolation from the socio-cultural setting within which it occurs. That is, there is little doubt that a number of factors, from financial constraints to values and beliefs, directly influence tourism decision making. Many of those factors themselves are influenced by wider, cultural factors; *consumption choices simply cannot be understood without considering the cultural context in which they are made* (Solomon 1994: 536). An understanding of the 'consumer culture' of tourism is also fundamental to the study of the demand for tourism, and is the focus of Chapter Six.

(i) The tourism demand process

At a basic level, tourism is a product that is purchased and consumed. Hence, tourists go through a process of *acquiring and organising information in the direction of a purchase decision and of using and evaluating products and services* (Moutinho 1987: 5). In other words, unless a trip or a holiday is an impulse purchase, tourists make a choice on the basis of their personal needs and desires and the extent to which they perceive those needs will be satisfied by a particular trip, holiday or destination. That choice will normally be influenced by factors such as the image or known attributes of the destination, the impact of advertising, the distance and mode of travel to the destination, previous experience, the advice of family and friends and so on. Additionally, holiday choice is constrained by factors such as family and work commitments, financial considerations and, of course, the range of products supplied by the tourism industry.

Together, these stages that the tourist goes through represent the tourism demand process. This has been conceptualised by a number of authors. For example, Mathieson and Wall (1982) propose that the tourism demand process involves five sequential phases. These can be expressed diagrammatically (see Figure 1, below).

Figure 1: Stages of the tourism demand process

Stage 1: Felt need or travel desire	Stage 2: Information collection and evaluation	Stage 3: Travel decisions	Stage 4: Travel preparations and travel experience	Stage 5: Travel satisfaction evaluation

Source: adapted from Mathieson and Wall (1982: 28)

Within this process, the motivation to participate in tourism is manifested in a 'felt need' to travel and only when the decision has been made to satisfy that need does the individual move on to the subsequent stages in the process. Similarly, Goodall (1991: 65) suggests that the holiday-decision process generally involves the five steps of problem identification (whether or not to take a holiday in the first place), the search for information, the evaluation of alternatives, the purchase decision and, finally, feedback, whereby the evaluation of the holiday experience becomes an additional factor in the next decision-making sequence.

Others have developed more complex models which attempt to define diagrammatically the varying factors that influence the final decision. Schmoll (1977), for example, utilises a four step sequential process from travel desires, through information search and the evaluation of alternatives, to the purchase decision. That final decision is influenced, according to Schmoll, by forces and pressures that emanate from four separate fields, namely travel stimuli, in the form of trade or personal information and recommendations; personal and social determinants, which shape motivations and expectations; external variables, such as the image of the destination, past travel experiences and the constraints of time and money; and characteristics of destinations. With the exception of personal/social determinants, each field has an influence on each stage of the decision process.

In a similar vein, Gilbert (1991: 79) identifies four elements of the tourism decision process:

(a)   *Energisers of Demand.* These are the forces, including motivation, which lead the tourist into deciding to take a holiday in the first place.

(b)   *Filterers of Demand.* Demand is constrained by a variety of demographic and socio-economic factors.

(c)   *Affectors of Demand.* The information about a destination and the tourist's image of it will affect the course of action taken.

(d)   *Roles.* The role of the tourist as a consumer (for example, as a family member) may determine the final choice of holiday.

Inevitably, these models all over-simplify what in practice is a complex, dynamic and multi-dimensional consumption process. The demand for tourism is, generally, neither a 'one-off' event nor a simple, uni-directional circular process whereby previous travel experiences influence the motivation for, and supplement the information in, the next holiday decision process. As Pearce (1992) points out, tourism consumption occurs over a life-time, during which tourists may progress up or climb a travel career ladder as they become more experienced tourists (see also Pearce and Caltabiano 1983). In the process, their attitudes, values, social relationships or life-style factors may all change, representing new influences on decision making. There is also a lack of clarity and distinction between the different stages in the decision process whilst there may, potentially, be a reverse flow of influences. For example, it may be an advertisement or a travel brochure (second stage factors) that creates the need or motivation. Moreover, models of tourism decision-making imply a logical and rational process, simplifying a complex process that frequently defies rationality and that has been described as *discretionary, episodic, future oriented, dynamic, socially influenced and evolving* (Pearce 1992: 114). But, they provide a useful foundation for understanding the demand for tourism, particularly in the way in which they highlight the role of motivation in the process. This is most commonly identified as motivational 'push' as opposed to destinational 'pull', a distinction which serves to separate the motivational stage from subsequent elements of the decision making process.

(ii) Push versus pull factors

If all the knowledge, information, images and perceptions of a particular holiday or destination are combined they add up to the overall attraction, or *pull*, of that holiday choice. Pull factors may be described as *destination-specific attributes* (Goodall 1991: 59) within the decision making process. For example, the destination-specific attributes of a skiing holiday might include accommodation, entertainment facilities, the probability of good snow, the availability of skiing instruction and so on. At the same time, there usually exists a variety of factors that influence, or *push*, an individual into making a purchase decision. These *person-specific motivations* are what push an individual into wanting a particular type of holiday or, indeed, a holiday as opposed to another product, such as a new washing machine. Thus, the skiing holiday might be chosen in preference to, say, a summer beach holiday because an individual has a need or preference for a healthy lifestyle.

The distinction between push and pull factors is of fundamental importance to understanding the role of motivation within the demand for tourism. Generally, it is the push factors, the needs and wants of an individual, that lead to the decision to purchase a holiday in the first place, the nature of those needs determining the type of holiday the individual wants. For example, a person might want to visit friends and relatives but may be motivated by a need for love and affection. Once the decision to take a particular type of holiday has been made, the pull factors of different destinations determine which one is chosen. Thus, *the key to understanding tourist motivation is to see vacation travel as a satisfier of needs and wants* (Mill and Morrison 1985: 4).

135

In short, motivation is the very basis of the demand for tourism. The distinction between push and pull factors may not, in practice, be always clear cut whilst, as suggested earlier, a whole host of other factors, including the socio-economic and psychographic characteristics of the individual and broader, cultural factors, may influence different stages of the process as well as the final choice of tourism product. But, it is effectively motivation that translates an individual's personal needs into goal-orientated behaviour, behaviour from which the tourism decision making process evolves and progresses. The motivation to satisfy needs, combined with personal preferences, pushes the tourist into considering alternative products; the final choice depends on the pull of alternative holidays or destinations.

An understanding of tourist motivation is of fundamental importance to the study of tourism demand; *an analysis of the motivational stage.. can reveal the way in which people set goals for their destination-choice and how these goals are reflected in both their choice and travel behaviour* (Mansfeld 1992). There is also great practical value in the explanation and analysis of tourist motivation. Those organisations which are best able to cater for and predict tourist motivation and demand, and hence satisfy the needs of tourists, are likely to be most successful in an increasingly diverse and competitive tourism market.

Perspectives on tourist motivation

The complexity of the concept of tourist motivation is reflected in the widespread and diverse treatment of the subject in the tourism literature. Despite the popularity of the subject, it has been observed that *no common understanding has yet emerged* (Jafari 1987: 152). This can be explained in part by the fact that much of the work concerned with tourist motivation has been theoretical in nature and drawn from a variety of disciplinary foundations. There have also been relatively few empirically-based attempts to verify these theories of motivation (Dann, Nash and Pearce 1988), a situation mirrored, according to Mansfeld (1992), by a corresponding lack of empirical studies in the wider context of consumer behaviour in general. Much of the research has been based upon content theory, focusing in particular on tourists' needs and, thus, overlooking the processes whereby these needs are transformed into goal-oriented behaviour; as Witt and Wright (1993) argue, needs undoubtedly arouse motivated behaviour, but they do not necessarily predict what that behaviour will be.

Generally, then, the literature on tourist motivation encompasses a variety of ideas and approaches. These are summarised by Dann (1981), who defines tourist motivation as *a meaningful state of mind which adequately disposes an actor or group of actors to travel, and which is subsequently interpretable by others as a valid explanation for such a decision.* What we are concerned with here are the ways in which this *meaningful state of mind* is determined or, more simply, how it is that people are motivated to be tourists. It must also be stressed that the study of tourist motivation is of most relevance to the category of what may be described as holiday tourism; that is, tourism that is generally non-essential and for pleasure. The demand for other forms of tourism, in particular business tourism, tends to result from the purpose of the trip rather than from the needs of the tourist.

In his review of the study of tourism motivation, Dann (1981) identifies seven different perspectives that have been adopted:

1. *Travel as a Response to What is Lacking Yet Desired*
The motivation for travel lies in the desire to experience something new or different. People become tourists because their own physical and cultural environment cannot fulfil this need.

2. *Destinational Pull in Response to Motivational Push*
 This approach highlights the importance of push factors in tourist motivation. Such factors may be determined by the tourist's home environment or by an individual's own psychological needs.

3. *Motivation as Fantasy*
Tourists may be motivated by the perceived opportunity to indulge in forms of behaviour that would not normally be socially sanctioned or acceptable in their home environment.

4. *Motivation as Classified Purpose*
In contrast to push factors, this approach views the purpose of a trip or holiday as the primary motivating factor.

5. *Motivational Typologies*
Typologies of tourists are often used as models of tourist motivation. Within the context of this book typologies and motivation, though connected, are treated as separate issues (see Chapter Four).

6. *Motivation and Tourist Experiences*
This approach suggests that tourist motivation is largely determined by the expected experience in relation to the home environment, in particular by the promise of authenticity.

7. *Motivation as Auto-Definition and Meaning*
The principles of social action theory, especially symbolic interactionism, can be usefully applied to tourist motivation. The ways in which tourists define and respond to situations is seen as a better way of explaining tourist motivation rather than simply examining their behaviour.

Within these seven perspectives, there are two distinct approaches which may be used as a basis for an examination of tourist motivation. The first is to consider ways in which motivation results from influences external to the tourist (extrinsic motivational factors) and the second is to consider the personal needs of tourists themselves (intrinsic motivational factors).

(i)   Extrinsic motivation

There are a variety of different forces and pressures which emanate from an individual's social and cultural environment and which may, to a lesser or greater extent, influence that individual's needs and motivations. These pressures may flow from sources such as social norms, the influence of family and friends, the work environment and so on. Therefore, although some may argue that *motivation is a purely psychological concept, not a sociological one* (Iso-Ahola 1982), there is little doubt that, in the case of tourism, motivation often results from societal values, norms and pressures which are internalised and become psychological needs. For example, the motivation for many people to take a holiday is to relax, to rest, to have a change and to get away from the routine, mundane constraints of everyday life. These needs can be grouped together under the general heading of escape, or *avoidance* (Iso-Ahola 1982) motivations which are, undoubtedly, rooted in society. In short, needs which underpin tourist motivation may be viewed *in terms of the (tourist) group of which the person deliberately or otherwise is a member* (Dann 1981: 199), rather than from the individual's psychological condition.

It would be logical to propose that, sociologically, a structural approach to extrinsic tourist motivation should be adopted in as much as certain categories of motivation, such as escape, result directly from the pressures and condition of life in a tourist's home society. MacCannell's assertion that for modern tourists, *reality and authenticity are thought to be elsewhere: in other historical periods and other cultures, in purer, simpler lifestyles* (1989: 3) and that tourism is a search for the authentic that results from the inauthentic, alienated condition of modern industrial society, is firmly based in structural sociology. More specifically, tourist motivation may be viewed from a functionalist perspective; whether motivated by the desire to rest and relax, to 're-create', or to seek authentic experiences, the function of tourism is to redress the balance and harmony of society: *tourism is social therapy, a safety valve keeping the everyday world in good working order* (Krippendorf 1986: 525). It is also important to bear in mind that overall tourism demand results from the needs and motivations of *individual* tourists who, together, comprise the market for tourism. Motivation is concerned with the individual tourist and, therefore, a micro, social action perspective is also of value to the study of motivation. (See Dann, 1981, for a discussion of the disciplinary treatment of motivation).

(a) The tourism-work relationship

Modern tourism and, more generally, leisure, originated as a result of the fundamental changes that occurred in the nature and structure of society from the early nineteenth century onwards. People were motivated to participate in leisure activities or to travel by the need to remove themselves physically or mentally from the conditions of life in the cities of the Industrial Revolution. In particular, leisure and tourism became the antithesis to work, a *status quo* that, for many people, continues to this day. Work is a primary extrinsic motivational factor for tourism.

Leisure, tourism and work cannot be separated; work provides both the means and the motivation for leisure and tourism and, up to a point, people need to participate in leisure and tourism to continue in work. (Importantly, work should not only be considered in the narrow sense of paid employment. Other commitments, including unpaid work and family/home responsibilities, should also be included.) Thus, work and leisure are not separate, distinct conditions. A relationship exists between the nature, or experience, of work and the leisure experience (see Parker 1983). For some people, work is boring, monotonous, repetitive and something to be endured; leisure and tourism represent freedom and escape from work and work, therefore, is a means to an end. For others, work is a way of life. It is exciting, stimulating and, perhaps, the dominant feature in an individual's life; the role of leisure may thus be subordinated to work. The important point is that different types of work produce different levels of satisfaction. Creative, challenging work arguably produces higher levels of satisfaction whereas more mundane, repetitive forms of work result, generally, in lower satisfaction for the individual. Different work environments produce different individual needs and, hence, different leisure and tourism motivations. In short, *the experience of work in industrial societies...forms the context for the experience of leisure* (Clarke and Critcher 1985:17).

Of course, it is not only the work environment which determines an individual's leisure and tourism needs. Nor, under certain circumstances, does the work-tourism relationship apply to particular groups in society, such as the retired or the unemployed (although involuntary non-work may be considered the same as work as a motivational factor in tourism). Parker (1983) suggests three basic ways in which the work-leisure (tourism) relationship manifests itself, thereby providing a framework for understanding the links between work and leisure experiences and requirements. Similarly, Zuzanek and Mannell (1983) propose four different hypotheses about the nature of the work-leisure relationship.

1. Work and tourism in opposition

Where work and tourism are in opposition, there is a sharp contrast between the experiences of each. The individual is motivated to seek out forms of tourism that offer a distinct change of experience, or even lifestyle, from that found at work. In theory this relationship should operate in both directions; that is, people in monotonous, production-line type employment are motivated to go on holidays which are stimulating and exciting and which allow them to escape, albeit temporarily, from the reality of everyday life. Conversely, it might be expected that those who are employed in challenging, stressful jobs would seek out quieter, restful or even monotonous types of tourism experience. It has been found, however, that this model is most applicable to those in lower status jobs and to whom tourism *compensates* (Zuzanek and Mannell 1983) for deficiencies at work and, by implication, at home. Hence, this model is also referred to as the compensation hypothesis (Ryan 1991: 20); tourism compensates for deficiencies in the nature of people's work.

Ryan (1991: 20) cites the leading role played by the textile workers of Lancashire and Yorkshire, in the formation of cycling and rambling clubs at the end of the nineteenth and in the early twentieth centuries, as an historical example of the compensatory nature of leisure experiences. For them, the countryside became a refuge from the conditions of life and work in industrial urban centres. He goes on to describe a situation where the tourist escapes to a fantasy life, the life of the 'idle rich', staying in hotels and enjoying standards of service that could normally only be dreamed of. By saving for the holiday, the tourist is able to indulge in a life-style that is in direct contrast to normal life; in compensation for what is missing at work and at home, the holiday represents an inversion of everyday reality. Thus, the tourist is motivated to search out the opposite of the work/home experience. The worker-as-tourist seeks to be a *king/queen for a day*, whilst the middle or upper class tourist seeks to be a *peasant for a day* in an inversion of their normal work and social environments (Gottlieb 1982).

The opposition/compensation model of tourist motivation is also applicable to the lifestyle or constraints that are imposed by different types of work, rather than the deficiencies of the work itself. People are constrained by time commitments and codes of dress and behaviour; in contrast, tourism offers the opportunity to escape from these constraining rules and norms, to indulge in 'ludic' behaviour (that is, behaviour that can be described as play). For example, Lett (1983) describes how charter yacht tourists in the Caribbean behave in a manner which is *an inverted expression of many of the pervasive values and attitudes of middle-class U.S. culture* (1983: 54). Constrained only by time, the tourists ignore the social rules and conventions of their home society and indulge in excessive drinking and sexual activities, behaviour which is *licenced and excused only because it is temporary and occurs away from home* (1983: 53). Lett emphasises the compensatory character of such behaviour and suggests that it not only refreshes and restores tourists but also prepares them to re-enter their structured, everyday existence.

If tourism presents the opportunity for inversion from condition (reality) to another (fantasy) and escape from the rules and norms of home society (an escape from responsibility), it is then logical to progress the argument to suggest that tourism, for the tourist, is a form of regression to a child-like existence (Dann 1996: 101-134). This may be manifested in a number of ways. For example, the freedom from responsibility and decision making, roles taken over by the travel agent or tour operator who, in effect, act *in loco parentis*, may represent a form of liberation which *becomes no more or less than a return to the realm of childhood* (Dann 1996: 104).

Equally, the choice of destination/attraction offers the opportunity for tourists to immerse themselves in a child-like world. It has been suggested, for example, that the popularity of rural heritage sites, such as Beatrix Potter's Hill Top Farm in the English Lake District, is evidence of tourists' desires to evoke childhood memories, to retrace their steps to childhood places, both real and imagined.

Similarly, particular types of holidays or attractions, such as theme parks, permit tourists to participate in child-like behaviour, to play, to enter a world of fantasy, to have fun. In short, the tourist as child is in opposition to, or compensates for, the tourist as adult; tourism is a journey back to a world of freedom, play and a lack of responsibility – of childhood.

142

2. Tourism as an extension of work

Where tourism and leisure are an extension of work there is, again, a direct link between the work experience and the tourism/leisure experience. Unlike the opposition/compensation model, however, where the individual is motivated to seek change and escape, the extension model proposes that there is little distinction between patterns of work and patterns of leisure. In other words, tourism and leisure complements, rather than contrasts with, work. Thus, people who have challenging, stimulating and satisfying jobs, who are in a position of some responsibility, are more likely to choose an independent and stimulating type of tourism. Conversely, those who work in highly regulated, routine and monotonous jobs, who have a passive work role, will adopt a similarly passive attitude towards their tourism and leisure activities. They will choose the mass produced, package holiday which, in effect, mirrors the production-line environment of the workplace. The extreme case would be the individual whose work is central to his or her life and for whom there is little or no distinction between tourism and work, no boundary between work and leisure. For example, a history teacher's holiday might be spent touring historical sites, an activity which could be described as both leisure and work.

The important implication of the theory of tourism motivated as an extension of work is that as work practices change and adapt, so too will the demand for tourism. Many of the main tourism generating countries are being rapidly transformed from industrial to post-industrial economies; primary, manufacturing industries are being superseded by service industries, traditional production lines are becoming increasingly automated. For example, Glasgow has lost virtually all its traditional manufacturing industries and is basing its economic regeneration on the development of the tertiary, service sector, including tourism.

Some would argue that the move towards service industry dominated economies is resulting in more widespread job satisfaction, whilst others would argue that although technology has advanced, the system of production (that is, capitalism) remains unchanged. Whichever viewpoint

143

is adopted, there is little doubt that changes in work practices and environments will impact upon tourism motivation and demand.

3. Neutrality between tourism and work

Both the opposition/compensation and the extension models of the relationship between leisure and work highlight the role of work itself in determining tourist motivation. That is, a causal relationship exists between work and tourism and leisure. In contrast, the third model occupies the mid-point between opposition and extension, suggesting that work has little or no effect on leisure patterns and *vice versa*. In effect, the experience of work and the experience of leisure remain independent; there is no link between the two. As Clarke and Critcher (1985: 19) point out, in this situation it is likely that leisure is seen to be more fulfilling, that work loses its perceived importance and becomes a means to an end. For example, during the 1980s in Britain the work ethic was dominant; by the start of the 1990s, quality of life had become a more widely accepted motivation. The importance of work has diminished and the implication is that the influence of work as an extrinsic factor in tourist motivation is also diminishing in terms of the type of tourism chosen. But, the position of tourism, in particular the annual summer holiday, as the accepted (or even expected) form of leisure activity is such that the role of work as the prime extrinsic motivator of tourism is virtually unassailable.

(b) Social influences

In addition to work and the work environment as a major factor in influencing tourist motivation, a variety of other extrinsic pressures may affect the individual. These pressures are exerted by other people and together may be termed social influences (Moutinho 1987: 5). There are four main sources of social influence in an individual's tourist motivation, each of which requires brief explanation:

1. Family influences

The family can play a significant role in the detrmination of tourist type (see Chapter Four); irrespective of other factors, the family may be a powerful constraint on the choice of tourism product. Equally, the family can have a significant influence on tourist motivation. It is through the family that, initially, most people acquire and internalise their values, beliefs and expectations. Thus, if an individual was brought up in a family which enjoyed regular overseas holidays, it is likely that he or she will be motivated to continue the tradition. Conversely, a negative experience or impression of family holidays may motivate an individual family member into becoming an independent tourist. The VFR (visiting friends and relatives) market is, of course, largely influenced by the family with the desire to visit relatives, both domestically and overseas, being a powerful tourism motivator.

2. Reference groups

A reference group is any group that an individual turns to as a point of reference for beliefs and attitudes. That is, it is a group against which an individual can judge his or her own beliefs and behaviour. Reference groups may take various forms, such as religious or ethnic groups, work colleagues, or the local neighbourhood, and are either normative (influence general values) or comparative (influence specific attitudes). The level of contact with or adherence to a particular reference group will determine the influence that group has on an individual.

3. Social class

Social class is *a relatively permanent division of categories in a society, a division that brings about some restrictions of behaviour between individuals in different classes* (Moutinho 1987: 7). As discussed in Chapter Three, the concept of social class is becoming of less relevance in postmodern societies. That is, the process of de-differentiation is breaking down the traditional distinctions or roles, such as work or gender roles, parameters which distinguished one class from another. As a result, new social groups are emerging which pay little respect to more traditional class boundaries. But, members of a particular social class or group tend to have similar values and lifestyles and it is likely that they will follow standards of behaviour acceptable to that class or group. Therefore, social class/grouping is an important factor in tourist motivation. For example, many destinations are categorised by the social

TOURISM AND TOURIST MOTIVATION

class of the majority of visitors, some being seen as 'up-market', others as 'down-market'. Different types of tourism may also be class motivated; the working classes have traditionally tended to be attracted by mass tourism or crowds of other tourists, whereas a more solitary approach, what Walter (1982) refers to as *romantic tourism*, is of greater appeal to the middle class. Similarly, newer types of tourism appeal to newer (postmodern) social groupings. For example, eco-tourism is ostensibly designed to appeal to that group of tourists whose motivation/behaviour is framed by their shared environmental beliefs and concerns. As discussed shortly and following on from the discussion of the 'good' tourist in the preceding chapter, research has shown that environmental concern is not in fact a major motivational factor amongst eco-tourists.

4. Culture

The culture of a society is the combination of its values, morals, behavioural norms, dress, cuisine, artefacts and language. In short, a society's culture is its way of life which is passed on from generation to generation. The culture of a society is dynamic; it may change and adapt over time. Such transformations may be evident in tangible elements, such as tastes in food or music, or in new styles of clothing or architecture; they may also be intangible, as in the alleged emergence of postmodernity (see Chapter Three).

In either case, a society's culture influences the attitudes and behaviour of the individual members of that society. In the context of tourist motivation, the culture of a particular society can be a strong influence on the determination of tourism demand. For example, travel and tourism is more deeply rooted in some cultures than others, or more acceptable in some countries than others. Similarly, different cultures motivate different types of tourism, such as the importance of religious tourism and pilgrimage within Islamic culture whilst, as discussed in the next chapter, the role or meaning of tourism as one form of consumption may also be directly influenced by cultural factors.

Social influences on tourist motivation are not mutually exclusive. Indeed, it is likely that a combination, if not all, of these four sources of pressure and influence have a bearing on an individual's decision making process. Some, such as the influence of family, may be more explicit, whilst class or cultural characteristics may be so ingrained as to be unrecognised as positive or negative motivational factors. They may also be combined with motivational forces arising from the work-leisure relationship, so that it may be impossible to highlight any one dominant source of motivation.

(c) Modern society and tourism motivation

Leisure in general and tourism in particular have become institutionalised within modern, industrial societies. For the majority of the populations of the main tourism generating countries, the summer holiday is an accepted, or even expected, part of life, celebrated as vigorously as other more traditional festivals in the annual calendar. Rapid advances in technology, economic growth and greater amounts of time available for leisure activities have brought to the masses a degree of freedom and mobility once reserved for the privileged minority. Indeed, it has been argued that *mobility, vacations and travel are social victories* (Krippendorf 1986).

Paradoxically, however, those societies which provide the opportunity for travel and tourism also provide the motivation; modern, industrial society has created not only the means of, but also the need for, tourism. For many tourists, the annual holiday represents the chance to rest, to recover from the stresses and strains of everyday life, to get away from it all: *a hurried mobility has obsessed most of the inhabitants of the industrialised nations. One seizes every opportunity to free oneself from the boredom of everyday life as often as possible* (Krippendorf 1986). Tourism has become an essential ingredient in a person's life cycle in modern society. In order to survive in modern society, an individual must, periodically, escape from it. Thus, from a structural point of view, tourism is motivated by society and, at the same time, plays an essential function within it. In other words, society itself determines, arguably, the ultimate motivation for tourism.

It is the character of life in modern societies, an amalgamation of the activities, work practices, demands, technological advances, expectations and social values which, together, constitute the modern 'way of life', that has created the need to escape. This need has been satisfied by increasingly fast, economical and widely available forms of transport. Since the beginning of the industrialisation and urbanisation of societies, people have become increasingly alienated. The division of labour, mass production and automation have alienated people from their work and the product of their labour; greater mobility and communication have alienated people from their friends and families; cities have alienated people from nature; people have even become alienated from themselves. Immersed in a world dominated and guided by the economy and economic growth, people have lost their sense of place and belonging; independence and freedom have replaced community, having has replaced giving, materialism has replaced contentment. Manufacturers introduce new products to make every task easier, faster and more painless, yet every technological advance diminishes human contact and reduces the need for social interaction. As life gets faster, people have less time. The realities of modern life, for many, are a source of stress, constraint, disenchantment and dissatisfaction. People have lost their sense of time and place, they have lost their self-identity. In short, life in modern, industrial society is typified by a sense of 'anomie'.

Anomie is a word used by sociologists to describe *a situation of perceived normlessness and meaninglessness in the origin* [tourist generating] *country* (Dann 1981). According to Dann (1977), anomie is a major extrinsic tourism motivator. Adrift in modern society's headlong rush to achieve economic and material growth, people find themselves wanting to say 'stop the world, I want to get off'. Whether to simply rest for a couple of weeks on a beach, to participate in physical or cultural activities which the hectic pace of life at home does not allow for, or to search for meaning, fulfilment and authenticity in other places and cultures (MacCannell 1989), people are motivated to escape, temporarily, from their society. Every year, millions of people join together in a kind of migration, *seemingly of their own free will, but appearing as if they were obeying an order* (Krippendorf 1986). They willingly subject themselves to traffic jams, delays at airports and all the other problems associated with modern, mass travel in order to refresh themselves, to prepare themselves for work or simply just to convince themselves that, compared to life in other places or countries, things are not too bad after all. Motivated by the realities of everyday life and spurred on by the efforts of the tourism industry, *people learn to desire vacations...for escape purposes and come to think of such vacations as essential for their psychological well-being* (Mannell and Iso-Ahola 1987).

In short, tourism has become a fact of modern society. Society has created the need and the motivation for tourism, it has created the means by which the great majority of the population may participate in tourism and, in a sense, society sustains tourism as an essential function in the work-leisure cycle. It is for these reasons that some authors (for example, Krippendorf 1987) maintain that the root of the 'problem' of tourism, as a mass phenomenon that impacts physically and culturally on destination areas, lies not in tourism itself but in the societies that generate tourists. They argue that, unlike early travel, modern tourism is motivated by the need to escape rather than a desire to discover and, therefore, the only way to minimise the impacts of tourism is to remove the need for tourism in the first place. By fundamentally altering the way of life in modern societies, people will no longer feel the need to escape and, by implication, will not participate in tourism. The position of tourism as a socially motivated and maintained activity is such that, unless technological advance in areas like 'virtual reality' can offer a viable and realistic alternative, people will increasingly feel the need to take holidays away from their everyday society.

(ii)   Intrinsic motivation

The study of motivation has, traditionally, been concerned with the needs and desires of the individual. It is an individual's personal and deep-rooted needs that lead to motivated, goal-orientated behaviour, the goal being to satisfy those needs. The study of motivation has, therefore, been guided by the assumption that *in order to understand human motivation it is necessary to discover what needs people have and how they can be fulfilled* (Witt and Wright 1992: 34). Every individual has personal and unique needs, needs which may go unrecognised by, but are still intrinsic to, the individual. In short, the notion of intrinsic need satisfaction has long been considered the primary arousal factor in motivated behaviour and, in the context of tourism, a number of attempts have been made to

149

link intrinsic, psychological needs with identified goal-oriented touristic behaviour.

(a) Maslow's hierarchy of needs

One of the best known theories of motivation is Maslow's hierarchy of needs (Maslow 1943). It was originally developed by Maslow in connection with his work in clinical psychology during the 1940s but since that time it has been applied widely as a general theory of motivation. It has also been used in specific fields of research, such as motivation in business, and it also forms the basis for much of the work concerned with tourist motivation.

Underlying Maslow's theory of motivation is the concept that all individuals have a number of needs which fall into five broad classifications:

Physiological Needs: hunger, thirst, rest, sex, etc.

Safety Needs: freedom from threat, fear and anxiety, etc.

Love (Social) Needs: friendship, affection, receiving love, etc.

Esteem Needs: self-esteem, self-confidence, reputation, prestige, etc.

Self-actualisation Needs: self-fulfilment, etc.

In addition, Maslow originally proposed that these five classes of needs form a hierarchy (as shown in Figure 2 on page 151), each of which must be satisfied before an individual will be motivated by the next class of need in the hierarchy. If none of the needs in the hierarchy have been satisfied, then the basic, physiological needs take precedence and dominate behaviour. Once this need has been satisfied, then it no longer motivates behaviour and the individual will move up to the next level of the hierarchy. This process continues until the final level is reached, the implication being that self-actualisation is the level to which people should aspire (see Cooper *et al* 1993: 21).

Figure 2: Maslow's Hierarchy of Needs

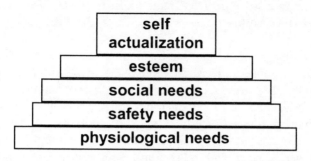

The appeal of Maslow's theory lies, no doubt, in its simplicity. Maslow himself has recognised the limitations of his model, in particular its relevance and adaptability to the work situation. He has also suggested that the linear progression from one set of needs to the next does not necessarily occur in all cases; not only does he identify seven different 'routes' through the hierarchy but he also states that each set of needs may only be partially satisfied before the next set begins to dominate behaviour. Because of these limitations, Witt and Wright (1992: 36) suggest that Murray's classification of human needs, developed in 1938, provides a better, although more complicated, basis for understanding and explaining tourist motivation. But, Maslow's model has been widely adapted by tourism researchers, perhaps because of the way in which a wide range of differing human needs are presented in a simple and understandable framework (Cooper *et al* 1993).

For example, Pearce (1988) and Pearce and Caltabiano (1983) have developed a framework for the study of tourist motivation that is initially based on Maslow's hierarchical model. They describe five different levels of motivation, namely, a concern with biological needs, safety and security needs, relationship needs, special interest needs and, finally, self-actualisation needs. They argue that such a framework allows for both biological motives (for example, rest and recuperation) and social motives to be included and, unlike other theories of tourist motivation, it recognises that motivations may change over time and that tourists may also have more than one motivation. Also, tourist motivation is viewed as a dynamic process; people have a tourism 'career' and move up the tourist ladder at different stages of their life-cycle (see Pearce 1992). At any stage they may also retire from their tourism career; that is, they may decide not to take holidays.

There is, of course, the danger that the application of Maslow's hierarchy to the specific context of tourist motivation over-simplifies a complex process, providing tidy explanations for observed tourist behaviour without considering a range of other forces and influences on the decision-making process. Certain types of tourism can be related to specific needs; summer-sun package holidays, for example, might satisfy biological needs (rest and relaxation), safety needs (the security of organised, institutionalised travel) and self-esteem needs (being able to display a suntan on returning home), yet intrinsic need satisfaction cannot fully explain tourist motivation. It tells only part of the story. But, it draws attention to the fact that people have psychological needs that may be satisfied through tourism, needs which may, in fact, go unrecognised by the individual concerned.

(b) Psychological motives for tourism

Dann (1977) suggests that tourism is motivated both socially by the anomic condition of society and psychologically by the need for ego-enhancement. A similar position is adopted by Iso-Ahola (see Mannell and Iso-Ahola 1987) who subdivides psychological motivational forces into two simultaneous influences. On the one hand, motivation results from the need to escape from personal or interpersonal environments whilst, on the other hand, there also exists the tendency to seek intrinsic psychological rewards from participation in tourism. The difference between Dann's and Iso-Ahola's position is that the former asserts that escape and the search for reality/meaning is socially determined, whilst the latter argues that tourist seek escape-avoidance from personal, psychological environments. In both cases tourists are motivated by the prospect of 'reward'; in other words, people feel the need to travel not only because of the sense of normlessness and meaninglessness imposed upon them by modern society but also by the need to be recognised, to have their ego or confidence boosted, to personally and psychologically gain from tourism. Thus, whilst on holiday, away from their usual surroundings and friends, people are able to act out an alien personality, similar to the *king/queen for a day* situation described by Gottlieb (1982). It is more than simply an inversion of the normal and more than indulgence in ludic behaviour. The opportunity for ego-enhancement, for status enhancement, links directly to the potential satisfaction of Maslow's concept of self esteem needs, achieved through the suntan, showing photographs of places visited, or sending a postcard as the ultimate status of symbol of 'I am here but you are there'. Equally, anomie as a tourist motivator can also be related to Maslow's hierarchy, participation in tourism resulting from the need for love and a sense of belonging.

For example, Dann's theory of tourist motivation is based upon research amongst tourists visiting Barbados. He found that anomic tourists were married and tended to belong to higher socio-economic groups, whereas ego-enhancement tourists were from a lower socio-economic group and more likely to be female. The demographic characteristics of the latter group related to lower status roles in the tourists' home countries, thus confirming the ego-enhancement motivation of travel. A major criticism of Dann's approach, as argued by Pearce (1982), is that, in addition to ignoring other possible motivations, it is unclear whether the findings are based upon the tourists' own explanations or the researcher's interpretation of the situation. Such criticism is understandable when it is considered that tourists themselves may have difficulty in recognising or articulating the real, underlying motivations for travel. For example, Crompton (1979) found that respondents to his research had difficulty in explaining the true reasons for destination choice. However, he identified seven psychological push motives for travel: escape from a perceived mundane environment, exploration and evaluation of self, relaxation, prestige, regression, enhancement of kinship relationships, and facilitation of social interaction. These psychological motives represented, according to Crompton (1979: 415), *a hidden agenda* for tourist motivation.

The same problem in determining the true psychological motivation for tourism has been recognised by Mill and Morrison: *tourists themselves may be unaware of the true reasons for their travel behaviour. Individuals are often unaware of the real reasons for doing certain things* (1985: 2). Additionally, people may not always be willing to reveal the real reason for their holiday, such wanting to impress their neighbours or work colleagues by showing off their suntans. Likewise, Krippendorf (1987: 22) suggests that an individual's motivation to travel will normally repeat *all the reasons that feature in advertising and which are repeated over and over again in all tourist brochures and catalogues*, whilst the true motivations lie hidden in the subconscious. But, Krippendorf lists eight different travel motivations that can be identified from the literature: recuperation and regeneration; compensation and social integration; escape; communication; broadening the mind; freedom and self-determination; self-realisation; happiness.

(c) Motivation by purpose

Owing, perhaps, to the difficulty in ascertaining an individual's underlying motivations for tourism, some authors relate motivation to the purpose of the trip rather than the satisfaction of an identified or hidden psychological need. These may be regarded as intrinsic inasmuch as they relate to the individual tourist's desire for personal reward or achievement of a goal through tourism. For example, McIntosh and Goeldner (1990: 131) list four categories of what they term basic travel motivators:

1. Physical motivators.
These relate to the need for rest, participation in sport, relaxing entertainment and other motivations which are connected with health. Common to all physical motivators is the reduction in tension and the refreshment of body and mind through physical activities.

2. Cultural motivators.
These are manifested in the desire to see and learn about other countries, their music, food, history, religion, art and so on.

3. Interpersonal motivators.
These include visiting friends and relatives, the desire to meet new people and to make new friendships, and escape from the everyday social environment.

4. Status and prestige motivators.
These concern ego-enhancement and the desire for recognition, appreciation and attention, and personal improvement. Trips may be related to education or study, the pursuit of hobbies, or business and conference type tourism.

The major problem associated with the motivation by purpose approach is that it describes the outcome or the goal orientated behaviour that results from a specific need, rather than the actual motivation itself. Thus, the desire to learn about other cultures may, in fact, be the outcome of a need to make up for a lack of culture in the home environment, or wanting to make new friends may result from a deeper motivation to avoid loneliness.

Similarly, it would be logical to assume that participation in eco-tourism is motivated by the attributes of such tourism (for example, low impact, optimising benefits to local communities and so on); in short, wanting to be a 'good' tourist. However, the true motivation for eco-tourism may have little, if anything, to do with environmental concerns.

The unclear relationship between environmentalism and 'good' tourism has already been discussed in general (Chapter Four). More specifically, studies into the motivation for eco-tourism are inconclusive, yet tend to support the argument that eco-tourists seek to satisfy needs other than behaving in an environmentally appropriate fashion (see Eagles 1992; Eagles and Cascagnette 1995; Wight 1996).

It was found that, although the motivation for eco-tourism vacations is diverse and related to a multitude of variables, eco-tourists are, generally, most interested in the physical attractions of destinations and the activities that such destinations offer. Enjoying wilderness scenery and undisturbed nature is the most frequently cited reason for participating in eco-tourism, followed by a variety of natural environment, physical or cultural activity motivations. (For example, see Figure 3, on page 156.)

Figure 3: Motivations of significant importance to eco-tourists

Motivations	Rank
Wilderness and undisturbed	1
nature	2
Lakes and streams	3
Be physically active	4
Mountains	5
National or provincial parks	6
Experience new lifestyles	7
Rural areas	8
Oceanside	8
Meet people with similar interest	9
Simpler lifestyle	11
Visit historical places	12
Outdoor recreation	13
Be daring and adventurous	14
Cultural activities	15
See maximum in time available	

Source: Eagles (1992: 6)

Thus, not surprisingly, it is evident that the setting is of greatest importance to the experience of eco-tourists. Unfortunately, most of the studies confuse push and pull factors. They relate motivations to the pull, or attraction, of particular settings whilst revealing little about what pushes or motivates eco-tourists in the first place. As Wight (1996: 7) argues, *it may be, however, that the setting is also critical to other, more traditional types of travellers... It is important, therefore, to... determine the benefits that eco-tourists seek.* She goes on to identify a number of 'discriminant characteristics' of the benefits sought by eco-tourists. These include the avoidance of crowds, the experience of wilderness, learning about nature, the opportunity for physical challenges and, importantly, the potential for bringing benefits to local communities.

Similarly, in an investigation into the psychographic characteristics of nature-based tourists, Silverberg *et al* (1996) found that although a conservationist attitude may be a discriminant factor between different clusters of tourists, many of the benefits sought by nature-based tourists are unrelated to environmental concern. For example, the desire to enjoy nature and unspoilt places, to experience wilderness and solitude, relate more to anomie or avoidance needs, whilst it has been argued that eco-tourism is both a niche and an expensive product, and is therefore better described as *ego-tourism* (Wheeller 1992a). From the available evidence, there is little to suggest that the motivations of eco-tourists differ markedly from other tourists and that their true needs bear little relationship to the overt purpose of eco-tourism.

(d) Tourism as a sacred journey

Anthropological research into tourism has been divided into two broad areas: assessing the impacts of tourism development on host cultures and societies, and analysing the meaning of tourism to the tourist. Whilst the first area falls under the heading of the social impacts of tourism (see Chapter Ten), the second is, essentially, an anthropological study of tourist motivation and is of relevance within the context of this chapter.

According to Graburn (1989: 22), *tourism...is functionally and symbolically equivalent to other institutions that humans use to embellish and add meaning to their lives*. If this is so, then it immediately becomes apparent that there is a potential link between the role of tourism as a secular ritual in modern life and more traditional, religious forms of travel, such as pilgrimage. Indeed, as Graburn (1983) asks, *if tourism has the quality of a leisure ritual that takes place outside of everyday life and involves travel, is not it identical to pilgrimage?* Similarly, MacCannell views the tourist's search for meaning and authenticity as a modern form of pilgrimage, with present day tourist sights being the equivalent to *the religious symbolism of primitive people* (1989: 2). It is important to note that we are concerned here with holiday tourism as opposed to the specific category of religious tourism; in the latter case, tourism and pilgrimage or sacred journeys become one and the same thing (see Vukonic 1996).

Even at a more mundane level, the manner in which thousands of people each year are drawn, as if by some invisible power, to the popular tourist sights around the world is directly analogous to a form of pilgrimage. Many tourist sights or attractions are accorded the status of a religious icon or symbol; they have to be seen by tourists, they are *famous for being famous...*[and]...*entail a kind of pilgrimage to a sacred centre, which is often a capital or major city* (Urry 1990: 12). It is not the actual sight, nor the original motivation, but the meaning to the individual tourist that is important. In other words, a religious pilgrimage is normally considered to be something serious, legitimate, authentic and of spiritual significance to the participant, whereas tourism, by comparison, is frivolous and superficial (Pfaffenberger 1983). Yet, if the labels attached to each are stripped away, it becomes apparent that the experience of seeing, for example, the Taj Mahal, may be of equal significance to a tourist as is a visit to, say, Lourdes, for a pilgrim. *The difference between tourism and pilgrimage lies not so much in any radical phenomenological difference between them... but rather in the culturally-supplied language of symbols in which travellers are obliged to express their peregrinations* (Pfaffenberger 1983).

The argument that tourism is a form of sacred journey is based upon the relationship between work and play (tourism) and, in particular, the location of each. Compulsory activities, such as making a living, take place in the ordinary, home environment, whereas tourism is voluntary and takes place in the non-ordinary environment, away from home. It is, perhaps, for this reason that staying at home during time off from work is not considered to be a true holiday; to stay at home is to do nothing whilst to go away is to do something (Graburn 1989: 23). It also lends credence to the adage that a change (in this case, of location) is as good as a rest. Thus, it is considered proper that people work at home and go away for their holidays.

If work takes place in the ordinary environment then, logically, it represents the ordinary experience. It also represents the passing of ordinary time. Normally, the passage of time is marked by regular festivals or events which, traditionally, have a religious or sacred significance. Thus, festivals such as Christmas or Easter represent a temporary shift from ordinary, secular, profane time into sacred time. During these periods of sacred time, the individual is also transferred from the ordinary, profane existence (usually dominated by compulsory activities) into another, non-ordinary state of existence. In modern, secular societies the annual summer holiday is one such event which has come to be equated with the religious festivals in more traditional societies. The week or fortnight away marks a shift from the profane experience of everyday life to the non-ordinary, sacred experience of the holiday. Thus, by comparing the function of religious festivals in traditional societies to that of holidays in modern society, tourism becomes, logically, a sacred journey.

A number of authors have linked the concept of tourism as a kind of sacred journey with Turner's work on pilgrims (see Turner 1973; Turner and Turner 1978). This, in turn, represents an extension to the concept that the passage of time alternated between profane (ordinary) and sacred (non-ordinary) time. It also builds upon the notion introduced in Chapter Four that tourist behaviour is dependent, up to a point, upon the location of an individual's 'spiritual centre' and that tourism is a form of personal transition (Nash 1996: 39-57). Turner develops the idea that, by taking part in religious rituals or undertaking a pilgrimage, people become divorced from everyday social and economic structures and constraints. Typically, this involves a three-stage process. Initially, people go through the *separation* stage, where they become separated from their ordinary home environment and society. In terms of tourism, this is the equivalent of travelling to, and arriving at, the destination. They then move into the second stage, into a condition which Turner describes as *liminality*. That is, people (or tourists) cross the threshold or boundary (from the Latin *limen*) of their normal, ordered and structured society and enter into a state of anti-structure (that is, a situation where the structure and order of everyday life have disappeared). Normal obligations, such as work, no longer exist and new types of relationships, unaffected by the usual social constraints of status and role, are established between individuals and groups. So, tourists, while on holiday, are temporarily freed from the demands of their jobs, household chores, social commitments and, generally, the behavioural norms and values of their society. Unrestricted by social barriers, they are able to form groups or relationships with people with whom they would not, perhaps, normally mix and together enjoy the sense of freedom and escape offered by the holiday. Turner describes this sense of togetherness, of sharing, in his context, a religious, spiritual experience, as a state of *communitas*.

Passariello (1983) and Lett (1983) use this concept as a basis for explaining the behaviour of, respectively, weekend domestic tourists at a Mexican coastal resort and North American charter yacht tourists in the Caribbean.

The third and final stage is *reintegration*; people return to their ordinary home environment and social structure. In traditional societies, it is likely that the return from a sacred ritual or pilgrimage, such as a Muslim having completed his pilgrimage, or *hadj*, to Mecca, is signified by reintegration into the social group at a higher status. For a tourist, the experience of liminality is more likely to be of a compensatory nature. That is, he or she returns refreshed, renewed and ready to accept the responsibilities and constraints of everyday life. Reintegration is at the same social status or level as separation but the tourist has been spiritually uplifted by the liminal (or *liminoid*, the word used by Turner and Turner (1978) to distinguish between secular and liminal, religious experiences) benefits of the holiday. The tourist is motivated in the first place by the psychological need for spiritual regeneration, a need that may be satisfied by a temporary shift away from the ordinary, profane existence into sacred time. The tourist is able to look at life from the outside, from the freedom of the holiday, from the *Centre Out There* (Turner, 1973).

(iii)   Tourist motivation and the tourist gaze

Urry (1990a; 1990b; 1992) describes the activity of tourism as gazing or, more specifically, the tourist 'gaze'. *What is the minimal characteristic of tourist activity is the fact that we look at, or gaze upon, particular objects* (1990b). The actual physical purchases, such as transport, accommodation and food are incidental to this central feature of tourism; the consumption of these goods and services allows the tourist to gaze upon *features of landscape and townscape which separate them off from everyday experience* (1990a: 3). Tourist motivation results from the need to gaze on sights, places and peoples that are unusual, that are removed from the experience and routine of normal, everyday life; by implication, tourist activity (gazing) is motivated by the need to collect gazes.

There are two different ways in which tourist gazes may be collected, depending on the needs of the individual tourist (see Urry 1990a):

(a) The romantic gaze

The romantic gaze (see also Walter 1982) is motivated by the desire for solitary enjoyment and experience. It is the equivalent to the search for authenticity and the sacred journey to the 'centre out there'. The romantic tourist seeks reality in other cultures and societies and, broadly, tries to recreate the 'lost art of travel'.

(b) The collective gaze

The collective gaze is communal tourism. It is motivated by the need to gaze at the familiar or to share the non-ordinary with other people. Indeed, it is the shared experience that is of fundamental importance to the collective gaze.

Tourist motivation: conclusions

Throughout this chapter, tourist motivation has been identified with the satisfaction of an individual's needs, needs which push, or motivate, the individual into particular types of behaviour. These needs may result from pressures and forces which are external to the individual, such as the work experience, family obligations or societal norms, from deep-rooted, psychological needs, such as self-esteem or a need for companionship, or from a combination of both. As such, this approach has provided an indication of the enormous range and variety of forces that have the potential to motivate an individual into goal orientated (specifically, touristic) behaviour. However, as Witt and Wright (1992: 44) argue, *the study of needs can at best only provide a partial explanation of motivated behaviour*. Other factors must also be taken into consideration if the explanation of tourist motivation is to be of use in predicting tourist behaviour. In particular, it is necessary to look at tourist motivation over time and the way in which an individual's needs may be translated into motivated behaviour.

In theory, tourist decision making follows a logical process which commences with the translation of needs into motivated behaviour. This behaviour takes the form of a consideration of the different products related to the satisfaction of needs and, based upon the available information and the overall image of the destination, the tourist then makes a decision and purchases a holiday. Thus, each stage can be

161

assigned a separate and identifiable position and function within the overall decision making process. In practice, this process may not be quite so simple and straightforward. The dividing line between different stages is not always distinct and, in particular, the *meaning* of a holiday to the consumer should also be considered. In other words, tourists experience and purchase more than the actual one or two week break. Prior to departure, the process of choosing, of anticipating the holiday (see Parrinello 1993) is all part of the tourism experience and people may be motivated as much by the prospect of having a holiday as by the potential benefits of the holiday itself. Holidays are often purchased many months in advance and the thought of having a holiday, having something to look forward to and to dream about, can be as equally exciting and beneficial (and in many cases more so) than the holiday itself. Thus, tourist motivation can *be strictly linked with anticipation* (Parrinello 1993).

Nor does the process finish when the tourist returns home from a holiday. Although the physical state of being on holiday has come to an end, the memories and images of a holiday may remain with an individual for much longer, particularly if photographs have been taken or souvenirs bought. In a sense, the holiday lasts much longer than the actual period spent away and a tourist might also be motivated by the thought of being able to look back on his or her holiday whilst, at the same time, anticipating and planning the next one. So, the stages of motivation, choice, holiday purchase and the actual trip become merged into a continual process of anticipation, experience and memory, a process which sustains itself in modern, tourism generating societies which are *literally saturated with tourist culture* (Parrinello 1993).

Again departing from the basic notion of needs resulting in motivated behaviour, tourist motivation is also dependent on the extent to which people *expect* a particular choice of action to lead to certain outcomes. For example, an individual might want to go on a beach holiday to get a suntan, motivated by the self-esteem need, perhaps, of being able to show off his or her tan. The choice of destination will be motivated, not only by the original need to get a tan, but also by the extent to which the individual expects to achieve that goal. The individual will thus be motivated to choose a destination that offers the best opportunity for sunbathing and also, perhaps, at a time of year when a suntan is most noticeable (that is, a winter sun destination). The same principle can also be applied to the influence of socio-economic restrictions on holiday choice. Thus, a person who has a low expectation of being able to afford a particular holiday, will be motivated to choose another type of holiday or, if there is a low expectation of satisfying needs on the alternative holiday, to stay at home.

This approach to motivation is known as *expectancy theory* (see Witt and Wright, 1992 for more detail). It is a complicated method of analysing motivation, yet it serves to highlight that tourist motivation is, itself, a complex subject. There is a huge variety of push factors that may motivate tourism, and these factors vary between different people. If people's expectations are also taken into account it becomes evident that destination pull factors can play an equally important role in motivation. The implication is, therefore, that to be able to fully understand and predict any one person's motivation for tourism it is necessary to concentrate on that person's preferences, experience, desires and social and economic circumstances.

The situation is further complicated by the fact that tourists may not always be able or wish to reflect upon or express their real motives for travel (Dann 1981). There is, also, no saying that particular groups of people behave in particular ways, or that particular types of tourism or destinations appeal to particular types of tourist. Essentially, tourist motivation results from a variety of social, economic, demographic and psychological factors peculiar to each individual tourist but, nevertheless, the influence of society and sociological factors, both external and intrinsic to the individual, provide a solid foundation for an understanding of tourist motivation.

Six

The Consumption of Tourism

Introduction

The demand for tourism is a complex, dynamic and multi-dimensional process. It is a process whereby tourists, as consumers of tourism experiences, progress through a number of stages, from the initial identification of the need or desire to travel (the motivational stage) to the final, evaluation and feedback stage. Each stage potentially feeds backwards or forwards into preceding or subsequent stages and, at the same time, a variety of external variables influence of the process. To complicate matters further, for the individual tourist each tourism experience links into subsequent tourism demand processes in a continuous and evolving process. This occurs as long as the tourist continues to participate in tourism and, throughout this 'travel career', it is likely that the tourist's increasing experience and knowledge of tourism will further influence and shape the demand process. It is not surprising that the demand for tourism has been described as *discretionary, episodic, future oriented, dynamic, socially influenced and evolving* (Pearce 1992: 114).

Despite this complexity, there are a variety of ways in which the outcome of the tourism demand process may be predicted. As discussed in Chapter Four, early attempts focused upon the construction of tourist typologies which, although suffering a number of shortcomings, provide a basis for understanding how particular types of tourists are likely to behave. That is, they ascribe different styles of tourism consumption to different types of people according to a variety of psychographic variables. As we have seen, these typologies do little to explain *why* people choose to consume tourism in the first place. Therefore, researchers have long been concerned with the analysis of tourist

164

motivation, exploring those social and psychological factors which influence tourists' wants and needs.

An understanding of the tourism demand process and the study of tourist motivation as a primary, integral element of that process, is important, but of equal, if not greater importance, is the recognition that the demand for tourism should not be viewed in isolation from the broader cultural context within which it occurs. That is, tourism is just one of a whole host of goods and services that people in modern societies consume. The relative importance of different goods and services, their meaning or significance, and the manner in which they are consumed is determined as much by the cultural condition of society as it is by the needs and desires of individual consumers. So, an analysis of the demand for tourism is not complete without considering how the consumption of tourism in particular is influenced and framed by what is termed 'consumer culture' in general.

Thus, the purpose of this chapter is to explore the link between tourism and the cultural context of consumption. First, it introduces an important group of variables which potentially shape or impinge upon the overall consumption of tourism: the attitudes and values of tourists.

Values and the consumption of tourism

Although motivation is widely considered to be the trigger, or the primary energising factor in the tourism consumption process, most tourism demand models recognise the existence of other factors, or *affectors* of demand (Gilbert 1991: 79), that may also influence the behaviour of tourists. A number of these variables may play a direct role at the motivational stage, determining people's needs and wants and thus being translated through motivation into goal-oriented (tourism consumption) behaviour. Many of these factors are highlighted in Chapter Five.

The subsequent stages of the demand process, such as the information search, the comparison of alternatives and final choice, as well as the actual and evaluated experience of the holiday, are also influenced by a variety of factors. These may include past experiences, the advice of friends and relatives and, in particular, demographic variables. It is *commonly believed that tourist behaviour...[is]...affected, if not determined, by the tourist's age, sex, marital status, education, disposable income, place of origin and other similar factors* (Pizam and Calantone 1987: 177). In much the same way that tourist typologies are formulated according to the observed behaviour of different types of tourists, such variables are for the most part descriptive. That is, although they are of use in segmenting tourist markets and as a basic predictor of how certain groups may consume tourism, they reveal little about why tourists behave in particular ways.

As a result, some commentators believe that so-called psychographic or life-style variables, including values, attitudes, opinions and interests, are more important factors in the tourism decision-making process (Luk *et al* 1993). Potentially revealing *more meaningful information* about tourists' behaviour (Cha *et al* 1995: 38), psychographic analysis has been used by a number of researchers in segmenting tourist markets and explaining behaviour (for example, Mayo 1975; Woodside and Pitts 1976). For the purposes of this chapter it is important to distinguish between concepts such as attitudes, interests and values. The reason for this is that, although they are frequently and collectively referred to as affectors of demand, and are often used interchangeably, there are fundamental differences in what constitutes them and how they may influence behaviour. Moreover, it is values, in particular, that may reflect a society's beliefs or value systems and thus be structurally determined, and which may influence the demand for tourism.

According to Rokeach (1973: 18), *an attitude differs from a value in that an attitude refers to an organisation of several beliefs around a specific object or situation. A value, on the other hand, refers to a single belief of a very specific kind.* In other words, *values transcend specific objects and situations* (Feather 1975: 10) and are concerned with desirable or acceptable forms of behaviour or end-states, whereas attitudes are commonly related to specific objects or situations. The implication of this is that values are the dominant force in shaping people's ideas, attitudes and opinions. That is, values precede or guide attitudes and behaviour, serving as standards or criteria for personally and socially preferable conduct or outcomes of behaviour (Kamakura and Mazzon 1991). Values *govern a person's lifestyle and provide a direct and useful explanation of the multitude of interests, outlooks on life, consumption practices, and activities that define a lifestyle* (Müller 1991: 57). Thus, tourists may have different attitudes towards different destinations or types of tourism. Overall, the way in which they consume tourism is likely to be influenced by their personal values with respect to, for example, the importance they attach to leisure as opposed to work or to the experiences they seek through tourism.

Concern for the role of values has long been an integral element of the study of consumer behaviour in general; surprisingly, perhaps, less attention has been paid to the role of values on the consumption of tourism in particular. Much of the research into the link between values and consumer behaviour is based upon the pioneering work of Rokeach (1973). He defines a value as an *enduring belief that a specific mode of conduct or end-state of existence is personally or socially preferable to an opposite or converse mode of conduct or end-state of existence* (1973: 5). Values represent a set of prescriptive beliefs that guide the choice or evaluation of potential behaviour. It is also evident that, to be socially preferable, some values are structurally formulated; that is, some values represent socially acceptable behaviour and are thus internalised by the individual through the socialisation process (see Chapter One). Conversely, it is likely that some personal values may result from social interaction.

Not only do individuals carry these beliefs or values which determine their modes of behaviour, they also organise these beliefs into a value system which represents a continuum of the relative importance of the different values they hold. In other words, most people possess multiple values which they prioritise into a system or hierarchy which is *stable enough to reflect the fact of sameness and continuity of a unique personality socialised within a given culture and society, yet unstable enough to permit rearrangements of value priorities as a result of changes in culture, society, and personal experience* (Rokeach 1973: 11). Thus, an individual tourist's value system may, in theory, adapt according to social or cultural influences. For example, the increasingly widespread belief that sunbathing may be harmful in the longer term might influence the individual to put 'health' values before 'pleasure' values. Similarly, the alleged increase in environmental awareness throughout society might encourage tourists to place environmental values in a higher position in the value system. In the context of tourism this does not yet appear to be the case, suggesting that more personal, hedonistic values dominate, in general, the consumption of tourism.

According to Rokeach, it is also important to distinguish between so-called *instrumental* values, which guide modes of conduct and may be seen, therefore, as means to an end, and *terminal* values, which relate to the desired end-state. Instrumental values, which include concepts such as honesty and responsibility, can be sub-divided into either moral or competence/self-actualisation values, whilst terminal values, such as freedom, self-respect or equality, may similarly have either a social or personal focus. Implicitly, instrumental values are, literally, instrumental in the attainment of terminal, end-state values, although the distinction or causal links between the two are not always clear. For example, honesty might be instrumental achieving self-respect, whilst environmentally appropriate behaviour might be instrumental in achieving a world of beauty (the latter identified by Rokeach as a terminal value). But, both of these instrumental values may become goals in themselves, whilst other single or combinations of modes of behaviour may be instrumental in achieving any one terminal goal. Thus, the terminal value of self-respect may be achieved through a combination of honesty, courage and environmental awareness. Despite this ambiguity, the concept of a value system based upon means and end values provides a useful conceptual framework for understanding how values influence behaviour in a variety of situations, including the consumption of tourism.

In order to try to measure values, Rokeach developed his Rokeach Value Survey (RVS), which consists of 18 instrumental values and 18 terminal values. (See Figure 4 on page 169.) It is immediately apparent from this list of instrumental and terminal values that there is a close link or relationship between values and motivations as determinants of human behaviour, suggesting that values do indeed play an important role as determinants or predictors of behaviour. For example, the five hierarchical needs identified by Maslow (1943) – physiological, safety, love, esteem and self-actualisation – and which were discussed in the context of tourist motivation in Chapter Five, are generally reflected in many of Rokeach's terminal values.

Figure 4: The Rokeach Value Survey

Instrumental Values	Terminal Values
Ambitious *(hard-working, aspiring)*	A comfortable life *(a prosperous life)*
Broadminded *(open-minded)*	An exciting life *(a stimulating, active life)*
Capable *(competent, effective)*	A sense of accomplishment *(lasting contribution)*
Cheerful *(light-hearted, joyful)*	A world at peace *(free of war and conflict)*
Clean (neat, tidy)	A world of beauty *(beauty of nature and arts)*
Courageous *(Standing up for your beliefs)*	Equality *(brotherhood, equal opportunity for all)*
Forgiving *(willing to pardon others)*	Family security *(taking care of loved ones)*
Helpful *(working for the welfare of others)*	Freedom *(independence, free choice)*
Honest *(sincere, truthful)*	Happiness *(contentedness)*
Imaginative *(daring, creative)*	Inner Harmony *(freedom from inner conflict)*
Independent *(self-reliant, self-sufficient)*	Mature love *(sexual and spiritual intimacy)*
Intellectual *(intelligent, reflective)*	National security *(protection from attack)*
Logical *(consistent, rational)*	Pleasure *(an enjoyable, leisurely life)*
Loving *(affectionate, tender)*	Salvation *(saved, eternal life)*
Obedient *(dutiful, respectful)*	Self-respect *(self-esteem)*
Polite *(courteous, well-mannered)*	Self-recognition *(respect, admiration)*
Responsible *(dependable, reliable)*	True friendship *(close companionship)*
Self-controlled *(restrained, self-disciplined)*	Wisdom *(a mature understanding of life)*

Source: Rokeach (1973: 359-40)

At the same time, and more specifically, the two primary tourism motivational factors, namely avoidance/escape and self-reward/ego-enhancement (Dann 1977; Mannell and Iso-Ahola 1987), are also implicitly encompassed by terminal values such as pleasure, self-respect and freedom. Equally, many of the other terminal values identified by Rokeach can be transposed onto tourist motivation and behaviour. For example, tourism may satisfy, either directly or through the process of inversion, the 'comfortable life' value, whilst 'happiness' is likely to be a dominant influencing value in many people's tourism decision making process.

The RVS has been used in a variety of applications (see Kamakura and Mazzon 1991), including Luk *et al*'s (1993) segmentation of tourists' service quality expectations. In its original form it is somewhat complex and, more recently, it has been simplified and adapted into new value scales for the specific purpose of market research/segmentation and the analysis of consumer behaviour. One example of this is the List of Values (LOV) Scale, a simplified and shortened version of the RVS which is used to identify nine consumer segments based upon the values they endorse.

Similarly, the Values and Lifestyle Scale (VALS), in Figure 5 below, divides American consumers into nine lifestyles or types under four categories based upon their self-images, aspirations, values and beliefs.

Figure 5: VALS Categories

Need Driven Groups: Survivor lifestyle Sustainer lifestyle	**Outer Directed Groups:** Belongers lifestyle Emulator lifestyle Achiever lifestyle
Inner Directed Groups: I-am-me lifestyle Experiential lifestyle Societally-conscious lifestyle Self-directed lifestyle	**Outer/Inner Directed Groups:** Integrated lifestyle

Source: adapted from Shih (1986)

Again, there are evident links between these groups and sub-groups of consumer-types and different forms of tourist behaviour, suggesting that the VALS scale represents a useful predictor of tourism demand. For example, the inner-directed socially conscious lifestyle group is made up of *consumers who are mission-or cause-oriented and have a sense of social responsibility. They favor* [sic] *appeals stressing conservation, simplicity, frugality, and environmental concerns* (Shih 1986: 4). This suggests that the societally-conscious group will seek out appropriate forms of tourism, such as eco-tourism. Similarly, the outer-directed sub-group of emulators might be expected to participate in forms of tourism which enhance their status.

Interestingly, although value scales have been found to be reliable predictors of consumer behaviour in general, with the LOV scale being found to be the more accurate (Kahle *et al* 1986; Novak and MacEvoy 1990), there have been relatively few empirical studies into the effect of values on tourist behaviour in particular. Boote (1981) discovered that consumer preferences for different chains of family restaurants could be revealed by value-based segmentation methods, whilst Pitts and Woodside linked ten recreation and leisure choice criteria to a number of instrumental and terminal values in the context of different tourism settings and attractions. They found that *values were shown to be related to differences in choice criteria and to actual behaviour* (Pitts and Woodside 1986: 23). Madrigal and Kahle considered the role of value systems, as opposed to single values, in tourist behaviour and concluded that what they termed value domains *may be an important set of variables to be considered in predicting what lures tourists to a destination* (Madrigal and Kahle 1994: 27).

They also suggested that values alone are not a sufficient criterion for predicting behaviour, destination attributes and tourists' demographic characteristics and needs also being important variables. Similarly, studies by Pizam and Calantone (1987), Müller (1991), Dalen (1989), Thrane (1997 also support of the general argument that *travel behaviour is significantly associated with a person's general values and vacation-specific values, therefore lending support to the...theory that values can act as predictors of travel behaviour* (Pizam and Calantone 1987: 180).

The role of values in determining tourist behaviour must still be considered within the overall context of the decision making process. That is, although values may be a powerful and influential force in consumer behaviour, there are many other factors which, as we have already seen, may shape tourist preferences and behaviour. More specifically, there is little evidence to suggest that the values that people hold have an effect on all forms of consumption. To put it another way, different types of consumption may be influenced by different values and, therefore, the consumption of tourism may not follow the pattern of other activities. This supports the argument that individuals possess a variety of values, each of which may be more or less influential in different situations. As Madrigal and Kahle (1994) observe, a number of different values may be relevant to particular situations or decisions. These different values are hierarchically ordered in a value system and *an individual relies on his/her value system to maintain self-esteem or consistency in those situations where one or more conflicting values are activated* (Madrigal and Kahle 1994: 23). Within the tourism consumption process, the likelihood of value conflict is high, particularly between personal terminal values (for example, pleasure, freedom, happiness) and social values that serve as guidelines for socially acceptable behaviour. In many cases tourism may provide the opportunity for people to behave in ways that are directly in conflict with their normal values; that is, tourism allows people to escape not only from their home social environment but also from the constraints of their normal social life, constraints which may include many of the socially-constructed values that they hold. As a result, it is important to now consider what may be described as the meaning of tourism as a form of consumption in modern (or culturally postmodern) societies.

Tourism and consumer culture

As discussed in Chapter Five, it is motivation that triggers the tourism consumption process. In other words, if there is to be a demand for tourism, there must also exist needs and wants, or energisers of demand, which through the motivational process become translated into goal-oriented behaviour. Moreover, the manner in which individuals attempt to satisfy these needs and wants through the consumption of tourism – or, the character of their goal-oriented behaviour - is to a great extent shaped or modified by a variety of deterministic influences, including demographic factors, roles, and values.

Given this primary and fundamental role of motivation and the potentially significant influence of those factors which affect, shape or filter the demand for tourism, it is not surprising that researchers have long been concerned with analysing and attempting to develop an understanding of tourist motivation and the overall tourism demand process. The purpose of such research has been primarily to enable the prediction of tourist behaviour, with evident practical applications in terms of product design, market segmentation, and so on.

One inherent weakness of much of the work concerned with the demand for, or consumption of, tourism is that it has adopted an overly tourism-centric perspective. That is, most commentators have, traditionally, approached the consumption of tourism in isolation from other forms of consumption and from the broader social and cultural influences that pattern or shape consumer behaviour as a whole; little or no reference is made to the influence of consumer culture on the consumption of tourism in particular. Thus, the existence of tourism as a specific form of consumer behaviour is not questioned. It is tacitly accepted that ever increasing numbers of people participate in tourism and attention is focused largely on how the demand for tourism is determined by motivational and other factors. As a result, less importance has, until recently, been attached to the explanation of the significance and meaning of tourism as a form of consumption in general, and the ways in which the consumption or styles of tourism may be influenced by cultural transformations and developments in the tourist's home environment in particular.

To put it another way, the analysis of tourism demand and motivation in the literature is, for the most part, based on the premise that tourism is a satisfier of needs and wants (Mill and Morrison 1985: 4). The inward, tourism-centric focus of much of the relevant research has meant that, whilst attention has been directed at identifying those needs and wants and how they may be satisfied, in a utilitarian sense, by tourism, less emphasis has been placed on addressing broader, culturally-related issues. For example, why is tourism, as opposed to other modes of behaviour, chosen as a form of consumption? Why has international tourism, over the space of some forty years, been transformed from a luxury into a perceived 'necessity'? Why do styles of tourism consumption change? Many of the needs relevant to tourist motivation, such as the physiological needs of rest and relaxation, or the ego-enhancement needs referred to in the preceding chapter, may be satisfied by a variety of different activities, yet tourism remains an increasingly popular activity, with ever greater demands for specialised, niche products. This suggests that the widely held belief, 'I need a holiday', is as much a cultural construct as it is a rational, need-satisfying course of action. It also suggests, of course, that the consumption of tourism encompasses a meaning and purpose beyond basic, utilitarian need satisfaction.

In short, tourism as a form of consumption central to the modern leisure experience cannot, or should not, be considered in isolation from the wider cultural framework within which it occurs. This is particularly so in those tourism generating societies which have experienced a cultural shift towards the condition of postmodernity because, as proposed in Chapter Three, consumption patterns have become one of the defining characteristics of postmodernity. Whereas, in the modern era, an individual's position or identity was commensurate with his or her work, social class and so on, the de-differentiating process of modernity has required alternative methods of creating or achieving self-identity. This role has been filled by consumption; indeed, *consumption has been seen as epitomising this move into postmodernity* (Bocock 1993: 4) and postmodern culture is very much identified with consumer culture. So, it is important to explore how the consumption of tourism is influenced by this broader, postmodern consumer culture within which it occurs.

The evolution of consumer culture

Consumer culture may be defined as the character, significance and role of the consumption of commodities, services and experiences within modern societies. Its existence as a cultural phenomenon implies that consumption, as a social activity, has become culturally significant, particularly in contrast to the role of its opposing phenomenon, production, which was dominant during the modern era. Indeed, as Pretes observes, a fundamental feature of postmodern culture is that *consumption, rather than production, becomes dominant* (Pretes 1995: 2). This has not always been the case.

It has long been recognised that a relationship exists between production and consumption of goods and services, a relationship which, as Miller (1987: 134) observes, was traditionally characterised by viewing consumption activities *as the result of, or as a process secondary to, the development of manufacturing and other forms of production*. Certainly within the context of tourism, recent years have witnessed a change in the nature of the production-consumption relationship as demonstrated by, for example, increases in the number of specialist tour operators, the promotion of niche markets, or the development of more individual, flexible forms of tourism. This change may, in turn, be linked to shifts in consumer culture and the increasingly dominant role of consumers, meaning that, conversely, the role of the producer has been weakened. Thus, consumer culture has evolved and is directly related to the changing production-consumption relationship. Three stages in the evolution of consumer culture have been suggested by Featherstone (1990; 1991).

(a) The production of consumption

From the production of consumption perspective, reflecting the traditional view of the production-consumption relationship, consumer culture is related to and emerges from the mass production of goods and services for purchase and consumption, with the producers being able to dictate styles, fashion and taste. As a result of this culture of mass production and consumption, and the inherent need for all commodities to appeal to the widest possible market, high and low culture become merged with the cultural value of commodities tending towards the lowest common denominator. Thus, from this perspective on consumption, the dominant role of the producer leads, perhaps inevitably, to a diluted and homogeneous cultural value of mass goods and services which, in a differentiated, modernist society, serves to reflect *given social*

175

hierarchies (Miller 1987: 135). Described elsewhere as a process of 'McDonaldisation' (Ritzer 1996), this approach is of most relevance in the context of tourism to the analysis of earlier forms of mass, package tourism; through developing efficient and predictable means of transporting large numbers of tourists, the producers of package tourism were, to a great extent, able to control the development and style of the mass consumption of tourism and (cultural) product quality was sacrificed to price. Thus, in short, this perspective proposes that goods (and services) are produced and then consumed as and when individuals have wants or needs that require satisfaction. In this sense, then, consumption can be viewed on the basis of the utility or 'use-value' of commodities (Warde 1992: 17). It is also, in a cultural sense, production-led. Through Fordist production methods and as an essential prere quisite for such forms of production, producers are able to dictate what, when and how consumers consume (see McCracken 1986).

(b) The mode of consumption

In contrast, the second approach or stage focuses upon the mode of consumption, highlighting the culture of consumption rather than simply viewing consumption as the inevitable result of production. It is based upon the notion that, within postmodern, post-industrial society (or, societies where tertiary, service industries increasingly dominate the economy) traditional social groupings are being replaced by a new and expanding middle or 'service' class (see Urry 1988; Featherstone 1990; Voase 1995). No longer enjoying a sense of self-identity through traditional roles, these new 'service classes' have turned to what and how they consume as markers of identity. Producers have had to respond, leading to a corresponding reversal of power in the production-consumption relationship. This 'use' of consumption is considered in more detail shortly.

(c) The consumption of dreams

Of particular relevance to the postmodern consumption of tourism, the third perspective on consumer culture concentrates on *the emotional pleasures of consumption, the dreams and desires which become celebrated in consumer cultural imagery* (Featherstone 1990). In this case, consumption neither flows logically from production, nor does it play a role in the determination of social status; the production-consumption relationship becomes irrelevant. Rather, consumption is viewed as the fulfilment of dreams, as a search for pleasurable experiences, as a means of escaping from the rigidity and structure of day-to-day culture and society. Reference is frequently made to the traditional role of fairs and carnivals in the pre-industrial era – they were both local markets and places to indulge in pleasure, to experience unusual or exotic images. It is not surprising that tourism is seen by some as a continuation of the carnivalesque tradition into postmodern consumer culture; the spectacle of mass tourism at the seaside resorts in the late nineteenth and early twentieth centuries and, more recently, the popularity of, for example, theme parks are both seen as evidence of this trend (Urry 1990a). More generally, of course, the desire to escape from the ordinary and mundane, to consume the dreams and fantasy of travel, is also considered to be a major tourism motivating factor (Dann 1981).

If these three perspectives on consumer culture are applied to tourism, it is evident that, in recent years, the nature of the consumption of tourism has developed from a producer-led to a consumer-led form of consumption. Earlier forms of tourism leading, in particular, to the development of mass package tourism were symptomatic of the dominant role of tour operators in shaping holiday tastes and styles based upon the modernist, 'Fordist' approach to mass production. More recently, however, the tourism industry has been obliged to become increasingly responsive to the changing demands of the consumer. What this signifies, in the more general context of consumption, is that the culture of consumption has come to occupy the dominant position in the production-consumption relationship. This has come about, in part, from a variety of factors and transformations within the wider social and economic system in post-industrial societies that have enabled the practice of consumption to assume a leading role in people's lives. Such factors include the large, widely-available and ever-increasing range of consumer goods and services, the popularity of 'leisure shopping', the emergence of consumer groups and consumer legislation, pervasive advertising, widely available credit facilities and *the impossibility of avoiding making choices in relation to consumer goods* (Lury 1996: 36).

However, it is not only the *practice* but also the *significance* of consumption that is of vital importance in the emergence of a dominant consumer culture. We recognise that commodities, whether goods or services, have a meaning beyond their economic exchange or use value. As Lury (1996: 11) explains, *the utility of goods is always framed by a cultural context, that even the use of the most mundane objects in daily life has cultural meaning... material goods are not only used to do things, but they also have a meaning, and act as meaningful markers of social relationships.* In fact, it has been argued that consumption results only from the inherent meaning or significance of goods, their use-value being irrelevant (Baudrillard 1988), although this is disputed by others (Warde 1992: 26). Nevertheless, social lives are, in short, patterned, or indeed created, by the acquisition and use (that is, consumption) of things. A well-used example is that of the motor car. In simple utilitarian terms, the car is no more than a convenient, independent, motorised means of travelling from one point to another quickly and in comfort. But, for most people, the choice involved in purchasing a car goes well beyond the practical advantages of car transport; the car is, arguably, one of the most powerful status symbols of the twentieth century.

The combined practice and significance of consumption can, thus, be conceptualised as the *active ideology that the meaning of life is to be found in buying things and pre-packed experiences* (Bocock 1993: 50). In other words, consumption in late twentieth century capitalist economies *must not be understood as the consumption of use-values, a material utility, but primarily as the consumption of signs* (Featherstone 1991: 85). Also, within postmodern culture in particular, this symbolic process inherent in consumption is considered by many to be its role in creating a sense of identity and status or, as Bourdieu (1986) proposes, in establishing distinctions between different social groups. As Miller (1987: 135) argues:

> *In a period of strong social stratification, objects tend to reflect given social hierarchies... When, however, this [stratification]*

178

> *breaks down, goods can change from being relatively static symbols to being more directly constitutive of social status... In other words, demand for goods may flourish in the context of ambiguity in social hierarchy.*

Such 'ambiguity in social hierarchy' connotes the de-differentiation of social groups in postmodern societies (see Chapter Three); groups which were previously identified and demarcated by work roles now seek identity and status through consumption.

Although much of the consumer behaviour literature is concerned primarily with the role of consumption in identity-construction or group-distinction, it is not the only symbolic or social role of consumption. In other words, the *act of consuming is a varied and effortful accomplishment undetermined by the characteristics of the object. A given consumption object (for example, a food, a sports activity, a television programme, or an art object) is typically consumed in a variety of ways by different groups of consumers* (Holt 1995: 1). In other words, although some individual's consumption practices may be identity or status driven – what Holt describes as 'consuming-as-classification' – the same consumption objects, including tourism, may be consumed by others in different ways. Different objects of consumption, whether goods (for example, a car or an item of clothing) or services (for example, a meal in a restaurant) mean different things to different people. Varying significance may be attached to the same object and it is consumed in different ways. Holt (1995) identifies a total of four categories of consumption:

(a) consuming as experience

(b) consuming as play

(c) consuming as integration

(d) consuming as classification.

These four categories provide a useful basis and framework for looking at the different ways in which tourism in particular may be consumed.

Before doing so, it is important to emphasise that the main point to emerge from this discussion is that not only have tourists, as in all forms of postmodern consumption, assumed the leading role in the tourism production-consumption relationship, but also the style of tourism they desire and their behaviour as consumers (tourists) will be influenced by the significance attached to the consumption of tourism. In other words, the tourism industry is no longer in the position of being able to dictate the supply of tourism. Tourists are demanding an ever-increasing variety of tourism experiences, experiences which, moreover, have a significance beyond their utility value. That is, tourism provides more than escape, more than two weeks on a beach, more than the chance to explore new places and cultures. Tourism plays a much broader role in people's lives, a role which influences how they consume tourism.

To return to Holt's four-fold categorisation of consumption practices, he suggests that there are two ways of conceptualising consumption – the *purpose* of consumption and the *structure* of consumption. In terms of purpose, consumers' actions may be ends in themselves (autotelic) or means to an end (instrumental). Structurally, consumption may be focused directly upon the object of consumption or, conversely, the objects of consumption may serve as a focal point for interpersonal actions. These two dimensions form a grid within which a typology of consumption may be located (see Figure 6 on page 181), the purpose being to provide a framework for analysing the different ways in which consumers interact with particular consumption objects.

As suggested above, tourism is no different from other consumption objects in that, depending on the significance that people attach to it, they will consume it in different ways. Therefore, this typology can be applied to tourism to reveal the different meaning or significance that culturally frames the consumption of tourism.

(a) Consuming tourism as experience

The consumption-as-experience perspective focuses upon the subjective or emotional reactions of consumers to particular consumption objects. It

Figure 6: A typology of consumption

PURPOSE OF ACTION

		Autotelic Actions	*Instrumental Actions*
	Object Actions	**CONSUMING AS EXPERIENCE**	**CONSUMING AS INTEGRATION**
STRUCTURE OF ACTION	*Inter-personal Actions*	**CONSUMING AS PLAY**	**CONSUMING AS CLASSIFICATION**

Source: Holt (1995)

is concerned with the ways in which people experience, or make sense of, different objects, or as Holbrook and Hirschman (1982: 132) put it, *this experiential perspective is phenomenological in spirit and regards consumption as a primarily subjective state of consciousness.* Moreover, *how consumers experience consumption objects is structured by the interpretative framework(s) that they apply to engage the object* (Holt 1995: 3). More simply stated, many consumption objects (goods and services) are located or are provided within a social world which provides the framework for their definition, meaning or understanding.

Tourism is no exception to this process. As a form of consumption it is firmly embedded in tourists' social world and the ways in which people experience, or consume, tourism will depend very much on their interpretation of the role or meaning of tourism within that social world. For example, tourism may be interpreted as a form of sacred consumption (Graburn 1989). It occurs outside normal (profane) times and places – it *is a festive, liminal time when behaviour is different from ordinary work time* (Belk *et al* 1989: 12) and is consumed as a sacred or spiritual experience. Tourists' behaviour will, therefore, be framed by this sacralisation of tourism and may be manifested in different ways. Thus, some may seek the spiritual refreshment of solitary, romantic tourist places, regarding *as quintessentially sacred those places...that are exceptionally natural, uncrowded, and unspoiled by other tourists. Such places are sacred not only because they are perceived as authentic and unspoiled; there is also some naturism or reverence for nature reflected* (Belk *et al* 1989: 17; Walter 1982). Conversely, for others the sacred nature of tourism may be reflected in their collective or communal experience of tourist sites and destinations. In other words, the annual holiday becomes a kind of ritualistic gathering where tourists participate in particular types of behaviour; for example, the mass migration of young people to places such as Ibiza, where they indulge in various forms of excessive behaviour, may be described as a cultural ritual no different from, say, the annual family gathering at Christmas.

Importantly, the consumption of tourism is also framed by the experiential aspect of modern consumption as a whole, namely, that *the consumption experience...[is]...a phenomenon directed towards the pursuit of fantasies, feelings, and fun* (Holbrook and Hirschman 1982: 132). In other words, consumption is directed towards the hedonistic pursuit of pleasure, pleasure which, according to Campbell, results not from physical satisfaction but from romantic day-dreaming:

> *The essential activity of consumption is thus not the actual selection, purchase or use of products, but the imaginative pleasure-seeking to which the product image lends itself, 'real' consumption being largely a resultant of the 'mentalistic' hedonism* (Campbell 1987: 89).

Tourism in particular lends itself to this concept of consumption as the pursuit of illusory pleasure, especially as day-dreaming suggests desires for the novel, different or 'other' (see also Featherstone's (1991: 21) discussion of consuming dreams, images and pleasure). Indeed, novelty seeking has been a fruitful area of research in the context of tourism consumer behaviour (Dimanche and Havitz 1994). The implication of this is that, for the most part, the experiential consumption of tourism represents, most frequently, the consumption of dreams, an escape to the non-ordinary, sacred, novel 'other'. It is the experiential participation in the ritual of tourism, a ritual that, however defined by the individual tourist, is the antithesis to the normal or ordinary existence. Thus, if tourists are seeking authenticity (see Chapter Seven), that authenticity must also represent 'The Other'.

(b) Consuming tourism as integration

According to Holt, consuming-as-integration is an instrumental action through which consumers are able to *integrate self and object, thereby allowing themselves access to the object's symbolic properties* (Holt 1995: 2). The object becomes a constituent element of their identity, either by merging external objects into their self-concept, or by adapting their self-concept to align it with the socially or institutionally defined identity of the object.

In the case of the consumption of tourism, integration is automatic as tourists play an integral role in the production of tourism experiences – as with all services, production and consumption are inseparable and instantaneous and tourists cannot be separated from the 'product' (see Middleton 1988: 26). But, much depends upon the direction of that integration. A tourist who wishes to be identified with a particular destination's culture or society or with a particular form of tourism may adapt his/her self-concept to 'fit' the identity of the destination or tourism-type. Thus, for example, individuals who see themselves as 'good', environmentally aware tourists will adapt their behaviour by consuming particular types of tourism or by assimilating into the local area; the self is integrated into the object. Conversely, to return to the example of the island of Ibiza, young tourists may behave in a certain way because they wish to integrate themselves into the local tourism cultural scene; they fit themselves to the image of the destination. On the other hand, certain types of tourism or tourist experience may be integrated into the individual's self-concept in a process of self-extension (see Arnould and Price 1993 for an analysis of white-water rafting as an example of one such form of tourism); here, the object is integrated into the self.

(c) Consuming tourism as play

The consuming-as-play perspective suggests that people utilise objects as a resource or focus for interaction with other consumers, rather than referring specifically to the experiential characteristics of the consumption object. Thus, in the context of tourism, consuming-as-play does not refer, for example, to the ludic or 'tourist-as-child' (Dann 1996) character of certain experiences, but to the fact that tourism is used as a vehicle for socialising with fellow consumers of tourism or sharing particular experiences.

This draws attention to the fact that tourism is, frequently, a social experience, an element of which is *to be able to consume particular commodities in the company of others. Part of what people buy is in effect a particular social composition of other consumers* (Urry 1990b: 25). In this sense, tourism provides the focus for people to socialise or to fulfil a more *performative, reciprocal* (Holt 1995: 9) role in entertaining each other. Equally, tourism may also be a means of sharing unusual or extraordinary experiences; the communal interaction with the consumption object allows tourists to commune or experience communitas (again, see Arnould and Price 1993). In either case, however, the focus is on the communal, social nature of the consumption experience rather than the object of consumption. Up to a point, it becomes less important where tourism is being consumed and, indeed, what the nature of the tourism experience is. More important is the fact that the consumption of tourism is a shared experience, where tourists consume tourism to be themselves, to escape from themselves or to share the unusual with others. In the last of these, the true consumption experience may be the shared 'looking forward to looking back'; that is, the shared experience of something different or even dangerous that will be re-lived in later conversations.

(d) Consuming tourism as classification

Most commonly, consumption is considered a means of classification. Particularly within de-differentiated, postmodern societies, consumers utilise consumption objects to create self-identity and to *classify themselves in relation to relevant others* (Holt 1995: 10). It has been argued, for example, that traditional social groupings are being replaced by a new and expanding middle or 'service' class (Featherstone 1990; Voase 1995). Within this new social class, there are two identifiable groups, namely, those who possess both economic and cultural capital in significant quantities (the new bourgeoisie), and those who possess cultural capital but less economic capital - the new 'petit bourgeoisie' (Bourdieu 1986). The latter, larger group are seen as the new taste-makers; having less financial resources, their consumption practices are guided by the identity value of goods and services. *Style, status, group identification, etc., are aspects of identity-value* (Warde 1992) and they seek social differentiation and status through different styles, rather than values, of consumption. Different goods and services have different social and cultural values and serve as markers of taste and style. For the new middle classes as a whole, consumption has become one of the primary means of demarcating social status and relationships in a postmodern era where traditional social markers no longer exist.

In the context of tourism, the consuming-as-classification perspective points to the role of tourism consumption in identity and status formation. Tourism has long been a marker of social status and the history of tourism is little more than the story of how tourists have sought social status through emulating the touristic practices of the higher or wealthier classes. Yet, *while travel has remained an expression of taste since the eighteenth century, it has never been so widely used as at present* (Munt 1994: 109). In response, the travel industry is developing more specialised, niche products, such as eco (or 'ego') tourism, or styles of tourism which, though relatively affordable, have the aura of status or luxury. An example of the latter is the relatively recent introduction of cruise holidays by some of the larger British tour operators, bringing the 'exclusivity' of cruising within the economic reach of the mass tourist.

Together, these different forms or approaches to consumption in general suggest that a variety of different meanings can be attached to the consumption of tourism in particular. This, in turn, suggests that an understanding of tourist typologies and motivation is not in itself sufficient to have a complete appreciation of the demand process. In other words, there is no doubt that, for many tourists, the prime objective remains the ego-centric desire to escape, rest, relax and have fun. Equally, the way in which they fulfil that desire will be dictated, up to a point, by their individual psychographic characteristics and by particular constraining factors. But, there is also no doubt that tourism, as a form of consumption, is culturally framed; the societies which generate tourists can have a major influence on the significance of tourism as a form of consumption in those societies, and are likely to do so as long as consumer culture remains dominant.

Seven

Tourism and Authenticity

Introduction

The links between authenticity and tourism have been explored by commentators and tourism researchers almost for as long as modern tourism itself has existed. During the nineteenth century attention was initially focused on the way in which emerging forms of mass transport, in particular the railways, diluted the perceived authenticity of the travel experience.

At the same time, the early pioneers of package tourism, such as Thomas Cook, also attracted criticism. For example, Charles Lever, writing in *Blackwoods Magazine* in 1865 about Cook's tourists in Italy, described cities as being *deluged with droves of these creatures, for they never separate, and you see them forty in number pouring along a street with their director, now in front, now at the rear, circling them like a sheepdog.* Implicit in this statement is the perceived inauthenticity of the tourists' experience, a theme which Boorstin continues and develops in his essay *From Traveller to Tourist: The Lost Art of Travel* (1964).

In contrast to Boorstin's thesis that tourists are satisfied with inauthentic, pseudo-events, MacCannell (1989) adopts a more positive perspective. He argues that living in modern, alienated societies, tourists are motivated by the need to experience authenticity: *modern man has been condemned to look elsewhere, everywhere, for his authenticity, to see if he can catch a glimpse of it reflected in the simplicity, poverty, chastity or purity of others* (1989: 41). Thus, for MacCannell, the entire phenomenon of tourism hinges on a quest for authenticity and reflects the deficiencies of modern life; the tourist is a model for *modern-man-in-general* (1989: 1).

187

The widely quoted Boorstin/MacCannell debate on the meaning and importance of authenticity has largely dominated the sociological treatment of tourism since the late 1960s. As a result, it has tended to overshadow other equally relevant issues concerned with the connection between authenticity and the tourist experience. For example, the concept of authenticity is frequently used as a marketing tool; holidays are advertised as offering the chance to experience the 'real' Africa, the 'hidden' Asia or, more generally, 'genuine' travel. In many cases, however, the authenticity on offer bears more relation to tourists' expectations (or what tour operators believe tourists want to see) than to what actually exists.

This then leads onto the question: what is an authentic tourist experience? Visitors to India on a typical Delhi-Jaipur-Agra (Taj Mahal) tour may well believe that they have experienced the 'real' India but, whilst there is no doubting the authenticity of individual sights, collectively they *represent* one particular image or perception of India; the India of the Moghuls, of royal palaces, of the Raj. That is, they are a sign of 'Indian-ness', a physical manifestation of an image that is, arguably, far removed from the reality of modern India. Thus, the authenticity of the destination is, in a sense, a myth (see Selwyn 1996).

Another problem to be considered is the extent to which any tourist site or experience may be considered authentic once it becomes packaged and sold as part of the overall tourist product. In other words, once a destination, an event or even a cultural artefact becomes caught up in the tourism system it becomes a commodity. Commodities have a value, normally measured by price, and once culture has become commoditised it can lose its meaning and significance for local people and, potentially, its authenticity to tourists (see Greenwood 1989).

Thus, the relevance of authenticity to tourism and the tourist experience is much broader than might at first be imagined. This chapter examines the relationship between authenticity and tourism and considers, in particular, the way in which tourists look to heritage and the past in their search for the authentic.

Authenticity

(i)   What is authenticity?

Before looking at the various ways in which authenticity is linked to the tourist experience, it is important to consider what is actually meant by authenticity. It is a word that is frequently used in the academic literature to describe the tourism experience, tourism attractions and events or the motivation for tourism. Equally, it often appears in tourist brochures, advertisements and other travel industry publications, perhaps one of the most over-used words in the 'language of tourism' (Dann 1996). Despite the widespread use of the word, scant attention is paid to explaining or defining authenticity in relation to tourism. This may in fact be because it is so widely used and because its meaning or interpretation varies according to its use: as Trilling (1974: 11) states, *the word 'authenticity' comes so readily to the tongue these days and in so many connections that it may very well resist... efforts of definition.* He goes on to assert, however, that its original usage was in the context of the museum to describe objects which are *what they appear to be or are claimed to be* (1974: 93), a usage which continues to be the most widely accepted and understood.

Within the context of tourism, the concept of authenticity has become rather more ambiguous. On one hand, the word 'authentic' is frequently used to describe products, works of art, cuisine, dress, language, festivals, rituals, architecture and so on - in short, everything which comprises a country's culture. Generally, something is considered to be authentic if it is made, produced or enacted by local people according to custom or tradition. Thus, in one sense, authenticity connotes traditional culture and origin, a sense of the genuine, the real or the unique. On the other hand, within tourism, it is also used to describe (and sell!) different types of travel, certain journeys or even entire holidays. Importantly, it is generally used to distinguish between specialist or niche-market tourism products and mass tourism products, the implication being that mass tourism is, somehow, inauthentic. For example, tour operators which organise adventure travel holidays or overland trips typically refer to the implicit authenticity of the travel experiences they offer. Thus, the

189

plore brochure states that *whether a seasoned traveller or a first-timer, avelling five hundred miles or five thousand, we're all explorers, discovering what's new, unusual and extraordinary about the world we live in* (Explore 1997).

Immediately, then, a difference appears between the two applications of authenticity within tourism. One is based upon the tangible origin of something; a cultural object or event is either real, genuine and authentic, or it is false, or a fake. The second application is based upon a less tangible comparison. For a holiday, a journey or a particular tourism experience to be authentic, it must be perceived to be so in comparison to another experience that is inauthentic. For MacCannell (1989), the inauthentic is modern society and tourism, therefore, becomes a search for the authentic. It is easy, then, to see how certain forms of travel and tourism come to be described as authentic because, in a sense, mass, package tourism is an extension of modern society and, hence, inauthentic.

Cohen (1988a), in his discussion of authenticity and commoditisation in tourism, furthers the debate by explaining how a word that is normally used to describe something that is real or genuine has also become a socially constructed concept (that is, a description of the condition of modern society). Following Trilling's origination of the word 'authentic' in the museum, curators and ethnographers have tended to view the authenticity of primitive and ethnic art in strict terms; to be authentic, things must have been created by traditional craftsmen using traditional materials. In particular, authentic items must have been made for the use of local people rather than for trade or selling on to strangers; *the absence of commoditisation...[is]...a crucial consideration in judgements of authenticity* (Cohen 1988a).

Most importantly, authenticity is a quality that is perceived to be firmly rooted in pre-modern life, a quality *of cultural products produced prior to the penetration of modern Western influences* (Cohen 1988a). In other words, things can only be authentic if they have been created without the aid of modern materials, tools or machinery. Thus, anything, including society, that has been adapted, influenced, altered or, as an anthropologist might describe, contaminated by the modern, Western world has lost its authenticity.

It is here that authenticity develops into a way of describing the state or condition of societies. If the origin of strictly authentic products lies in pre-modern societies then, by implication, modern Western society, with all its characteristics of alienation, materialism, mass production and consumption and so on, is inauthentic. Conversely, traditional countries or societies (by implication, those in the less developed parts of the world) are more authentic. For the tourist, authenticity or authentic experiences are to be found in pre-modern societies or societies that have yet to become Westernised and developed.

The question that then arises is: what are the characteristics of authentic, pre-modern or traditional societies that tourists seek? Is it, for example, simply symbols or signs of authenticity, such as the existence of traditional, non-mechanised farming methods, or do tourists wish to fully immerse themselves in traditional society, to experience a way of life that no longer exists in modern, developed societies

A full consideration of the characteristics of traditional (authentic)*versus* modern (inauthentic) societies is beyond the scope of this chapter, and much depends upon the perspective adopted. But, given the socio-cultural characteristics of traditional societies (see Figure 7 on page 192), it appears unlikely that a meaningful experience of traditional life could be included in the tourism experience.

As discussed later in this chapter, this does go some way to explaining the attraction of the British countryside as a symbol of the pre-industrial, pre-modern era (see Sharpley 1996) and, more generally, the current fascination with heritage and the past. In a touristic sense, if traditional, pre-industrial society is perceived to be authentic, then there is much truth in the suggestion that *the past is a foreign country* (Lowenthal 1990).

Figure 7: Characteristics of 'traditional' and 'modern' societies

Traditional	Modern
• Traditionalism: - orientation to the past/tradition - inability to adapt to new circumstances • Kinship system: - economic, social, legal position determined by kin relationships - ascription as opposed to achievement • Influence of emotion, superstition, fatalism	• Traditional values less dominant: - ability to change/adapt - challenge to obstacles of tradition • Open social system: - geographical/social mobility - economic, political, social freedom - achievement as opposed to ascription • Forward-looking society, demonstrating: - innovation, entrepreneurial spirit - objective, rational approach

Adapted from Webster (1990)

To summarise, then, authenticity within the context of tourism has two meanings:

(a) it is a description of the tangible *quality* of something (for example, an artefact, a meal, a festival, a building) which is associated with production methods or cultural foundations that are perceived to be pre-modern or traditional.

(b) it is a socially constructed, intangible perception of destination societies and cultures, of forms of travel, or of overall tourism experiences that appear to be pre-modern or traditional.

192

(ii)   The Boorstin-MacCannell debate

Both Boorstin and MacCannell take the inauthenticity of modern society as the starting point for their arguments. Indeed, both follow the structural line that the behaviour of modern tourists reflects and results from this inauthenticity, but their conclusions lie at opposite ends of what may be described as the authenticity-inauthenticity continuum. For Boorstin (1964), modern (American) society is contrived, illusory and unreal. People thrive on pseudo-events and this is reflected in the way that the modern, mass tourist is satisfied with contrived, meaningless events which can be viewed, preferably, from the comfort and surrounding of the familiar world. As Boorstin argues, the tourist...

> ... has come to believe that he can have a lifetime of adventure in two weeks and all the thrills of risking his life without any real risk at all. He expects that the exotic and the familiar can be made to order... expecting all this, he demands that it be supplied to him. Having paid for it, he likes to think he has got his money's worth. He has demanded that the whole world be made a stage for pseudo-events. (Boorstin 1964: 80)

The events are supplied by the tourism industry, images of new destinations are contrived by the media and every effort is made to make the tourist feel at home; one of the aims of Conrad Hilton was to create 'a little America' in each of the countries where he opened one of his hotels. As a result, the tourist is increasingly removed from the reality and authenticity of the destination society and *tourism turns into a closed, self-perpetuating system of illusions* (Cohen 1988b).

MacCannell (1989) adopts the opposite perspective. Rather than simply reflecting or representing the embodiment of the inauthenticity of modern life, the tourist recognises it and becomes a kind of secular pilgrim (MacCannell 1973) on a quest for authenticity. The very motive for tourism becomes a search for the authentic: *sightseeing is a kind of collective striving for a transcendence of the modern totality, a way of attempting to overcome the discontinuity of modernity* (MacCannell 1989: 13). The modern tourist looks for meaning in the reality of the life of other people in other places yet, at the same time, accepts the inauthentic condition of modernity. As if to perpetuate the differentiation between the modern and the pre-modern, modern society collects and preserves the pre-modern in museums and heritage centres, in arts, music, fashion and decor, in order to provide havens of reality and authenticity in the turmoil of modern life. For the tourist, the challenge lies in the extent to which he or she is allowed, by the destination tourism industry, to experience the real lives of others. Inevitably, events are staged for tourists but any resulting inauthenticity of experience results not from the demands of tourists for pseudo-events, as Boorstin argues, but rather as *a structural consequence of the development of tourism* (Cohen 1988b).

(iii)   Authenticity and the individual tourist

The arguments of Boorstin and MacCannell represent two extremes and, in reality, it is highly unlikely that tourists who conform to their descriptions exist in any great number, if at all. MacCannell's characterisation of the tourist is more in keeping with a description of an anthropologist and, as McKercher (1993) points out, *it is a mistake to assume that most tourists are anything more than consumers, whose primary goal is the consumption of a tourism experience.* More simply stated, tourism is most frequently motivated by the desire to escape from, not by the need to become involved in other societies, as suggested by MacCannell. Equally, it is widely accepted that tourists are becoming more discerning and more quality conscious and the tourism industry is having to provide an ever increasing variety of destinations and products to satisfy demand (for example, see Jenkins 1990; Lickorish 1990). Boorstin's tourist, therefore, bears more relation to a caricature of a mass tourist than to anyone who actually exists although, at the same time, it is probable that some tourists come close to his description.

Undoubtedly there are the purists who seek to escape entirely into authentic cultures and societies and others for whom the notion of authenticity does not even come into consideration in their holiday decision-making process. It would be safe to suggest that the great majority of tourists fall between these two extremes in terms of their search for authenticity. At the same time, the alienation that results from the condition of modern society is not necessarily recognised or experienced to a similar degree by all members of society (see Chapter Four and Cohen 1979b). For example, many people might be entirely satisfied with their lives, identifying with and accepting the characteristics of modern life, such as a routine job or materialism as a symbol of success. Their centre is firmly rooted in modernity and their sense of alienation is minimal. Other people may reflect on the meaning of their lives and may experience or be more aware of a sense of alienation from modern society. Such differences may result from occupational and educational factors. For example, Cohen (1988a) proposes that intellectuals are, generally, more aware of their alienation than *the rank-and-file middle-classes, and especially the lower middle class, who still strive to attain the material gains which those beyond them already enjoy.*

The important point is that, if there is indeed a link between alienation and the search for authenticity, then different tourists will be more or less disposed to seek authentic experiences elsewhere. Furthermore, the greater an individual's need to experience authenticity, the stricter will be the criteria by which that individual judges something to be authentic (Cohen 1988a). Thus, the greater a tourist's alienation from society, the greater will be the emphasis on finding and experiencing authenticity and the stricter will be the rules by which authenticity is judged. In other words, a recreational tourist may well perceive a particular attraction or event to be authentic whereas experiential tourists might see through the staged, contrived nature of the same attraction or event, perceiving it to be totally inauthentic. For example, two different tourists staying at a hotel at a beach resort in Spain may witness a show that includes some flamenco music and dancing. One of these tourists may be a non-alienated, recreational tourist with little desire to seek authenticity, the other a person seeking the 'real' Spain. The first, even recognising the staged nature of the show, may accept it as authentic whilst the second would almost certainly write it off as contrived, false and inauthentic. For the post-tourist, of course, the debate becomes irrelevant; all tourism is a game, all tourist experiences are part of that game and, in recognising this and the tourist's role in the game, the concept of authenticity is not considered.

To any individual tourist, then, authenticity is not a given, measurable quality that can be applied to a particular event or product, nor does it provide a simple scale against which a tourist experience may be judged. Rather, the perceived authenticity (or lack of authenticity) of a cultural product or of an overall tourist experience depends upon the relationship between the tourist as an individual and the product/experience with which he or she is concerned. It is not a fixed, static concept, but *negotiable* (Cohen 1988a). In other words, authenticity *must* be considered from the point of view of individual tourists, their expectations, their experience and their home socio-cultural environment. It is also argued that perceptions of authenticity are dependent on the relationships that tourists have with people in tourist settings (Pearce and Moscardo 1986). For example, a tourist in an inauthentic environment, such as a Western-style hotel, may still have an authentic experience by interacting with a local person who works in the hotel. Thus, *it is the relationship between the tourist and the host which determines authenticity* (Pearce and Moscardo 1986).

(iv)   Authenticity over time

Just as authenticity is a negotiable process based on the relationship between the individual tourist and the cultural product or event, so too is it possible to suggest that authenticity can develop over time. That is, it is feasible for a product or event that is originally inauthentic to become assimilated into local culture and to become authentic. No culture or society can be static; all cultures are dynamic, new cultural products emerge and, therefore, *emergent authenticity* (Cohen 1988a) is a valid and realistic process within the context of tourism. Thus, for example, festivals or events originally staged for the benefit of tourists may, over time, come to be accepted as a local, authentic custom. Similarly, crafts or products intended for tourist consumption may also achieve such a status. Tourism may also lead to the revival of old or forgotten rituals or crafts; the passage of time should not be viewed as a sign of diminished authenticity. For example, the traditional craft of greenstone carving in the southern Indian town of Mahabalipuram has been revitalised by the demand for souvenirs. The products, though intended for sale to tourists, are no less authentic than those produced by similar techniques hundreds of years ago:

> *Frequently arts, crafts and local culture have been revitalised as a direct result of tourism. A transformation of traditional forms often accompanies this development but does not necessarily lead to degeneration. To be authentic, arts and crafts must be rooted both in historical tradition and in present-day life; true authenticity cannot be achieved by conservation alone, since that leads to stultification.* (de Kadt 1979: 16)

Overall, then, authenticity is not simply the antithesis to modern life, something that motivates tourists. Nor is it just a label that may be attached to cultural products, events or tourist experiences as a means of comparing them with the inauthentic, the modern or the spurious. It is something that is unique to each individual tourist, possessing a meaning and importance that can only be assessed alongside an understanding of a tourist's experience, motivation, relationship to his or her home environment and reaction to the tourism environment. In other words, authenticity should be judged through the tourist's own eyes, *what he considers to be the essential marks of authenticity, and which sites, objects, and events on his trip do, in his opinion, possess these marks* (Cohen 1988b).

Staged authenticity

Of central importance to the consideration of the authenticity of tourist experiences is the notion of *staged authenticity* (MacCannell 1973 and 1989). MacCannell suggests that although the tourist is motivated by the desire for authentic experience and *may believe that he is moving in that direction* (1973), he is, nevertheless, frustrated in his ambition by the way in which experiences have been set up, or staged. In other words, although he may believe he is witnessing authenticity the tourist is, in fact, experiencing only what local people or the tourism industry are allowing him to see.

MacCannell's concept of staged authenticity is based upon the work of Goffman (1959) who divides the structure of social establishments into what he terms as the *front* and *back regions*. The front region is where the social interaction takes place, where hosts meet guests or where servers attend to customers. The back region is *the place where members of the home team retire between performances to relax and to prepare* (MacCannell 1989: 92). Performers (for example, hosts or waiters) appear in both regions, whereas the audience (guests, diners in a restaurant) are only allowed into the front region. Under this simple dichotomy the performance, the show, takes place in the front region but reality exists in the back region. For example, in a restaurant diners are served and eat their food in the front region, the dining room, but the food is prepared, the plates are washed and so on in the back region, the kitchen. Thus, the front region is removed from reality; the diners do not see their meals being cooked. Conversely, where customers are able to see their food being prepared, the dining out experience might be perceived to be more authentic.

In adapting Goffman's work to tourist settings, MacCannell suggests that the simple front-back dichotomy can be expanded into a continuum which starts at the front and ends at the back and it is from this that the notion of staged authenticity emerges. He proposes that there are six different stages on the continuum which, theoretically, may be identified (see MacCannell 1989: 101):

Stage One: this is Goffman's front region, the setting which tourists attempt to penetrate or get behind.

Stage Two: although still a front region, this stage has been given the superficial appearance of the back region by, for example, having wine racks on display in a restaurant.

Stage Three: this stage is still firmly embedded in the front region but it is totally organised to resemble a back region.

Stage Four: moving into the back region, tourists are permitted to see this stage. For example, tourists may be taken into the workshops to see the production process of local goods.

Stage Five: this is a back region to which tourists are occasionally permitted entry, such as the   flight   deck   on   an aeroplane.

Stage Six: this is Goffman's back region, the ultimate goal of the tourist but one which is rarely, if ever, reached.

When these six staged are applied to the setting for tourist experiences, it becomes evident that a tourist's quest for authenticity can progress along the continuum, but it is unlikely that the tourist will ever reach the sixth and final stage. Each stage offers the tourist apparently increasing opportunities for authentic experiences yet, from stages two through to five, what the tourist encounters is staged authenticity. The tourist is allowed glimpses of the back region, contrived events and attractions that are passed off as authentic, but the final stage of participating in the lives and culture of the host community is rarely experienced

The tourist, in his quest for authenticity, is doomed to failure. As more and more countries, regions, societies and cultures are caught up in the tourism net, the opportunity for authentic experience diminishes: *tourists make brave sorties...hoping, perhaps, for an authentic experience, but their paths can be traced in advance... Adventuresome tourists progress from stage to stage, always in the public eye, and greeted everywhere by their obliging hosts* (MacCannell 1989: 106).

One of the main criticisms of MacCannell's model is that it ignores the ability of tourists to understand and interpret the staged authenticity with which they are presented, although it does provide a useful framework for assessing the degree of authenticity inherent in tourist attractions and events. In order to achieve a more realistic model of staged authenticity, the structural approach adopted by MacCannell should be combined with a micro, social action perspective which takes into account the way in which tourists perceive and respond to the situation facing them. Cohen (1979a) combines two types of setting (staged and real) with tourists' impressions of the setting (again, staged and real) utilising a two dimensional approach to identify four different relationships between a tourist and the tourist setting:

(a) The setting is authentic and the tourist recognises it as such.

(b) The setting is staged but the tourist, believing it to be real, fails to recognise its contrived nature.

(c)   The setting is real, but the tourist believes it to be staged and is, therefore, suspicious of its authenticity

(d)   The setting is staged and the tourist recognises it as such.

Adding the impressions of tourists to the equation removes much of the finality of MacCannell's concept of staged authenticity. Whereas MacCannell's tourist is never likely to be satisfied and will continue to search for authenticity, tourists in Cohen's settings (a) and (d) recognise and accept their situation and will be less frustrated. This still represents a rather simplistic approach to the authenticity of tourist experiences and reference should again be made to the arguments presented by Pearce and Moscardo (1986). They identify nine different tourist experiences in which a tourist's relationship with people, with the setting (backstage or frontstage), or a combination of both can add to the authenticity of tourist experiences.

For example, meeting frontstage people in a fronstage setting, such as the performers in a tourist show, can be as equally authentic as meeting backstage people in a frontstage setting. In other words, authenticity is not dependent on the position along the back-front region continuum and nor is a tourist's recognition of a situation sufficient to determine the degree of authenticity experienced; a variety of other experiences may contribute to the authenticity of a holiday and, in many cases, the *backstage/frontstage distinction is irrelevant or not appropriate* (Pearce and Moscardo 1986).

In short, authenticity may or may not be staged; what tourists experience may be 'real' or it may be planned, a regularly repeated performance. What is important is the *total* tourist experience and what it means to the individual tourist. Different tourists have different motivations, expectations, knowledge and travel experience and the *whole issue of whether or not tourists are satisfied with their holiday experience demands a full consideration of the nature of the tourist environment, the tourists' perceptions of that environment and the tourists' need or preference for authenticity* (Pearce and Moscardo 1986).

The semiology of tourism

It is apparent that, within the context of tourism, authenticity is not a fixed, given quality or condition of a cultural product but something which is negotiable. In other words, the degree to which a sight or attraction is perceived to be authentic depends upon the relationship between an individual tourist and that sight or attraction. This relationship, in turn, depends to a great extent upon the attitudes, experience and so on of the tourist but, at the same time, the significance attached to a particular attraction or sight goes a long way to determining its authenticity. Something, such as an article of clothing, a souvenir or a festival, might be seen as authentic simply because it is unusual or different rather than because of its inherent quality or cultural meaning; its authenticity results from its difference or, to put it the other way round, its difference is a *sign* of its authenticity.

Arguably, *as soon as there is a society, every usage is converted into a sign of itself* (Barthes 1967, cited in Culler 1981); that is, everything has a sign as well an original purpose or meaning. For example, the basic purpose of a Rolls Royce motor car is transport, to carry its occupants from one place to another. To most people, however, a Rolls Royce is more than just a car; it is a sign of wealth, high status and success. Similarly, a Rottweiler is a dog, but it is also a sign of power and, perhaps, of danger; a passport is a legal, internationally recognised proof of nationality but it is also a sign of travel. The study of these signs, of the relationship between the *signifier* (a Rolls Royce) and the *signified* (wealth, status), is known as semiology and it is an approach which can be usefully applied to the consideration of the authenticity of tourist experiences.

Boorstin (1964: 106) complains that *the French chanteuse singing English with a French accent seems more charmingly French than one who simply sings in French. The American tourist in Japan looks less for what is Japanese than for what is Japanesey.* However, as Culler argues, most tourists are more concerned with finding and experiencing the image or sign of cultural practices and attractions rather than understanding their basic meaning or function: *all over the world the unsung armies of semiotics, the tourists, are fanning out in search of the signs of Frenchness, typical Italian behaviour, exemplary Oriental scenes, typical American thruways, traditional English pubs* (Culler 1981). It matters little that pubs are just convenient places for meeting and socialising or that high rise buildings are a logical way of housing a lot of people in a small area of land; for the tourist, the pub is a sign of Englishness, the skyscraper a sign of New York. As Culler (1981) again argues, *gondolas are the natural way to get around in a city full of canals..*[but]*...tourists persist in regarding these objects and practices as cultural signs.* What tourists want to see and to accept as authentic is something out of the ordinary, something beyond the threshold of their normal day-to-day existence that they can remember and relate to others when they return home. Thus, authenticity becomes a sign and tourism, rather than a search for authenticity, becomes a search for signs.

The relationship between a tourist and a sight is not a simple, two-way process. The tourist has to know that what is being looked at or experienced is an authentic sign, an attraction, that it is something worth visiting. For example, what is it that singles out the Empire State Building as a sign of New Yorkness, when there are many other skyscrapers (and higher ones, in the case of the World Trade Centre towers) in the city? The answer, according to MacCannell (1989), lies in a three way relationship. *The first contact a sightseer has with a sight is not the sight itself but with some representation thereof* (1989: 110). This representation may be in the form of a picture, a souvenir, a model or even just a name on a map and is what MacCannell calls a *marker*. A marker informs the tourist that a sight is worth seeing, that it is an attraction: *the 'real thing' must be marked as real, as sight-worthy; if it is not marked or differentiated, it is not a notable sight* (Culler 1981). Thus the tourist, in a triadic structure, links the marker with the sight in the process of sightseeing. The Empire State Building appears in all the brochures on New York; it is a symbol, a sign of the city. Therefore, to have an authentic experience of New York the tourist must visit the Empire State Building, along with other recognised symbols of New York, such as Central Park, Times Square and the Statue of Liberty. Preferably, the tourist also buys souvenirs and post cards as a reminder of the experience of New York.

It is the existence of pre-markers (for example, a picture in a brochure or a description in a guide book) and post-markers (souvenirs, photographs, post cards) that confirms a sight or experience as a sign of authenticity. Indeed, *the postcard, along with the photograph, is the most widely disseminated icon of tourist experience* (Edwards 1993). In other words, for a tourist experience or product to be authentic it needs to be certified as such. The paradox is that many experiences which conform more closely to the traditional meaning of authenticity go by untried or unnoticed if not marked. To continue the example of New York, using the subway is certainly a more authentic means of travelling round the city than joining a guided tour on an air-conditioned coach yet, because of the perceived danger, many tourists are quite happy to forego the experience of travelling on the subway. There is a limit to the New Yorkness they wish to experience, a limit which, as the following section considers, may frequently be dictated by the tourism industry.

The marketing of authenticity

It seems that tourists and indigenous peoples are incommensurably different within the touristic process, and indigenous peoples can only continue to be attractive to tourists so long as they remain undeveloped and, hence, in some way primitive. (Silver 1993: 310)

Authenticity is not only perceived by tourism researchers and others to be a prime motivator of tourism; it is recognised by the tourism industry as such. Also, it is widely accepted that the tourism industry plays an important role in shaping tourists' motivation and behaviour because, for many people, the travel brochure is the main source of information in planning holidays. Tourists frequently lack the knowledge, experience or access to information necessary to make travel purchase decisions and depend upon tour operators' marketing material, primarily brochures, for that information (Pritchard and Morgan 1995).

It is not only to tourists that brochures are important. The brochure is *probably the most important single item in the planning of tourism marketing* (Holloway and Plant 1992: 148). It is the medium through which tour operators sell their product, informing potential customers about the facilities, amenities and activities available, and how much they cost. However, as widely considered in the literature, brochures fulfil a broader function than the conveyance of factual information (Uzell 1984; Gilbert and Houghton 1991; Pritchard and Morgan 1995). They also have the power to shape tourists attitudes and expectations through what information is included or excluded and the way it is presented. In other words, brochures are also influential in determining how tourists perceive a destination: *there seems little reason to doubt that for many people tourist brochures...play a major role in forming their images* (Dilley 1986), images which result from the information and pictures that tour operators choose to include and, importantly, not to include in their brochures.

Tour operators are motivated by profit and market destinations to appeal to the greatest number of people who are likely to be attracted to their product. Thus, in most cases, there is a logical link between the destination and the potential market. Mediterranean countries are marketed to northern European customers primarily as sun, sea and sand destinations whereas to North Americans they are marketed as cultural and historical destinations, the reasoning being that most Americans go to resorts closer to home, such as the Caribbean, for beach holidays (see Buck 1977; Britton 1979; and Dilley 1986 for research into travel brochures). Beach holiday brochures primarily contain pictures and information about the beach, the hotel, the swimming pool and the nightlife, whereas cultural tourism will be marketed by pictures of historical architecture, traditional industries, information about special interest tours and so on. This is confirmed by recent research into the way in which British tour operators (both mainstream and specialist) market Cyprus – primarily a summer-sun destination – in their brochures. Despite the desire of the Cypriot tourism authorities to broaden the appeal of the island, Cyprus is typically represented in the brochures as a familiar, safe, welcoming destination with good beaches, plenty of sunshine and good nightlife. Reference is made to the cultural and historic attractions, particularly by the smaller, specialist operators, but even these strongly feature the sun and beach attributes of the island. Thus, for the most part, tour operators present the island as a sun-sea-sand destination, with the emphasis on fun, relaxation and a hint of romance (Sharpley 1998).

If this principle is applied to the marketing of authenticity, then it is logical to propose that tour operators represent destination countries in a way which potential tourists perceive them to be rather than the how they actually are. These perceptions are not always created by the tourism industry; in an age of mass information and communication, images of many countries in both the developing and the developed world appear regularly in magazines, in films and documentaries and in tourist advertisements. But, the tourism industry, through its brochures, may reinforce popularly held images of destinations, in particular of those destinations which offer tourists the opportunity to experience 'true' authenticity in the form of pre-industrial, primitive life styles. In other words, *the tourism industry only markets those images that it anticipates* [sic] *will be verified during travel, for tourists authenticity is not necessarily determined by gaining a genuine appreciation for another culture, but rather by verifying a marketed representation of it* (Silver 1993).

Inevitably, perhaps, as authenticity is seen to exist in other times and other places (MacCannell 1989), many destinations marketed on the basis of authenticity are in the developing world. Compared with rapid industrialisation and technological advance (and resultant alienation and inauthenticity) in the Western world, the countries of the developing world are seen as offering authentic, timeless experiences. Brochures describe destinations that have *many unusual and fascinating examples of human cultural activity, past and present; ...*[where]*...the pageant of human life is older, more varied, or just different from that at home* (Dilley 1986). They use clichés such as 'discover the undiscovered' or 'enjoy the unspoilt paradise' to emphasise that, although tourism has arrived, the modern world has yet to penetrate the destination. The images in the brochures tend to be selectively biased towards what a potential visitor expects to see in a country, an image of authenticity based upon pictures, films and historical associations. For example, travel brochures offering tours of India invariably include pictures of the Taj Mahal, the forts of Rajasthan, the houseboats on Dal Lake in Kashmir and of pilgrims bathing in the water of the River Ganges at Varanasi, attempting to recreate, perhaps, the days of the Raj. Furthermore, pictures of local people tend to conform to standard images, such as women wearing colourful saris and adorned with dramatic jewellery. Similarly, Britton (1979) found that *local residents are generally absent from illustrations; when they are shown, they likely appear as stereotyped stage props, such as a smiling Jamaican nimbly balancing a tray of cocktails on his head.*

What the brochures do not usually show are details and pictures of a destination's level of industrialisation, its problems of poverty, over-population and pollution, the signs that it is becoming Westernised. In other words, tourist brochures, not surprisingly, do not include images that are likely to deter visitors. Tourists, even those on a quest for authenticity, are trying to escape, albeit temporarily, from the pressures and problems of the modern world and the marketing of a destination and the tourism system within it tends to shield visitors from the realities of the country. In effect, the tourism industry markets and operates a sanitised authenticity; visitors to India may be aware of the poverty, but they do not wish to be reminded of it as they see the tourist sights.

As the countries of the developing world become more industrialised and more Westernised, the authenticity marketed by the tourism industry is increasingly divorced from the reality of the country; the authenticity marketed and sold becomes a myth, and will become more so as local people and local tourism industries recognise that their appeal and, more importantly, their value to tourists lies in their traditional culture rather than their emerging modernity.

Herein lies the paradox of tourism development in many countries. As discussed in Chapter Eight, the major rationale for promoting tourism is its potential contribution to social and economic development in destination areas. But, the appeal of many destinations, their authenticity, becomes challenged by the objective of that tourism-related development – modernisation. Thus, in the extreme, authenticity as demanded by tourists may be confined to themed centres, such as the Polynesian Cultural Centre in Hawaii, where *a satisfactory fiction emerges wherein a guest can imagine for a brief time that the idyllic life of Polynesia... described by Robert Louis Stevenson.....is a 'reality'* (Stanton 1989: 247).

Authenticity and the commoditisation of culture

A common thread throughout this chapter is that authenticity, within the context of tourism, is a product, a commodity. It is not a quality or a condition of something but, for many, an essential ingredient of the tourist experience. Tourists are motivated by a search for authenticity, whether as an actual experience or as a sign of something different from their ordinary, everyday existence, and the tourism industry markets authenticity as it would market any other tourism product. As tourism as a whole is a product that is produced, bought and sold then, logically, authenticity and the cultural products that represent it also have a value. It is important to consider the extent to which this centrality of authenticity to the tourism experience has led to what Cohen (1988a) describes as the *commoditisation* of culture. In particular, the question must be asked, does the commoditisation of culture dilute, or even destroy, its meaning and authenticity?

One of the most widely held assumptions about the development of tourism is that, generally, it leads to cultural change within the destination society. Mathieson and Wall (1982: 159) identify three major forms of culture which attract tourists and are, hence, susceptible to change:

(a) Inanimate forms of culture, such as historical buildings and monuments or traditional arts and crafts.

(b) Forms of culture which are reflected in the normal, day-to-day life and activities of people in destination societies.

(c) Animated forms of culture, involving the participation of people, such as religious events, carnivals, and traditional festivals.

All forms of culture are dynamic and liable to change over time, with or without the influence of tourism. Worldwide advances in information and communication technology, satellite television and the international spread of symbols of modern Western culture, such as MacDonald's, have a far greater influence on cultural change than tourism. But, following the onset of tourism the normal life of a host society, its values, lifestyles and customs, may adapt over time through processes known as acculturation and cultural drift. In other words, *when two cultures come into contact of any duration, each becomes somewhat like the other through a process of borrowing* (Nuñez 1989: 266). Generally, tourists are less likely to borrow from their hosts than *vice versa* (although there are exceptions) and tourism is perceived, therefore, to be a powerful agent of change, particularly in those societies with fragile or less dominant cultures. These issues are considered in greater depth in Chapter Ten.

In contrast to a gradual cultural change contributed to by the influence of tourism, certain forms of culture, in particular arts and crafts (that is, material forms of culture) and festivals or ritual events, can be changed or adapted specifically for tourists. They *come to be performed or produced for touristic consumption* (Cohen 1988a) or, in other words, they become commoditised. Such a process is inevitable as tourists, constrained by the short duration of their holidays, demand instant culture and authentic souvenirs to take home with them. Also, from the host society's point of view, if the most is to be made of culture as a commercial product, it must be *available and presentable; packaged for consumption into easily digestible and, preferably, photogenic chunks* (Simpson 1993). Thus, it is a process that is also often perceived as leading to the production of inauthentic, fake art and a loss of meaning to the producers: *local culture... is altered and often destroyed by the treatment of it as a tourist attraction. It is made meaningless to the people who once believed in it* (Greenwood 1989: 173). This need not always be the case.

(i) Arts and crafts

In many destinations both the purpose and the style of cultural products have been adapted to appeal to the tourist market. What were once religious or ceremonial artefacts are now mass produced and sold to tourists in a process of cultural commoditisation that can be identified in many countries around the world. Traditional art forms, designs and production techniques tend to disappear as simpler and less sophisticated replacements associated with the techniques of mass production are provided for tourist consumption. One such example are the *raksa* devil dance masks of Sri Lanka (see Simpson 1993). Originally used in a number of different contexts, such as folk dramas, festivals and rituals of exorcism and healing, the masks represent the images of a variety of deities and demons. They have a fundamental meaning and significance to the performance of such rituals and, at the same time, the production of the masks is also a recognised and socially important activity within the local community. But, the rapid growth of tourism to Sri Lanka during the late 1970s and early 1980s resulted in the masks being recognised as an appealing and commercially attractive representation of Sinhalese culture for the tourist market. As they became mass produced, not only did they lose their cultural meaning and authenticity as masks of different sizes, decoration and colours were produced to suit the taste of tourists, but also the status of the manufacturers in Sinhalese society deteriorated.

At best, the reproduction of cultural artefacts for tourism retains the quality and style, if not the meaning or authenticity, of the originals; at worst, they *consist of stylised works which bear only the most tenuous relationship to anything in the traditional culture* (Mathieson and Wall 1982: 168). In short, they typify what has been called 'airport art', manifested by a general deterioration in quality resulting, in particular, from the breaking of the connection between art forms and their original purpose. For example, Buddhist *tankas*, or paintings, which adorn Buddhist temples in Tibet and Nepal, are now mass produced and widely available for sale to tourists in Kathmandu. They can also be found in specialist shops and markets in the western world along with a huge variety of other cultural artefacts from areas such as Asia and South America. This export business has further severed the products from their cultural roots, although it can be argued that the internationalisation of culture also leads to a more widespread knowledge and appreciation of such art forms.

Despite the emphasis placed on the perceived negative impacts of the commoditisation of arts and crafts, tourism can also make a positive contribution to the continuation or re-emergence of traditional art forms. For example, Graburn (1976: 42) describes how tourists' demands for carvings made by the Canadian Inuit, or Eskimo, has led to a huge increase in production. Rather than resulting in a dilution of authenticity, the carvings are of a much higher standard than most souvenir crafts and are based upon aspects of the traditional Inuit lifestyle. Through their production of tourist souvenirs, the Eskimos are not only able to earn a living but also to preserve their cultural identity. In the case of the Indians of the south-western United States, a variety of art forms have been combined into a new, authentic artistic culture: *massive in-migration and mass tourism have not been disruptive. Rather, the contact with Anglo society offered extended markets that served to heighten artistic productivity and to revive old traditions* (Deitch 1989: 235).

In short, tourism can undoubtedly lead to the mass production of fake cultural objects that bear little resemblance, either in form or in meaning, to their original purpose and are, therefore, inauthentic. Equally, re-emergent or new arts and crafts also result from the demands of tourists for cultural souvenirs. Thus, just as all forms of culture are in a state of constant change and development, these new products are no less authentic to either the producers or the consumers than those from previous cultural periods (see also Ariel de Vidas 1995).

(ii) Festivals, events and rituals

Owing to the constraints that characterise tourism, cultural events which are based upon religious or traditional heritage, such as festivals, re-enactments of historical or mythical events and religious ceremonies, and which are intended as an attraction for tourists, will normally occur outside normal time and space. That is, the reason or tradition underlying the event becomes secondary to the event itself as the timing and content is adapted to suit the needs of tourists. For example, when researching Sinhalese devil dances, Simpson (1993) found that *the necessity for short, concise and essentially visual modes of presentation is at odds with the styles of performance the Berava adopt in their own ritual performances.* In this situation, it is highly likely that the meaning and significance of the event to the performers and local audiences is lost, even though to tourists it may appear authentic.

Examples of commoditised cultural performances occur all around the world, from staged dance performances given by African villagers to

'Hula' girls greeting tourists arriving at Honolulu airport in Hawaii. One of the first, and most widely quoted, studies into the tourism-related commoditisation of a cultural event was that by Greenwood (1989). He describes the way in which the *Alarde*, a public ritual in the Basque town of Fuenterrabia which commemorates the town's victory over the French in 1638, became a major tourist attraction as a result of its taking place during the height of the tourist season. The local authorities decreed in 1969 that, in order to allow large numbers of visitors to witness the *Alarde*, it should be performed twice on the same day. Within two years *what was a vital and exciting ritual had become an obligation to be avoided...*[and]...*the municipal government was considering payments to people for their participation in the Alarde* (Greenwood 1989: 178). It had become a commercial tourist attraction, devoid of all meaning to the participants. It is interesting to note, however, that, more recently, Greenwood accepts that the *Alarde* is once more a public event, but more significant now as a contemporary political statement than as a recreation of an historical event.

As with arts and crafts, there are also many situations where the commoditisation of cultural performances does not necessarily lead to a loss of meaning and authenticity. On the contrary, the opportunities and the financial rewards presented by the demands of tourists for authentic experiences can lead to the preservation and development of traditional, cultural events. Also, as Cohen (1988a) points out, the meaning of such events can change, but remain authentic, for the producers. For example, a festival might lose its religious significance through commercialisation but gain an equally important significance to the participants as a representation of local culture. McKean (1989) describes the case of Bali where ritual performances serve two distinct purposes within Balinese society. On one hand, festivals and rituals are performed for tourist consumption, providing a popular attraction at the same time as representing an important source of income. On the other hand, in a process of *cultural involution*, the commercial tourist version allows the Balinese to retain their traditional cultural skills and practices and to perform to local audiences, thereby preserving authentic cultural events within an increasingly modern social and economic context. Indeed, *younger Balinese find their identity as Balinese to be sharply framed by the mirror that tourism holds up to them, and has led many of them to celebrate their own traditions with continued vitality* (McKean 1989:132; see also Picard 1995).

In some cases, cultural events and festivals, whilst being major tourist attractions, retain their importance and authenticity within the host society. In other words, although attracting large numbers of tourists and, indirectly, generating tourist spending, their original function and purpose are not adapted or compromised by the demands of tourism but remain firmly rooted in the destination's cultural heritage. For example, the Changing of the Guards at Buckingham Palace in London draws large crowds but its role as a tourist attraction is incidental to its primary function. Similarly, the annual carnival in Rio de Janeiro, historically a celebration of freedom from slavery, is a festival performed by the people for the people. Again, the carnival is a major tourist attraction but it is neither motivated by, nor held for, tourists. It provides an authentic tourist experience but the importance and meaning of the carnival has been retained.

More generally, the commoditisation or commercialism of cultural performances cannot, and should not, lead to accusations of inauthenticity. People all around the world pay to see or experience performed cultural arts and events, from street buskers to major national theatre and dance companies and orchestras. Indeed, many art forms require financial support to survive and it is often tourism that provides that support. For example, it is often stated that many London theatres would go out of business if it were not for tourism. Yet it would be unheard of for a production of a Shakespeare play or a performance of Mozart's music to be described as inauthentic! Three points deserve emphasis when considering the link between the commoditisation of culture and the authenticity of tourist experiences.

(a) Different tourists, depending on their experience and expectations, have different perceptions of authenticity, but most adopt a broader, less purist stance than would, say, an anthropologist. Thus, many forms of cultural productions, whether performed or material artefacts, are accepted as authentic by tourists even if they have been adapted to the requirements of tourism.

(b) Very often, the tourism-induced commoditisation of culture leads to the preservation and recreation of traditional, authentic cultural art forms whilst those which are strongly rooted in local culture retain their integrity and meaning despite tourism. Furthermore, culture is not static but continually evolves and takes different forms.

Disneyland is as authentic as a traditional Buddhist festival and perceptions of authenticity or inauthenticity should not be clouded by what may be described as cultural arrogance.

(c) Generally, the decision to commoditise culture lies with the producers, not the consumers. In the extreme, as in the case of the Himalayan kingdom of Bhutan, the number of tourists and where they may go in the country is strictly controlled to protect the authenticity and integrity of religious festivals and ceremonies. As Cohen (1988a) argues, in order to avoid the blanket condemnation of the assumed negative impacts of cultural commoditisation, research should be emic (that is, from the point of view of the host society) and should assess over time the perceptions of both locals and tourists.

Authenticity, the past and nostalgia

If the past is a foreign country, nostalgia has made it the foreign country with the healthiest tourist trade of all.(Lowenthal 1990: 4)

One of the major themes throughout this chapter is that the notion of authenticity, within the context of tourism, is inextricably linked to the past, to an earlier, pre-modern era. For MacCannell, *reality and authenticity are thought to be elsewhere: in other historical periods and other cultures* (1989: 3); that is, in times and places which offer a sense of tradition and authenticity that has been lost in modern society. Similarly, the tourism industry implies, with its promises of 'unspoilt paradise', 'undiscovered peoples and places' and 'authentic culture', that tourists can, somehow, become time travellers; by boarding an aeroplane they can be transported back in time to places which offer the chance to experience life as it used to be. Thus, tourists are motivated by the inauthenticity of modern life, by the alienated, anomic condition of industrialised society, to seek meaning and reality elsewhere. In effect, the past has become a tourist destination.

The past has also become big business, for this concentration on the past is not limited only to tourism. Indeed, tourism is symptomatic within the modern world of a much broader and deeper-rooted concern for, and interest in, history and heritage. *Today a great deal of time and energy is dedicated to looking backwards, toward capturing a past which, in many ways, is considered superior to the chaotic present and the dreaded future* (Dann 1994: 55). In many aspects of life, from home decor to clothing fashions, from architecture to advertising, images, designs and styles of the past are used and recreated to signify an era that is, somehow, better than the present. For example, the use of festoon blinds, William Morris style wallpaper, Laura Ashley fabrics, brass lamps and Victorian pine furniture are popular ways of recreating a more traditional, familiar and friendly style of home furnishing in contrast to the perceived stark, characterless quality of many modern homes.

At the same time, saving, conserving and presenting the past is becoming a more widespread concern and activity. Landscape conservation was originally motivated by the desire to protect the natural environment from encroaching urbanisation and industrialisation; nowadays, symbols and relics of that industrialisation are themselves conserved and protected. Moreover, the past that is protected, recreated or simply looked back upon with nostalgia is becoming increasingly close to the present. For example, it is not uncommon for relatively modern, twentieth century buildings, such as Southwark bus station in London, to be added to the ever growing collection of listed buildings in Britain. Indeed, it is in Britain that interest in the past is most prevalent. Almost every town and city boasts a museum or heritage centre and *it seems that a new museum opens every week or so* (Urry 1990a: 104). The National Trust, with over two million members and eleven million visits to its properties each year, is the largest conservation organisation in Europe and the British government spends over £100 million a year on conserving the built environment (Urry 1990a: 106), to say nothing of the financial support provided for landscape conservation.

This ever-increasing interest in the past, feeding what has developed into the heritage industry (Hewison 1987), is widely believed to be caused by nostalgia, a condition which *now attracts or afflicts most levels of society* (Lowenthal 1990: 11). Nostalgia was once looked upon as a physical illness and even during the Second World War it appeared on the U.S. Surgeon General's list of standard illnesses suffered by American army personnel. Nowadays it is accepted that nostalgia is not simply an interest in or yearning for the past but, rather, *a positively toned evocation of a lived past in the context of some negative feeling toward the present or impending circumstances* (Davis 1979:18, quoted in Dann 1994: 65). In other words, nostalgia results from dissatisfaction with the present and concern for the future, a situation that Hewison (1987) links to *Britain in a climate of decline.* Thus, *in the face of apparent decline and disintegration, it is not surprising that the past seems a better place* (Hewison 1987: 43).

Reflecting the enormous increase in both the number and the diversity of heritage attractions, there has been a corresponding and growing debate surrounding the development, marketing and role of heritage. A full consideration of the relevant issues is beyond the scope of this chapter (see, for example, Herbert 1995), although a number of important questions are linked to the notion of authenticity. Primarily, many would argue that heritage sites or attractions do not present 'real' history. That is, they represent the past in a way that is attractive to (paying) visitors; they portray a sanitised past, a golden age with the 'bad bits' taken out. In other words, the more traditional role of history (education) has been replaced by 'infotainment'. This argument is further strengthened when the heritage site itself becomes the attraction. That is, many heritage centres represent the past through a variety of modern interpretative methods, from static displays, videos and 'talking heads' to the recreation of 'authentic' sounds and smells and journeys back in time in 'time capsules'. In many cases, there is little if any evidence of historical remains, the heritage attraction being created on the sites of past events or even mythical, literary associations. In short, it is the display, the interpretation that becomes the attraction, not the history it represents.

It is also important, within the context of authenticity, to consider whose heritage is being represented. For example, according to Tunbridge and Ashworth (1996), much heritage is 'dissonant'; that is, the heritage presented bears more relation to the heritage of visitors and, hence, what they expect to see or experience, rather than the 'true' history of the site. Also, the purpose of presenting heritage might be to achieve political objectives, to convey impressions or messages that go beyond the original significance of the site or event.

In the present context, it is useful to consider how the tourism industry, recognising and attempting to satisfy the tourist's nostalgic yearnings, has appropriated heritage. Dann (1994) suggests four ways in which nostalgia is linked to tourism and in which the tourism industry attempts to evoke, for the tourist, a sense of authenticity rooted in the past:

(a) Hotels
In an era when hotels are becoming increasingly similar and standardised, when one hotel lobby or room looks much the same as any other irrespective of the city or country in which it is located, a sense of authenticity, distinction and the luxury of a golden age can be achieved by recreating an image of the past. For example, Indian hotels which utilise buildings which were once, and in some cases still are, the palaces of maharajahs, transport guests back to the days of colonial India. Similarly, the famous Raffles Hotel in Singapore has recently been refurbished to recreate the atmosphere of the early 1900s. Most cities can boast an hotel noted for its individuality and authentic atmosphere, but such authenticity is only available to those who can afford it.

(b) Museums
MacCannell writes *the best indication of the final victory of modernity over other socio-cultural arrangements is not the disappearance of the non-modern world, but its artificial preservation and reconstruction in modern society* (1989: 8). One of the major physical manifestations of the power of nostalgia within the context of tourism is the proliferation of museums and, in particular, heritage centres which attempt to present not only artefacts from the past but also life as it was in days gone by. Modern methods of interpretation, such as audio-visual displays, re-enactments using actors, 'living museums' (for example, Beamish in County Durham or Williamsburg, Virginia) and the use of 'time cars' to carry visitors back in time through a heritage display (as at the Jorvik

Viking Centre in York or The Oxford Story in Oxford), are frequently used to recreate the past.

But, a major problem, as mentioned above, is that nostalgia acts as a kind of rose-tinted filter, creating a past that safe, secure and devoid of unsavoury facts of past times, such as poverty, illness, dangerous working conditions, child labour and so on. In other words, *myths of the past are created – the past is seen in the way in which we would like to see it, and not the way it was* (Wheeler 1992). Thus, tourists find a reality based not in the past, but on a modern representation of the past. (See Hewison 1987; Wright 1985; Lumley 1988; and Walsh, 1992).

(c) Infamous sites

Whilst the popularity of infamous sites, such as the Auschwitz visitor centre in Poland, the Bloody Tower in London and the Bridge over the River Kwai in Thailand, may be explained by morbid curiosity, as may the seven mile traffic jams of sightseers on the main road to Lockerbie the day after the explosion of Pan Am Fight 103 (see Rojek 1993: 137 and for a discussion of tourism to 'black spots'), Dann (1994: 61) relates it to the ability of nostalgia to discard unpleasant experiences. The reality of the attractions then lies in the evidence they present of past threats to society, to ordered life, to continuity and to identity. In other words, people visit infamous sites to confirm their own survival.

(d) Industrial centres

Much of the growth in the number of heritage centres and museums has been based upon the representation of the industrial past. New Lanark in the Scottish Clyde Valley, the Wigan Pier Heritage Centre, and the Rhondda Heritage Park in South Wales are just three examples of the over 460 museums in Britain (Urry 1990: 104) which display industrial material. Certainly, much of the popularity of such centres is based upon a nostalgia for industrial machinery and processes, such as the steam engine, which are no longer used. However, by drawing attention to the work of others, in other times and under conditions that are unacceptable today, they also represent a yardstick against which the reality and authenticity of modern and post-industrial society may be measured. Importantly, modern industrial heritage centres may also fulfil a political objective; the opening of the visitor centre at the Sellafield nuclear power station on the north-west coast of England was as much a public relations exercise as an attempt to inform or educate.

Perhaps the best example of the link between tourism and the experience of authenticity as represented by the past is the popularity of the British countryside as a tourist destination (see Sharpley 1996). If tourism is, indeed, a search for the authentic motivated by the inauthenticity and meaninglessness of modern society, then the countryside is the ultimate representation of the pre-industrial life. The countryside originally emerged as an identifiable, distinct tourist destination during the rapid industrialisation and urbanisation of British society during the nineteenth century. Romanticised by the poets and artists of the late eighteenth and early nineteenth centuries, it became the symbol of a life lost to the demands of industry and the capitalists. In the twentieth century, the countryside has come to be seen as the antithesis to modernism; visually and socially it has escaped the regulation and regimentation of modern urban life, representing freedom, nature and reality. But, the tourists' rural landscape is idealised by nostalgia. Modern machinery, housing, motorways, electric power cables and, more recently, wind farms, have no place in authentic countryside (Urry 1990a: 98) and the efforts of conservation organisations are firmly directed towards the maintenance of a kind of Wordsworthian image of the countryside within the framework of late twentieth century society. The countryside *has become so imbued with literary and painterly associations that we do not really see the landscape that lies before us. We substitute a countryside of the mind, shaped by our cultural perspectives and reflecting our psychological needs* (Hewison 1993).

The same criticism may be directed towards the perceived authenticity of tourist attractions and destinations as a whole. By continuing to look to the past for authenticity, reality and meaning, the tourist experience will be increasingly caught in a time warp and the culture that is packaged and presented to tourists will bear less and less resemblance to the reality of the destination. The challenge for the future, for both tourists and the tourism industry, is to view the culture and authenticity of destinations and host societies in their own right, rather than in comparison to the tourists own culture and society. In other words, authenticity is rooted as much in the present as it is in the past and, as more and more countries develop and modernise, their emerging culture and modernity must be accepted as authentic. To do otherwise, to perceive authenticity as being in other times and places (that is, the past), would result in tourism becoming based on myth and fantasy, the representations of authenticity in the host societies becoming as meaningless and inauthentic as the societies from which tourists, temporarily, escape.

Eight

Tourism and Development

Introduction

A two-way relationship exists between tourism and society. On the one hand, tourism and tourists are influenced by society; that is, society creates both the ability and the desire amongst its members to participate in tourism whilst also influencing how people behave as tourists. On the other hand, tourism and tourists impact upon society. As an export industry, international tourism is unique in that the customer (the tourist) travels to where the product is 'made'; tourism is consumed, as it were, on site. Domestic tourism, too, involves the movement of large numbers of people from one place to another and, in both cases, a wide range of activities, facilities, attractions and amenities are provided to satisfy their needs. Inevitably, then, tourism impacts upon the environments and societies within which it occurs. Of these two types of tourism-society relationship, this book has so far been concerned with the former – the influence of society of tourism. In this and subsequent chapters, attention is now focused upon the ways in which, conversely, tourism impacts upon societies.

It has long been recognised that the development and growth of tourism, in particular mass tourism, can result in a variety of negative consequences for destination environments and societies. During the 1960s, what Jafari (1989) refers to as the 'advocacy' stage or period of tourism development, tourism was for the most part viewed favourably as a means of creating income and employment, particularly in disadvantaged or less developed countries or regions. By the 1970s, however, as mass tourism grew dramatically in both scale and scope, increasing concern was voiced over the potential impacts of tourism (Jafari's 'cautionary' stage). A number of authors drew attention to these impacts (for example, Young 1973; Turner and Ash 1975; de Kadt 1979), their approach epitomised perhaps by Mishan, an economist, who wrote:

220

Travel on this scale with the annual need to accommodate tens of millions, rapidly and inevitably disrupts the character of the affected regions, their populations and ways of living. As swarms of holiday-makers arrive by air, sea and land, by coach train and private automobile, as concrete is poured over the earth, as hotels, caravans, casinos, night-clubs, chalets, blocks of sun-flats crowd into the area and retreat into the hinterland, local life and industry shrivel, hospitality vanishes, and indigenous populations drift into a quasi-parasitic way of life catering with contemptuous servility to the unsophisticated multitude. (Mishan 1967: 142)

Primarily, attention was and, by and large, remains directed towards two areas of concern: the nature of the relationship between tourists as 'guests' and the destination societies that play host to them, and the impacts of tourism on the physical environment. A number of early texts explored both of these areas, whilst one of the first texts to address specifically the socio-cultural aspects of tourism development was *Hosts and Guests: The Anthropology of Tourism* (Smith 1979). Since then, an increasingly large number of books and articles have considered the cause and nature of the impacts of tourism on the physical and socio-cultural environments in destination areas, providing the foundation for an equally large and diverse literature on the potential solution to these 'problems' of tourism, namely, sustainable tourism development.

In the context of this book it is the tourist-host relationship and socio-cultural impacts of tourism that are of greatest relevance. These separate yet inter-related issues are discussed in Chapters Nine and Ten. Of equal importance, but less widely considered in the literature, is the potential role of tourism in the overall development of destination areas. That is, the justification for promoting tourism is generally that it makes a positive contribution towards economic and social 'development'. The objectives and processes inherent in achieving such development are, however, rarely touched upon in the tourism literature, notable exceptions being Britton (1982); Erisman (1983); Pearce (1989); Opperman (1993); Opperman and Chon (1997); and Wahab and Pigram (1997). In other words, the general and widely held assumption is that tourism plays a positive role in the development of destination areas and societies; the primary challenge then becomes minimising the negative consequences of tourism in order to optimise that developmental role. Less often asked are the questions: what is development? What processes lead to development? And, can tourism play an effective role in development?

The purpose of this chapter is to address these questions, assessing in particular the potential for social development through tourism. In so doing, it provides a broader foundation for understanding and explaining the characteristics of the tourist-host relationship and for exploring the inevitability of the socio-cultural consequences of tourism.

Tourism: a tool for development?

Given the rapid and continuing growth in both domestic and international tourism, it is not surprising that many countries it is regarded *as an important and integral aspect of their development policies* (Jenkins 1991: 61). This potential role of tourism in promoting or encouraging development springs primarily from the economic benefits that result from the development of tourism itself. Not only does international tourism generate in excess of US$450 billion in tourist spending, contributing significantly to the income and foreign exchange earnings of destination areas, but it also supports a large and diverse industry. As a result, tourism is estimated to account for over ten per cent of global GDP and 10.6 per cent of global employment (WTTC 1994), figures which are, by any standards, impressive.

It is in the lesser developed, peripheral countries in particular that tourism is considered an important and effective means of achieving development. Though it is difficult to define or characterise less developed or developing countries (see Opperman and Chon 1997: 4-5), typically they suffer a number of problems. These include the economic problems of low *per capita* income, high levels of unemployment, dependence upon a declining agricultural sector, few or no manufacturing industries, a high level of imports and, consequently, high levels of foreign debt. Social indicators of under-development, directly and indirectly related to these economic problems, include low literacy levels, poor sanitation and health-care, and relatively low life expectancy.

Tourism is considered a way of combating many of these challenges; as Roche (1992: 566) comments:

> *whether for good or ill, the development of tourism has long been seen as both a vehicle and a symbol at least of westernisation, but also, more importantly, of progress and modernisation.   This has particularly been the case in Third World countries.*

In this context, the emphasis is placed on the potential economic benefits accruing from the development of tourism mentioned above, in particular its contributions to foreign exchange earnings and the creation of income and employment, and on the benefits of utilising tourism, as opposed to other economic activities or industries, as a vehicle for development (see Bull 1995). For example, Jenkins (1980) suggests a number of reasons why tourism may be seen as an attractive development option for less developed countries (LDCs):

(a)   International tourism has demonstrated consistent growth since the 1960s and long – haul travel, in particular, is becoming increasingly popular yet appears to be less price and income sensitive than more traditional, short-haul tourism.

(b)   Tourism to LDCs has, in theory, the effect of redistributing income from richer to poorer countries, although it has long been recognised that the net retention of tourist expenditures varies considerably from one destination to another.

(c)   Unlike other forms of international trade, tourism is relatively free of trade restrictions, a position that is likely to be strengthened by the inclusion of tourism in the General Agreement on Trade in Services (GATS) which became operational in January 1995.

(d)   World-wide, the growth in demand for international tourism both to and between LDCs is likely to continue.

(e)   Compared with other industries, tourism is often considered to have relatively low 'start-up' costs. Indeed, many attractions, such as natural scenery, beaches, mountains and climate, are, in effect, 'free'. But, as standards, expectations and competition grow, successful tourism development is becoming increasingly dependent on high levels of infra- and super-structural investment.

It is not only in LDCs that tourism's development potential has been recognised; tourism is also an important economic sector in most industrialised countries. In western Europe, for example, there has long been evidence of national government support of the tourism sector, in some cases dating back to the 1920s and 1930s (Shaw and Williams 1994: 67). More recently, *tourism – along with some other select activities such as financial services and telecommunications – has become a major component of economic strategies* (Williams and Shaw 1991: 1), particularly in the context of the development of peripheral regions and the socio-economic regeneration of rural areas (Hoggart *et al* 1995; Cavaco 1995). Similarly, there is a huge potential for tourism development in eastern Europe, although *the question of the nature, speed and quality of international tourism development...is likely to be one of the more critical components of the region's precarious post-communist pathway* (Hall 1993: 356).

In short, it is widely held that tourism can play a significant and positive role in national, regional and local development. This developmental role of tourism is frequently referred to in generalised terms, perhaps best summarised by the WTO's assertion in the Manila Declaration on World Tourism (WTO 1980: 1) that:

> *world tourism can contribute to the establishment of a new international economic order that will help to eliminate the widening economic gap between developed and developing countries and ensure the steady acceleration of economic and social development and progress, in particular in developing countries.*

But, no reference is made to the meaning, process and objectives of that 'development'.

At the same time, much empirical research has been undertaken into the economic, social and cultural impacts, both positive and negative, of tourism development. Rarely, however, are such studies located within the broader context of development as a whole. As Pearce (1989: 15) argues, research into the impacts of tourism development has, for the most part, been *divorced from the processes which have created them* and little reference is made to the *changing framework within which all development strategies, including tourism, have been formulated over the last fifty years* (Harrison 1992a: 10).

As a result, many important issues and questions about the role, meaning and process of tourism-induced development have been left unanswered, particularly about the extent to which tourism does in fact encourage or lead to development. The first task, then, is to consider what is meant by 'development'.

Development

(i) What is development?

Development is a term that is widely used yet, despite numerous attempts to do so, appears to defy definition. Part of the problem is that it is an ambiguous term that is used to describe both a process through which a society moves (or, implicitly, progresses, although progress itself is not synonymous with development) from one condition to another, and also the goal of that process; the development process in a society may result in it achieving the state or condition of development.

Dev. is a plan and not a single action

Yet development does not refer to a single process or set of events, nor does it imply a single, static condition. Thus, development may be seen as a term *bereft of precise meaning... [and]... little more than the lazy thinkers catch-all term, used to mean anything from broad, undefined change to quite specific events* (Welch 1984). As Wall (1997: 34) summarises, development can be referred to *as a philosophy, as a process, as a plan and as a product.*

225

Traditionally, development has been defined in terms of western-style modernisation achieved through economic growth. As the national economy grows, the national productive capacity increases and, as long as output expands at a rate faster than the population growth rate, then development is said to be occurring. This perceived role of economic growth acting as a catalyst for development meant that, initially, economic growth and development were one and the same. Indeed, throughout the 1950s and 1960s, the path from underdevelopment to development was seen to lie along a series of economic steps or stages which all nations, both developing and developed, must proceed (Rostow 1960). Within this context, development and underdevelopment came to be defined according to economic measurements, such as gross national product or per capita GNP, or according to economic structural criteria. But, this narrow economics-based definition, giving primacy to production and output, overlooked 'human element' of development. The emphasis on economic development and the inherent assumption that economic benefits would trickle down or diffuse to the wider population meant that problems of health, education, income distribution, unemployment and so on had become secondary to the drive for growth.

By the late 1960s it became clear that, in many countries, economic growth was not only failing to solve social and political problems but was actually causing or exacerbating them. As a result, the aims of development became more broadly redefined. Initially, development came to be seen as a process of modernisation with the emphasis on *how to inculcate wealth-oriented behaviour and values in individuals* (Mabogunje 1980: 38). Characterised by investment in education, housing and health facilities (with corresponding 'social indicator' measurements), modernisation was nevertheless still firmly rooted in the economic growth perspective. To be modern was to desire and consume goods and services normally produced in developed countries and, therefore, development was dependent on increased production and consumption.

By the 1970s, the pendulum was beginning to swing away from development as an economic phenomenon towards the broader concept of development as the reduction of widespread poverty, unemployment and inequality. Indeed, many policy makers rejected economic growth as the objective of development; people, rather than things, became the focus of attention. Seers (1969), in particular, challenged the traditional economic development arguments when he asserted:

The questions to ask about a country's development are therefore: What has been happening to poverty? What has been happening to unemployment? What has been happening to inequality? If all three of these have declined from high levels, then beyond doubt this has been a period of development for the country concerned.

To these three conditions he later added a fourth: self reliance. The oil crisis of the early 1970s had revealed the cost of dependence of many countries and, for Seers, development now implied *reducing cultural dependence on one or more of the great powers* (Seers 1977). Thus, not only had the concept of development expanded beyond economic growth and industrial expansion to include broader social objectives collectively described by Mabogunje (1980: 39) as *distributive justice*, but the notion of self-determination was also being introduced. No longer was development considered to be a process lying in the control of, or to be guided by, the advanced, Western nations; *development can be properly assessed only in terms of the total human needs, values, and standards of the good life and the good society perceived by the very societies undergoing change* (Goulet 1968).

In short, in the space of some thirty years the concept of development has evolved from a process narrowly defined (by the Western, industrialised nations) as economic development to a complex, multidimensional process requiring the transformation of social and political structures as well more traditional developmental goals. It has evolved into the process whereby a whole society or social system advances from a condition of life that is deemed to be unsatisfactory (by the members of that society) to a condition that, according to that society's values, better provides for the overall well-being of its members. It is the process for obtaining 'the good life' (Goulet 1968), central to which, according to Goulet, are three basic values representing the condition of life sought by all individuals and all societies:

(a) *the sustenance of life*: all people have basic requirements, such as food, shelter and health, without which a state of underdevelopment exists.

(b) *esteem*: all individuals seek self-esteem, a sense of identity, self-respect or dignity. The nature of esteem varies from one society to the next and may be manifested in increased wealth and material well-being or, conversely, in the strengthening of spiritual or cultural values.

(c) *freedom*: in the context of development, freedom represents increased choice for the individual members of society and freedom from servitude to ignorance, nature, other societies, beliefs and institutions.

Similarly, the UNDP's *Human Development Report* (UNDP 1990) defines development as the enlargement of people's choices, the most critical being to lead a long, healthy life, to acquire knowledge and to have access to the resources needed for a decent standard of living. It is, thus, a process within which at least five dimensions are identifiable (see Goulet 1992):

(a) an *economic* component: the creation of wealth and the equitable access to resources and material goods.

(b) a *social* component: health, education, employment and housing opportunities.

(c) a *political* dimension: human rights, political freedom and the ability on the part of   societies   to   select   and   operate political systems that best suit their needs or structure.

(d) a *cultural* dimension: the protection or affirmation of cultural identity and self-esteem.

(e) the *full-life paradigm*: the meaning systems, symbols and beliefs of a society.

To these should be added, perhaps, the *ecological* dimension, reflecting the emergence of environmental concern and the concept of ecological sustainability as a guiding principle of all development processes.

Overall, then, the concept of development has evolved over time from a process or condition defined according to strict economic criteria to a continual, global process of human development. For the purpose of this chapter, development can thus be defined as: the continuous and positive change in the economic, social, political and cultural dimensions of the human condition, guided by the principle of freedom of choice and limited by the capacity of the environment to sustain such change. The question then to be addressed is, how does this process come about (and, implicitly, how can tourism, in particular, contribute to it)? This is best answered by referring to what are known as the theories or paradigms of development.

(ii) Theories of development

Development theories are, essentially, broad philosophies which guide development plans and strategies. Modern development thinking evolved out of the global climate of political and economic change following the end of the Second World War. The economic reconstruction of Europe supported by the Marshall Aid programme, the emergence of the two 'super-powers' and resulting international tensions and, culminating in the Cold War, the rapid and widespread retreat of colonialism and the desire for development in the underdeveloped countries themselves were all instrumental factors in the emergence of development economics. Thus, reflecting the initial concepts of development discussed in the previous section, early development policy was influenced by the success of European reconstruction based on economic growth, aid and intervention and it was taken for granted that the Western, capitalist process of development was a necessary path to be followed by the underdeveloped countries in their transition towards becoming developed.

Since then, four main schools of development thought, or development theories, have evolved, each of which, by and large, has emerged as a result of increasing knowledge and understanding of the developmental process and a consequential rejection of preceding theories.

Economic based

(a) Modernisation theory

The basis of modernisation theory is that modernisation is an endogenous, or internal process which realises the potential for development in all societies. Different societies may be identified as being at different points on the traditional-modern continuum, or having reached different stages in the process of transforming from a traditional to a modern society. The position of different societies in this process is determined by measures such as GNP, *per capita* income, various social indicators and acceptance of modern values (for example, the desire to progress, to acquire, and so on), but the important point is that all societies are considered to be following this evolutionary path to modernisation. Harrison (1992a: 9) describes this as a process of *Westernisation, whereby the internal structures of 'developing' societies become more like those of the West, allegedly by emulating Western development patterns.* This is manifested in increasing urbanisation and industrialisation, the emergence of modern values and institutions and greater rationalisation and differentiation of social structures and roles. Implicitly, therefore, modernisation depends upon a transformation in the values and norms in traditional societies, values and norms which may, at the same time, represent barriers to development. Once those barriers have been removed or minimised, then modernisation, based upon economic growth, occurs. (See also Harrison 1988: 30.)

The evolutionary stages model of modernisation was translated into economic theory by Rostow (1960: 4) who claimed that:

> *It is possible to identify all societies, in their economic dimensions, as lying within one of five categories: the traditional society, the preconditions for take-off, the take-off, the drive to maturity, and the age of high mass-consumption.*

He argued that developing countries are at either of the first two stages but the decisive stage, the *great watershed in the life of modern societies*

(1960: 7) is the take-off stage where one or more significant manufacturing sectors emerge and induce growth in associated sectors and industries. For developing countries, the benefits of such economic growth 'trickle down' or diffuse through the spread of 'growth impulses', such as capital, technology or value systems, from the more developed to the less developed areas, eventually leading to an adjustment in regional disparities. The ways in which this necessary economic growth, leading to development, can be sustained has been the subject of debate amongst economic growth theorists. Some, for example, propose the 'big push' theory, whereby a wide range of industries in a country are helped and supported; others, conversely, suggest that economic growth and, hence, development occurs through backward linkages resulting from the establishment of particular sectors or industries.

Modernisation theory has been criticised on a number of grounds, in particular its use of 'traditional' and 'modern' as vague, ambiguous, ideal type classifications of societies, the implied mutual exclusivity of the two conditions and the inevitability of the replacement of tradition with modernity. It has also been criticised for its Western ethnocentricity and its fundamental doctrine of economic growth but, above all, for its failure to consider development in terms of global inter-relations and the way in which the term diffusion *serves as a code word for capitalist expansion in its economic, political, cultural guises* (Fitzgerald 1983: 14).

But, it is evident that there are strong links between modernisation and tourism; the justification for tourism related development is based upon the economic growth potential of tourism. That is, tourism (as a sector or actual resort) is seen as a growth pole from which economic benefits diffuse through the economy; tourism is promoted on the basis of its contribution to income and employment generation and the creation of backward linkages throughout the economy, concepts which are firmly rooted in modernisation theory. Implicitly, development occurs as a result of tourism-related economic growth. In practice this theory has guided a number of tourism development projects, such as Cancun in Mexico (see Wall 1997), yet, more often than not, the expected benefits have not accrued to destination areas. This can be partly explained by the second development theory: dependency theory.

231

(b) Dependency theory

Dependency theory, often more broadly termed underdevelopment theory (UDT), arose in the 1960s as a critique of the modernisation paradigm; its roots, however, lie in the structuralist economic policies adopted in Latin America during the preceding decade. Following the Great Depression, the export-oriented Latin American nations were suffering severe economic problems, the fundamental cause of which was identified as the continent's disadvantaged position in the world capitalist system. As a result, the UN's Economic Commission for Latin America (ECLA) advocated a strategy of import substitution supported by state planning and intervention. The policy of import substitution based upon state support soon proved to be unsuitable as a development strategy, inasmuch as it did little to improve the situation. But, it provided the foundation for the emergence of dependency theory, a school of thought based on Marxist theory (see Chapter One).

Dependency has been defined by Dos Santos (1970: 231) as

> *a conditioning situation in which the economies of one group of countries are conditioned by the development and expansion of others. A relationship of interdependence between two or more economies...becomes a dependent relationship when some countries can expand only as a reflection of the expansion of the dominant countries.*

In other words, it is argued that the diffusion of Western capital, technology and value systems achieves essentially the opposite of what modernisation theory proposes. This is because, within global economic and political structures, the wealthier, Western nations utilise their dominant position to exploit weaker, peripheral nations (mirroring earlier colonial ties). As a result, the ownership of enterprises in LDCs frequently lies with Western companies, expatriate workers occupy managerial positions and profits are returned to the parent company, thereby restricting developmental opportunities in LDCs. In short, the external economic and political structure of LDCs means that they are unable to *break out of a state of economic dependency and advance to an economic position beside the major capitalist industrial powers* (Palma

232

1995: 162). In effect, capitalist development in the core, metropolitan centres perpetuates underdevelopment in the periphery.

Some of the earliest thinking about dependency theory reflected the basis of Marxist structural-conflict theory. For example, Baran (1973) argued that, in much the same way that the capitalists are able to exploit the workers as discussed in Chapter One, the actual economic surplus produced by LDCs is either expropriated by foreign enterprises, misused by the state or squandered by the traditional élites. The possibilities for development are thus limited and *for backward countries to enter the road of economic growth and social progress, the political framework of their existence has to be drastically revamped* (Baran 1963). That is, the solution lies in withdrawal from the world capitalist system and development guided by a socialist political system.

This position is expanded upon by Frank (1969) who bases his arguments on the assumption of a single, capitalist world system that has existed since the fifteenth century. Within this single capitalist system, underdevelopment results not from the particular socio-economic characteristics of LDCs (that is, the barriers to development suggested by modernisation theorists) but from the historical relations between metropolitan centres and underdeveloped satellites, relations that exist both within and between countries.

Thus, development and underdevelopment are part of the same economic process, the former being dependent on the latter and made possible through the economic exploitation of satellites by metropolitan centres. Within a country, *the hinterland supplies the city and is exploited by it; in turn, the city... is dependent on the metropolitan countries of the West* (Harrison 1988: 82). Therefore, the existence of the world capitalist system prevents the development of LDCs, resulting in underdevelopment.

A number of other contributions have been made to dependency theory, the different approaches to which have been summarised by Todaro (1994). He suggests that there are three distinctive models within dependency theory:

1. *Neo-colonial Dependence Model*: underdevelopment which results from the historic evolution of an unequal relationship between the core and the periphery.

2. *False Paradigm Model*: underdevelopment which results from the imposition of inappropriate, Western based development policies in the periphery.

3. *Dualistic Development Model*: development that re-inforces the dualistic, rich/poor nature of societies within and between underdeveloped and developed countries.

One of the major criticisms of dependency theory is that it does not hold true for all LDCs. In other words, some countries have been able to break out of the dependency / underdevelopment situation and, since the Second World War, many LDCs have experienced higher growth rates than developed countries. Moreover, other than proposing withdrawal from global economic and political systems, it does not provide any tangible methods of achieving development. But, important parallels can be drawn between dependency theory and tourism, parallels which, as discussed later in the chapter, raise significant doubts about the true effectiveness of tourism as a means of encouraging development.

In one particular sense, tourism reflects the dualistic development model as tourism, certainly to LDCs, tends to amplify or reinforce economic and socio-cultural differences between tourists and their hosts. This, in turn, is related to the way in which dependency theory more generally informs much of the research into the negative impacts of tourism on destination areas and communities. That is, it is widely recognised that international tourism *has evolved in a way which closely matches historical patterns of colonialism and economic dependency* (Lea 1988: 10). In terms of the structure and organisation of the international tourism industry, the ownership or control of the main sectors of the industry lies, for the most part, in the hands of western transnational corporations (McQueen 1983). Where LDCs have been unable to afford the development of attractions, facilities, tourism infrastructure and so, the investment has come from the West. Thus, tourism destinations become dependent on metropolitan centres for capital, technology and expertise and, as a result, tourism has come to be viewed as a form of neo-colonialism or imperialism (Nash 1989). At the same time, the fact that some 80 per cent of international tourists come from just twelve (wealthy) countries demonstrates the dependency of many destinations on the West for tourists themselves. Furthermore, this pattern of development is reinforced within many LDCs by common structural distortions in their social and economic organisation, particularly when they have been exposed to colonial or imperialist domination (Britton 1982).

The implications of this dependency for the tourist-host relationship in particular is explored in more detail in Chapter Nine. For now it is important to point out that the nature of tourism development in many countries can be explained by dependency theory. A number of authors have examined the so-called centre-periphery dependency model within the context of tourism in a general sense (for example, Høivik and Heiberg 1980; Britton 1982, 1987; Mathieson and Wall 1982), whilst others relate it to specific types of destination, such as small islands (Bastin 1984; Wilkinson 1989). Macnaught (1982), for example, considers the critical issue in tourism development in Pacific island communities to be not *the type of development but the extent to which the political and social autonomy of the destination area is undermined.* In either case, the conclusion is usually that the potential contribution of tourism to broader social and economic development is restricted or diminished by the political and economic framework of the tourism system.

(c) The 'neo-classical counter revolution'

During the 1970s, as dissatisfaction with dependency theory grew, a variety of new approaches emerged which served to redirect attention away from the more traditional economic growth models of development. In particular, issues such as environmental degradation and basic human needs came to the fore, whilst concepts such as 'spaceship earth' brought about a more global perspective on development. But, it was not until the 1980s and the Reagan-Thatcher era that a new

235

identifiable development theory emerged. Following neo-classical economic theory, which suggests that international trade can be a positive force in export-led economic development, the neo-liberal theorists of the New Right claimed that the path to economic, social and political development lay in the modern free-market capitalist system. The problems facing LDCs were seen as resulting not from market imperfections but from excessive state intervention (as proposed by dependency theorists) in the form of, for example, foreign exchange controls, pricing controls and unrealistic levels of state ownership and investment.

Influenced by the pro-market position, the neo-classical counter revolution was manifested in development policies that built upon the fundamental reliance on the free market and that favoured market liberalisation, the privatisation of state enterprises and overall reduction of state intervention. In particular, it has guided the policy of the World Bank and the International Monetary Fund (IMF) and their Structural Adjustment Lending programmes, which render loan facilities conditional on specific policy and economic structure changes in loan-receiving countries (Mosley and Toye 1988). Thus, Structural Adjustment Lending focuses on the need for micro and macroeconomic adjustments, specific policy instruments including:

- credit ceilings and control of the money supply;
- exchange rate adjustment and liberalisation;
- deregulation of prices of goods and services to remove pricing distortions;
- fiscal policy, especially reductions in public expenditure;
- trade and payment liberalisation, including the removal of import quotas;
- institutional reforms, with particular emphasis on privatisation and reducing state influence.

Implicitly, these pre-conditions imposed by lending programmes based upon structural adjustment are a reaffirmation of the role of capitalism and the marketplace in development. As a result, the neo-liberal policies of the 'counter revolution' have attracted criticism similar to that levelled

Based on lending programmes

at the modernisation paradigm with respect to the dominance of Western countries and social and environmental issues. Furthermore, it is generally agreed that structural adjustment programmes have not been successful (Harrigan and Mosely 1991); indeed, the conditions attached have tended to depress incomes and investment, whilst in many countries social and economic conditions have declined. Pastor (1987), for example, found that funding programmes in Latin America resulted in higher inflation and a real reduction in wages.

Tourism development in many countries has benefitted from international structural funding. For example, Inskeep and Kallenberger (1992) describe a number of resort developments, including Pomun Lake in Korea and Antalya in Turkey, that benefited from World Bank support. Diamond (1977) similarly evaluates investment in tourism in Turkey during the 1960s and early 1970s, whilst Lee (1987) outlines the way in which European financial aid for tourism development has been provided to the Africa, Caribbean and Pacific (ACP) region through the Lomé Convention.

Little attention has been paid in the literature to the effects of Structural Adjustment Lending programmes on tourism development in particular, a surprising omission given the economic value of tourism as a sector of international trade. Curry (1992) explored the effects of economic adjustment programmes on the hotel sector in Jamaica, identifying, in some instances, a negative impact on hotel profitability. More generally, Dieke (1995) assessed the implications of lending programmes on tourism in African economies, concluding that they served to highlight the *strategic importance of the private sector in tourism development* (1995: 87)

In many cases, this has actually strengthened existing dependency on the metropolitan dominated tourism system, such as in The Gambia where, at the same time, *per capita income actually fell between 1985 and 1994... whilst lower levels of public spending, the removal of subsidies and other policy measures... have led to deteriorating socio-economic conditions for the majority of Gambians* (Sharpley and Sharpley 1996: 29).

237

(d) The alternative development theory

The fourth and, chronologically, the most recent development theory to emerge is that of alternative development. Most recently manifested in the widespread acceptance and adoption of sustainable development, a concept which *has achieved virtual global endorsement as the new [tourism] industry paradigm since the late 1980s* (Godfrey 1996: 60), alternative development is a broad-based approach which has been born out of frustration with the failure of preceding and fundamentally Western-biased, economic growth-based development policies. In contrast to these, alternative development implies a break with the linear model of economic growth (Redclift 1987), adopting a resource-based, 'bottom-up' approach focused primarily on human and environmental concerns.

Alternative development embraces a number of principles which define its perspective and objectives. They are also clearly reflected on the principles of sustainable development in general and of sustainable tourism development in particular. Primarily, the theory of alternative development recognises that development is a complex, multi-layered process that is related to environmental, cultural, social, as well as more traditional economic factors. Also, it has as its starting point the belief that development should be endogenous. That is, it is a process that starts within, and is guided by the needs of, each society; it is not something that should be implemented, imposed or controlled by other societies. Thus, alternative development is centred upon the satisfaction of basic needs, it encourages self-reliance and it should be in harmony with the environment.

The idea of basic needs emerged at the 1976 International Labour Office (ILO) conference on world employment and was later adopted by institutions such as the World Bank. The ILO stressed the benefits of employment creation over economic growth, employment being a necessary prerequisite to the satisfaction not only of fundamental human physiological needs (the provision of shelter, warmth, food, and so on) but also social, cultural and political needs (Streeten 1977). Aimed at the world's poorest people, the basic needs approach suggests that development depends ultimately on the fulfillment of people's potential

238

to contribute to and benefit from their own community. The notion of a grassroots, community focus to development, building on Schumacher's (1974: 140) argument that *development does not start with goods; it starts with people and their education, organisation and discipline* is implicit in the alternative development approach, as is the requirement for self-reliance.

The concept of self-reliance is the antithesis to dependency theory. It argues that human development is not possible in the context of development programmes based on core-dominated economic growth, a situation that results in cultural dependency (Erisman 1983). Communities, therefore, should be allowed to assert their right to make their own decisions according to local needs. Galtung (1986: 101) suggests that, as a fundamental basis for achieving self-reliance, a society should:

> *produce what you need using your own resources, internalising the challenges this involves, growing with the challenges, neither giving the most challenging tasks... to somebody else on whom you become dependent, nor exporting negative externalities to somebody else to whom you do damage and who may become dependent on you.*

Importantly, this suggests that self-reliance does not imply isolation; rather, it should be the goal of local, regional and national communities in an interdependent world. Moreover, it also relates to another principle of fundamental importance to alternative development, namely, that the environmental constraints to development should be recognised and taken into account. This was a consideration not apparent in preceding development theories, but one that reflected increasing concern, certainly within the developed world, about the environmental problems of resource depletion, pollution and population growth. In other words, alternative development was the first development theory to embrace the notion that there is an intrinsic relationship between development and the physical and human environment; *many forms of development erode the environmental resources upon which they must be based, and environmental degradation can undermine economic development* (WCED 1987: 3).

In short, alternative development places the emphasis on development that satisfies local communities needs, that is controlled by that community and which is in harmony with the environment, principles which also underpin the notion of alternative tourism. Just as, during the 1970s, increasing public awareness of environmental issues in general led to the emergence of a global environmental movement, so too was increasing attention paid to the negative consequences of mass tourism development in particular. The 1970s was the decade *in which the potential conflicts of tourism and the natural environment were realised* (Dowling 1992: 37) and, in response to the growing recognition of the socio-cultural impacts of tourism, the early tourism literature reflected the emergence of alternative development thinking. For example, Emery (1981) considered 'alternative futures' in tourism, whilst Dernoi (1981) proposed alternative tourism as 'a new style in North-South relations'. The concept of environmental harmony and self-reliance, fundamental requirements of alternative development, also became the focus of research into alternative tourism, the latter manifested in what became known as the community approach to tourism development (Murphy 1985).

The primary justification of alternative tourism is that it is just that: an alternative to, specifically, mass tourism. Thus, the proponents of alternative tourism advocate tourism that is, for example, small scale, under local control, that is developed in harmony with the local physical and socio-cultural environment and that optimises the benefits to local communities. In short, it is a form of tourism that benefits, rather than exploits, destination societies. The concentration on small-scale, local projects has led to accusations that alternative tourism is a micro solution to a macro problem; it offers an alternative to mass tourism, but does not provide solutions to the alleged problems of mass tourism. As a result, the concept of alternative tourism has been widely criticised (for example, see Butler 1980; Smith and Eadington 1992). But, it provided the catalyst for the emergence of the concept of sustainable tourism development, arguably the most debated issue in tourism during the 1990s and certainly the most widely adopted set of principles and guidelines for the development of tourism. Therefore, it is important to consider how effective or viable sustainable tourism is as an approach to achieving development, a question that can only be answered by first looking at the concept of sustainable development itself.

Sustainable development

Sustainable development represents a development philosophy and set of principles that, throughout the 1990s, not only set the agenda for global development policies in general but also provided a framework for the planning and management of a multitude of economic activities and sectors, including tourism. Despite its popularity, the validity of both the overall concept of sustainable development and the specific proposals for its achievement contained within a variety of documents remain the subject of intense debate. This controversy surrounding the notion of sustainable development has arisen, in part, from a lack of agreement over the actual meaning of the term; indeed, more than 70 different definitions of the term have been suggested! But, the most popular and enduring remains the Brundtland Commission's definition of sustainable development as *development that meets the needs of the present without compromising the ability of future generations to meet their own needs* (WCED 1987: 48).

Though politically attractive and applicable to many forms of development, this definition does not explain what sustainable development is or how it can be achieved. This task is, perhaps, best approached by thinking of sustainable development as the fusion of two processes, namely 'development' plus 'sustainability' (see Lélé 1991). The development element has already been discussed in this chapter and, therefore, sustainable development may be thought of as alternative development that is 'sustainable'. What, then, is meant by sustainability?

In a strict sense, if something is sustainable, it can continue or be continued indefinitely. Within the context of this chapter, sustainability refers more specifically to the capacity of the earth to support human existence, also indefinitely. In other words, the earth is a closed, finite eco-system, within which the human economic system of production and consumption, or human activity supporting and leading to development, represents a sub-system. The global eco-system is, therefore, akin to a *single spaceship, without unlimited reservoirs of anything, either for extraction or for pollution, and in which, therefore, man must find his place in a cyclical ecological system* (Boulding 1992: 31). In short, the global eco-system is the *source of all material inputs feeding the economic subsystem, and is the sink for all wastes* (Goodland 1992: 16). These source and sink functions of the planet have a finite capacity to, respectively, supply the needs of production/consumption and absorb the wastes resulting from the production/consumption process. This means that, for any form of economic activity, such as tourism, to continue indefinitely, attention must be paid to three factors:

(i) the rate at which the stock of natural (non-renewable) resources is exploited or reduced by human economic activity must be balanced with the development of substitute, renewable resources.

(ii) the rate at which waste resulting from human economic activity is deposited back into the ecosystem must be within the capacity of the environment to assimilate, or absorb that waste.

(iii) global population levels and, perhaps more importantly, *per capita* levels of consumption. It is generally accepted that the level of consumption currently enjoyed by individuals in Western societies would be unsustainable if translated into *per capita* consumption on a global scale.

Sustainable development is development that not only recognises but works within the constraints of the environmental limits of human activities; it is an approach that accepts that development of any kind cannot be separated from concern for, and the protection of, the environment.

A number of attempts have been made to convert this philosophy into a global development strategy. One of the first was the Brundtland Commission's report *Our Common Future* (WCED 1987) which based its proposals on two fundamental concepts. Firstly, development should be directed towards meeting the needs of all, thereby extending to them the opportunity to fulfill their aspirations for a better life; subscribing to the principles of alternative development, the report states that *the satisfaction of human needs and aspirations is so obviously an objective of productive activity that it may appear redundant to assert its central role in the concept of sustainable development* (WCED 1987: 54). Secondly, development should occur within environmental limits which, importantly, are *imposed by the present state of technology and social organisation* (WCED 1987: 8) rather than by the environment itself. The means of achieving development remains, according to the report, economic growth. As a result, the report has been criticised as a return to classical growth theory disguised in the respectable garb of environmentalism. Conversely, *Caring for the Earth – A Strategy for Sustainable Living* (IUCN 1991) places the emphasis firmly on the necessary change in attitudes and practices amongst people in all societies. In other words, sustainable development is dependent upon sustainable lifestyles, recognising that *resource problems are not really environmental problems: they are human problems* (Ludwig *et al* 1993).

A complete discussion of these and other reports are beyond the scope of this chapter (see Reid 1995). But, based upon the focus and proposals of the main policy documents, it is possible to identify and summarise the basic principles and objectives of sustainable development. Essentially, the concept of sustainable development embraces three fundamental principles:

(i) **An holistic approach:** sustainable development demands an approach that embraces both developmental and environmental issues within a global social, economic, political and ecological context.

(ii) **Futurity:** the focus of sustainable development is upon the long-term capacity for continuance of the global eco-system, including the human sub-system.

(iii) **Equity:** sustainable development is development that is fair and equitable and which provides opportunities for access to and use of resources for all members of all societies; both in the present and future.

These principles underpin the objectives of sustainable development, which essentially embrace the objectives of alternative development (self-reliance, the satisfaction of basic needs, community-based development, leading to an overall improvement in the quality of life for all), whilst ensuring that the activities and processes supporting such development are, as discussed above, within the earth's environmental source and sink capacities. Importantly, in order to achieve these objectives, certain requirements must also be fulfilled:

(i) global sustainable development can only be achieved if national and international political and economic systems are dedicated to equitable development and resource use.

(ii) technological systems must be harnessed in order to search continuously for new solutions to environmental problems.

(iii) all societies need to adopt a new, sustainable lifestyle

The extent to which these are possible and, indeed, the extent to which sustainable development represents a viable method of achieving long-term, global development remains the subject of intense debate. But, many countries, societies and economic sectors are committed to working towards the stated objectives of sustainable development, building upon the 'Agenda 21' framework set out at the Rio de Janeiro Earth Summit in 1992. Tourism is no exception; the document *Agenda 21 for the Travel & Tourism Industry: Towards Environmentally Sustainable Development* (WTO/WTTC) sets out an agenda for the future global development of tourism. But, as with sustainable development in general, doubts remain about the viability of the concept of sustainable tourism development.

Sustainable tourism development

The concept of sustainable tourism development is as ambiguous and contradictory as the broader theory of sustainable development. For tourism academics and practitioners, it has become a catch-all phrase; *to some... [it is] all about new products or market segments, to others, it is a process of development, while still to others it represents a guiding principle to which all tourism should aspire* (Godfrey 1996: 61). It is also variously defined, although the WTO/WTTC document referred to above is one example of how the Brundtland Commission's definition is appropriated for specific sectors: sustainable tourism development is *development [which] meets the needs of present tourists and host regions while protecting and enhancing opportunity for the future* (WTO/WTTC 1996: 30). To complicate matters further, a variety of other terms, such as eco-tourism, rural tourism, low impact tourism (Lillywhite and Lillywhite 1991), alternative tourism, soft tourism (Kariel 1989), responsible tourism (Harrison and Husbands 1996), green tourism (Beioley 1995) and nature tourism (Whelan 1991) are also widely perceived to be synonymous with sustainable tourism.

Despite the variety of definitions and terminology, there are, generally, two broad interpretations of sustainable tourism development. On the one hand, it is possible to talk in terms of 'the development of sustainable tourism', a perspective which focuses on the tourism product with the overall objective being to sustain tourism itself. Referred to by Hunter (1995) as the *tourism-centric* approach, this is the most usual interpretation. On the other hand, a broader 'sustainable tourism development' approach may be adopted, which views tourism as a means of achieving overall sustainable development. The former term does not mean the same as the latter but, within the tourism literature, the two are frequently utilised inter-changeably. It is, arguably, the latter that should be the focus of sustainable tourism; if sustainable tourism is based upon the principles and objectives of sustainable development, then *tourism must be a recognised sustainable economic development option, considered equally with other economic activities when jurisdictions are making development decisions* (Cronin 1990). In other words, if tourism is to contribute to (sustainable) development, which is the primary purpose of promoting tourism in the first place, then it is the potential role of tourism in broader development policies, rather than sustaining tourism itself, that should be the focus of sustainable tourism development. This means that, rather than competing for scarce resources, the emphasis is placed on considering tourism in the context of the most appropriate and efficient shared use of resources, on a global basis, within overall developmental goals. In some cases, this may result in tourism being rejected as a development option.

The principles and practice of sustainable tourism are widely discussed in the literature. Since the late 1980s there has been a plethora of policy documents, planning guidelines, statements of 'good practice', case studies, codes of conduct for tourists and other publications concerned with the issue of sustainable tourism development. These have been produced at all levels and by an enormous variety of tourism organisations in the public, private and voluntary sectors. The general principles of sustainable tourism as embedded in these documents are summarised in Figure 8 on page 247.

At first sight, these overall principles of sustainable tourism development appear to conform to the broader principles of sustainable development. The sustainable use of natural resources and the development of tourism within physical and socio-cultural capacities is of fundamental importance, consideration is given to the equitable access to the benefits of tourism, and the concept of futurity is implicit within the principles. At the same time, the principle of community involvement appears to satisfy the specific requirements of self-reliance and endogenous development that are critical elements of the theory of sustainable development.

However, there are a number of ways in which tourism challenges the concept of sustainable development and which, following the central theme of this chapter, cast doubt on the overall contribution of tourism to development in destination areas. Firstly, in a general sense, it does not appear that tourism can be developed in accordance with the fundamental principles of sustainable development outlined earlier:

Figure 8: Sustainable tourism development: a summary of principles

- The conservation and sustainable use of natural, social and cultural resources is crucial. Therefore, tourism should be planned and managed within environmental limits and with due regard for the long term appropriate use of natural and human resources.

- Tourism planning, development and operation should be integrated into national and local sustainable development strategies. In particular, consideration should be given to different types of tourism development and the ways in which they link with existing land and resource uses and socio-cultural factors.

- Tourism should support a wide range of local economic activities, taking environmental costs and benefits into account, but it should not be permitted to become an activity which dominates the economic base of an area.

- Local communities should be encouraged and expected to participate in the planning, development and control of tourism with the support of government and the industry. Particular attention should be paid to involving indigenous people, women and minority groups to ensure the equitable distribution of the benefits of tourism.

- All organisations and individuals should respect the culture, the economy, the way of life, the environment and political structures in the destination area.

- All stakeholders within tourism should be educated about the need to develop more sustainable forms of tourism. This includes staff training and raising awareness, through education and marketing tourism responsibly, of sustainability issues amongst host communities and tourists themselves.

- Research should be undertaken throughout all stages of tourism development and operation to monitor impacts, to solve problems and to allow local people and others to respond to changes and to take advantages of opportunities.

- All agencies, organisations businesses and individuals should co-operate and work together to avoid potential conflict and to optimise the benefits to all involved in the development and management of tourism.

Source: Eber (1992); WTO (1993); ETB (1991);
WTO/WTTC (1996); EC (1993)

(i) An holistic approach

Despite the requirement that any form of development can only be sustainable if it is considered within a global socio-economic and ecological context, most sustainable tourism strategies in practice tend to focus almost exclusively on localised, relatively small scale development projects, rarely transcending local or regional boundaries, or on particular industry sectors. This is, perhaps, not surprising given the diverse and fragmented nature of the tourism industry, and it is certainly not to say that localised destination or sectoral strategies are not necessary. But, it is also vital to place such strategies within the wider, global picture. Most, if not all, sustainable tourism development strategies fail to do so. As a result, issues of both the scope of tourism in terms of resource exploitation and its scale as a global activity are overlooked. In effect, the entire world is tourism's resource base, yet a destination or sectoral focus means that broader questions of resource use are ignored. For example, eco-tourism development in Costa Rica or Belize may locally conform to sustainable principles (Weaver 1994), but the system of international air travel that carries tourists to those destinations may not. At the same time, an holistic approach would demand that attention is paid to all tourism.   Just as many environmental problems have become global, rather than national, issues, so too is tourism a global phenomenon. Thus, developing sustainable forms of tourism in some areas simply sweeps the problems of tourism under the carpet of other destinations and, as Klemm (1992) suggests, *the real challenge for the future is to provide sustainable tourism for the mass market.*

(ii) Futurity

There is little doubt that futurity is a primary concern of sustainable tourism development, yet it is the future viability of tourism itself rather than the contribution of tourism to long term sustainable development that predominates sustainable tourism strategies. There is, therefore, little evidence within sustainable tourism development principles of concern for the potential contribution of tourism to long term development goals.

(iii) Equity

Although most sustainable tourism development strategies emphasise the importance of community based, or collaborative, tourism planning, the objective being a more equitable share of the benefits accruing from tourism development, in reality both the flows and the structure of international tourism suggest that equitable development through tourism is unachievable. Despite the emergence of newer popular destinations and new tourism generating countries, the major international tourism flows and corresponding economic benefits remain highly polarised and regionalised. Europe and North America are, in particular, the main beneficiaries of tourism development, yet even within most Third World regions tourism has been monopolised by a few countries to the exclusion of the rest (Brohman 1996). Moreover, in many LDCs which are popular tourism destinations, tourism is frequently distributed unevenly, diminishing the opportunities for equitable development through tourism even on a national scale (Opperman 1993). Tourism is frequently concentrated within enclave resorts or tourist ghettos, contributing to socio-economic inequities through a developmental process which, ironically, is often promoted by the central governments of the countries in which the resorts are located (Pearce 1989: 95).

This situation is exacerbated by the structure of international tourism. Not only are tourist flows dominated by western, industrialised nations, but also the *three most lucrative components of...[international]... tourism (i.e. marketing and the procurement of customers, international transportation, and food and lodging) are normally handled by vertically integrated [western owned] global networks* (Brohman 1996). As a result, there tends to be a lack of local community control over resource use and, in particular, a significant proportion of tourism earnings is lost through overseas leakages. Studies have shown that such leakages, in the form of profit repatriation and payments for imports of goods and services, may often be substantial, especially in smaller, tourism dominated economies. For example, the import content of tourism in the Pacific Islands has generally been found to vary between 50 per cent and 90 per cent (Craig-Smith 1996: 43).

In short, the patterns and structures of international tourism, particularly between the metropolitan centres and peripheral developing nations, reinforce rather than diminish global socio-economic inequities. Thus, unsurprisingly, although localised, small-scale (alternative/sustainable) developments attempt to reverse this trend, much international tourism still reflects the problems of dependency.

This last issue, the inequity of tourism-related development, highlights an overall doubt about the potential contribution of tourism to development in destination areas. In other words, secondly and more specifically, the nature of tourism, in terms of both the ownership and control of the production system and the direction and scale of tourist flows, militates against the potential developmental benefits of tourism. Not only does the ownership or control of tourism services and facilities frequently lie in the hands of Western organisations (although, of course, this is not always the case), but also those organisations, particularly tour operators, are able to control tourist flows and, through their marketing and advertising strategies, the expectations and behaviour of tourists. Thus, the financial benefits of tourism are rarely fully realised in destination areas, whilst opportunities for development arising out of tourism remain subject to the activities of the organisations which control the tourism production system.

The activities of tourists themselves is an important factor in optimising the contribution of tourism to development. Sustainable development is dependent upon the adoption of sustainable lifestyles; similarly, sustainable tourism development is dependent upon sustainable (that is, appropriate or, as discussed in Chapter Four, 'good') tourist behaviour. However, as McKercher (1993) observes, tourists are consumers, not anthropologists, and they consume tourism for fun, entertainment and escape. In other words, for tourists themselves to make a positive contribution to development by, for example, travelling independently (that is, avoiding the Western owned tourist production system), staying in locally-owned accommodation, attempting to learn about and integrate into local communities and so on, requires them to work at tourism. But, as we have seen in the preceding chapters, this overlooks many of the realities of the consumption of tourism and the implications of this for the nature of the tourist-host relationship is considered in Chapter Nine.

Tourism and development - a summary

The justification for developing and promoting tourism, particularly in the lesser developed parts of the world, is that it represents an effective means of encouraging wider social and economic development in destination areas. This potential role of tourism is primarily based upon its economic contribution in terms of foreign exchange earnings, the generation of income and employment, the development of backward linkages throughout the local economy and so on, and there is little doubt that, in many countries, tourism has become a significant and, frequently, the largest economic sector. The economic development of Cyprus, for example, has almost entirely been based upon the successful growth of tourism sector which is now the backbone of the island's economy (Sharpley 1998b). This tourism-related developmental process remains firmly rooted in modernisation theory, a development paradigm which, as we have seen, has long been superceded by other theories. Development, as a process and a goal, embraces a much wider set of objectives than simply economic growth; it seeks equitable, fair and endogenous development based on self-reliance and the satisfaction of basic needs within sound ecological principles. That is, it seeks the social development goal of the 'good life'.

It is evident that tourism, as a potential contributor to this development process, has a number of characteristics that militate against achieving its objectives (see McKercher 1993). The tourism production system largely reflects the tenets of dependency theory and, although increasing attempts are being made by local and national governments and, indeed, by certain sectors of the tourism industry, to implement sustainable tourism development policies, significant doubts remain about the viability of this approach. The difficulties associated with achieving sustainable tourism development raise questions about the overall viability of sustainable development itself. Thus, although tourism undoubtedly makes a significant contribution to economic growth in many countries (and future policies should, arguably, be directed towards increasing this contribution), the nature of tourism is such that there is an inevitability about the social and cultural consequences of tourism, consequences which challenge tourism's contribution to social development. It is with these consequences that the following chapters are concerned.

Nine

The Tourist-Host Relationship

Introduction

It is virtually impossible to be a tourist in isolation. Unless travelling across uninhabited areas or regions it is inevitable that, sooner or later, tourists come into contact with other people. These may be either fellow tourists or members of local communities in tourism destinations; generally, it will be a combination of both types of contact, the extent or intensity of each being dependent on a variety of factors. For example, mass, institutionalised tourists on a two-week sun, sea and sand holiday are likely to have more inter-personal contact with fellow tourists than with local people, whilst an independent traveller or explorer may actively seek out contact with members of local communities. For the explorer, meeting local people and learning about their way of life may be a primary tourism motivator whereas, for the mass tourist, such contact may only be incidental to the holiday.

Whatever the type or extent of inter-personal contact that tourists experience, they will, almost certainly, come into contact with local people. Even if not actively seeking to meet locals (or, as is sometimes the case, making a positive effort to avoid contact), tourists in resort areas stay in hotels, eat in restaurants, drink in bars and buy souvenirs in shops and interact with members of the local community. In other words, even within a simple buying-selling context, tourists have a form of relationship with local people, one which is frequently referred to as the *host-guest* relationship (Smith 1989). For many tourists this relationship may be fleeting and, indeed, go unrecognised as such; for others, meaningful, two-way and authentic (see Chapter Seven) contact with local people may be the basis of the entire tourist experience. In either situation a variety of social processes are at work which not only determine the nature of the relationship itself but also go a long way towards indicating the potential positive or negative impacts of tourism development on destination communities. Thus, the main practical reason for developing an understanding of the processes involved in encounters between tourists and local people is to be able to plan and manage the development of tourism in a manner which minimises potential negative impacts on host communities.

This chapter examines the varying nature of the relationship between tourists and local people in destination areas. In particular, it considers whether tourism can lead to balanced and equal two-way relationships between tourists and locals, thereby acting, as some would desire, as a vehicle towards greater international harmony and understanding (WTO 1980), or whether it simply amplifies their social, cultural and economic differences, reinforcing existing attitudes and prejudices. This chapter also serves as a foundation to the discussion of the social and cultural impacts of tourism in Chapter Ten.

Characteristics of tourist-host encounters

Relationships between tourists and local people are almost infinitely variable (see Pearce 1994). Tourists are motivated by an enormous variety of factors, they carry with them different attitudes and expectations, they may be more or less experienced as tourists, they are on different types of holiday or trip, and they come from a variety of socio-economic backgrounds. Equally, the economic, social and technological conditions within a tourism destination country or region, the size, type and maturity of its tourism industry, and local cultural and religious factors will all have much bearing on the way in which local communities regard tourists. In short, such is the variety of factors which may influence the relationships that develop between tourists and local communities that it would be logical to conclude that there as many different types of tourist-host encounters as there are tourists and that, consequently, the analysis of such encounters is a difficult, if not impossible, task.

Despite this variety, it is possible to make some general observations about the nature of tourist-host encounters. For example, it would be logical to assume that the greater the economic, cultural and social differences between a tourist and a member of the destination community, the less balanced, or more unequal, will be the relationship between them. The relative wealth of Western visitors to developing countries is a particularly visible basis for an unequal relationship (and conforms to the dualistic development model of dependency introduced in the preceding chapter); in many instances, just the cost of the flight to some developing countries may be the equivalent of twice the average annual local income. Less obvious differences, such as conflicting attitudes towards punctuality, may also result in less tolerant contact. Conversely, the relationship between an American tourist and, say, a Canadian host is likely to benefit from a much greater degree of initial commonality in culture, language and outlook. Another general observation is that in most tourist-host encounters the tourist is on holiday whereas the host, more often than not, is employed in the tourist industry and is, therefore, at work. Again, cultural, social and economic distances are likely to amplify potential differences. Thus, links exists between the structure and nature of international tourism development as a whole and the types of tourist-host encounters that result in different destinations around the world. This issue is explored later in this chapter but, as a starting point, it is important to consider a number of characteristics which, to a lesser or greater extent, are applicable to all types of contact between tourists and local people.

One of the earliest attempts to analyse the nature of the contacts between tourists and local people in destination areas identified five particular characteristics common to most situations (see Sutton 1967). These refer, in particular to international tourism, although certain characteristics may also be applicable tourist-host encounters in the context of domestic tourism. It was argued that, as a rule, contact is transitory, that both parties seek instant satisfaction (for example, the tourist purchasing a souvenir, the shopkeeper making a sale), and that the relationship is asymmetrical or unbalanced (the tourist benefits from greater wealth, the shopkeeper from better knowledge about the value of his goods). Also, it was suggested that the encounter was a new or unusual experience for the tourist and, finally, that a cultural gulf usually existed between the parties involved in the encounter. A similar perspective was adopted by a

UNESCO report (1976) which highlights four characteristic features of tourist-host relationships, particularly within the context of mass tourism (for more detail, see Mathieson and Wall 1982:136):

(a) Most encounters between tourists and members of the local community are transitory. In other words, most tourists stay in a resort for only one or two weeks and although the encounter may be considered unusual, exciting and different from the tourist's point of view, for the host it may be simply 'business as usual'. As a result, the relationship is likely to be shallow, superficial and based upon different expectations. However, where visits are of a longer duration or, as is often the case, tourists return to the same resort year after year, more meaningful relationships may occur.

(b) Most encounters are constrained by temporal and spatial restrictions. Tourism is usually restricted to certain seasons of the year and, within those seasons, tourists are restricted by the length of their visit. Thus, they may try to see as much and do as much as is possible within the time available, a situation which local people may take advantage of by becoming exploitative, charging higher prices and so on. Tourist-host relationships may also be restricted by the location and spread of tourist-related services. Hotels, restaurants, bars, night-clubs and other facilities and attractions in resort areas are frequently concentrated in particular areas, sometimes in tourist zones or 'ghettos' located well away from towns and villages, making it difficult for less interested or motivated tourists to see the 'real' host country. Moreover, tourists are frequently discouraged from venturing out on their own and are sold tours, ensuring that the majority of tourists' spending is within the tourist area and minimising the opportunity for tourist-host encounters based upon anything but commercial interest. In the extreme, such as at self contained Club Med type destinations, tourists have no need to leave the confines of their resort and are unlikely to experience any encounter other than with resort staff.

(c) Tourism is an economic activity. The majority of people who work in the tourism industry do so to earn money and most interaction between tourists and local people is usually a form of economic transaction. As a result, many tourist-host encounters lack spontaneity; shows, tours and even visits to shops are frequently pre-planned to both fit in with tourists' tight schedules and to provide tourists with the maximum opportunity for spending money. Relationships which were once motivated by traditional hospitality may also become commercialised. For example, in the south eastern Turkish village of Harran, famous for its beehive-style houses and religious history, it is not unusual for tourists to be invited in to local people's homes for tea and then for payment to be demanded before departure. Conversely, when the Cyprus Tourism Organisation (CTO) proposed the development of agro-tourism in some mountain villages as part of its tourism diversification programme, local villagers were astounded by the suggestion that they should charge visitors for their hospitality.

(d) Tourist-host encounters, on the whole, tend to be unbalanced. That is, local people may feel inferior when faced with ostentatious displays of wealth, and may resent being in a subservient position to people who are on holiday.

A further characteristic applicable to many tourist-host encounters is an apparent lack of knowledge, understanding or sensitivity on the part of tourists to local culture and custom in tourism destination areas. Whilst of greater relevance to the potential impacts of tourism in general, such short-comings, often combined with preconceptions and stereotypical images of the host community and culture, further limit the opportunity for balanced or meaningful tourist-host encounters. Additionally, this characteristic is related to the broader issues of tourist motivation, the nature and structure of international tourism and, in particular, the way in which destinations are marketed to potential tourists. For example, one tour operator's brochure describes The Gambia as *perfect for sun lovers with palm studded beaches, friendly people and year round sunshine. With all its exotic charm, remember this is Africa: life here is slower, standards can vary and public services aren't as reliable as in other resort areas* (Thomson's 1994). No mention is made of the economic, religious or social structures of the country and first-time visitors to Africa will, almost undoubtedly, carry with them some preconceived images of 'Africa' based upon media images and the connection between

The Gambia and Alex Hailey's *Roots* rather than actual knowledge or experience.

This last point raises the question of whether it is the responsibility of the tourism industry to fully inform potential visitors or whether the onus should fall upon tourists themselves to find out as much as possible about their chosen destination (that is, to be 'good' tourists). For example, when the popular Caribbean destination of the Dominican Republic was devastated by hurricane Georges in 1998, a number of tourists expressed dissatisfaction that they had not been told that they were travelling in the hurricane season. Wherever that responsibility lies, it is certain that many tourists arrive at their destination totally unprepared for interaction or social contact with local people and, as a result, tourist-host encounters will be constrained and hampered by their lack of knowledge and understanding.

It is, of course, both easy and somewhat dangerous to generalise the varied and complex social processes and interaction involved in encounters between tourists and local people. Some or all of the above characteristics are likely to be identifiable in most tourist-host encounters and are equally applicable to both international and domestic tourism. For example, there is no reason why contact between a tourist and a local villager in the British countryside will not be as superficial, unbalanced, transitory and influenced by general preconceptions as such contacts in a developing country. Nevertheless, it is important to point out that encounters between tourists and local people occur in a variety of situations and may benefit from positive and informed perceptions and motivations on both sides. De Kadt (1979: 50) describes three principal contexts in which tourist-host encounters occur, namely, *where the tourist is purchasing some good or service from the host, where the tourist and host find themselves side by side, for example, on a sandy beach... and where the two parties come face to face with the object of exchanging information or ideas.* Of these, the first two situations are the most common contexts for tourist-host encounters and relate specifically to traditional, mass tourism. Conversely, the third situation, where both the tourist and the local person meet on the basis of equality, mutual respect and shared expectations, relates to the conditions under which tourism could lead, eventually, to greater international understanding. Although such two-way, meaningful and mutually satisfying encounters do occur, there is little doubt that they are relatively rare, largely as a result of mass tourism being of form of modern, mass consumption. In other words, in the majority of encounters, locals are perceived as part of the tourism product and tourists are seen as a potential source of profit; only in de Kadt's third scenario do individuality and personality enter the equation.

Host perceptions of tourists

It is widely accepted that *tourists are groups or populations with very different characteristics and attitudes, with clearly identifiable preferences, tastes, and perceptions* (Brougham and Butler 1981). These differences can lead to a variety of tourism impacts in destination areas and to different attitudes towards encounters with local people. It is not surprising, therefore, that a considerable amount of research has been undertaken into the desires, motivation and behaviour of tourists in relation to their impact on destination societies.

Much less research has been undertaken into the opinions and attitudes of local people with regard to tourism and tourists. Indeed, within the context of tourist-host relationships, the host is frequently assumed to be a fixed entity. In other words, whilst tourists are recognised as possessing a variety of characteristics, expectations and behavioural traits, the term host is used as a general description of members of local communities in tourist destination areas. The only distinction made between different categories of hosts is that, more often than not, it will be people who are involved in the local tourism industry who are most likely to come into contact with visitors. This relative lack of research is surprising since *the perceptions and attitudes of residents toward the impacts of tourism are likely to be an important planning and policy consideration for the successful development, marketing, and operation of existing and future tourism programs and projects* (Ap 1992). In particular, it is essential that local people are favourable towards tourists; if not, the possibility of a *community backlash* (Pearce 1994:104) may arise, leading to negative attitudes, such as an unwillingness to work within the tourism industry or even demonstrations of outright hostility towards tourists. By implication, therefore, the nature of the tourist-host relationship is as dependent on the different characteristics of local people themselves as it is on the varying perceptions, attitudes and so on that tourists bring to the encounter situation.

A number of attempts have been made to analyse the relationship between the different characteristics of host populations and their resulting perceptions of tourism and tourists. For example, Pizam (1978) looked at the attitudes of the residents of Cape Cod, Massachusetts, towards tourists, theorising that their perceptions would be a function of their economic dependency on tourism. He found, perhaps not surprisingly, that a positive correlation existed between residents' work and their attitudes towards tourism: *it was found that the more dependent a person was on tourism, as a means of livelihood, the more positive was his overall attitude towards tourism on Cape Cod.* In another study of resident perceptions, Belisle and Hoy (1980) discovered that local people's perceptions of tourism became less favourable the further their distance from the tourist zone, again indicating that those who are more directly involved in the tourism industry are more likely to have positive feelings towards tourism development. Similarly, Brougham and Butler's (1981) study of resident attitudes on the Sleat Peninsula, Isle of Skye, found that significant differences in perceptions of tourism were identifiable in relation to location of residence, but that other factors, such as age and language, also resulted in varying opinions of the benefits or disbenefits of tourism. More recently, Akis *et al* (1996) similarly found that in Cyprus a positive correlation exists between levels of income and attitudes towards tourism although, certainly in the case of the resort of Agia Napa, resentment is felt towards young tourists who attract complaints amongst local people of being noisy and frequently drunk.

A number of other studies are frequently quoted in the literature (for example, Rothman 1978; Sheldon and Var 1984; Perdue, Long and Allen 1987), the great majority of which tend to be largely descriptive. That is, the studies present the results of various research projects but do not fully explain *why* local people in tourist destination areas have either positive

259

or negative perceptions of tourism. More recently, Ap (1992) proposed that the theory of social exchange, a sociological concept firmly rooted in social action theory, provides a useful framework for the analysis of the tourist-host relationship.

Social exchange theory, which is generally concerned with explaining the exchange of resources (physical or symbolic) between people or groups of people, is similar to Nash's suggestion that *the relationship between tourists and their hosts includes certain understandings that must be agreed and acted upon* (1989: 44) or, in other words, is a sort of transaction. When applied to tourism, social exchange implies that both tourists and hosts undergo a process of negotiation or exchange, the ultimate aim of which is to maximise the benefit to each from the encounter. For the tourist, the benefit may be the purchase of a product or service or, more generally, a desired experience; for local people, the benefit may be economic gain.

The exchange process itself follows a sequence of events, commencing with the identification of *need satisfaction* (Ap 1992). That is, unless a need or a motivation exists, there is no reason for either party to initiate an exchange. Thus, unless a community has a need to develop tourism or sees tourism as a means of economic and social improvement, it is unlikely to be willing to become involved in or to welcome the development of tourism. The one exception may be where a community has a tradition of hospitality with no expectation of payment or reward, although such a tradition is likely to become rapidly commercialised with the advent of regular tourism. Once needs have been recognised, both the tourist and the host enter into an exchange situation that must be rational and that results in satisfactory benefits. In other words, both parties act in a rational manner that will result in the desired benefits, although those benefits will be satisficed rather than maximised. For example, as argued in Chapter Eight, tourism development is normally undertaken for the potential economic and social developmental benefits that it will bring to a community, such as improved standards of living, better transport services and so on. The greater the perceived benefits, the more positive will be local people's attitudes towards tourists. But, certain costs are involved, such as having to put up with crowds or higher costs in the shops during the tourist season. Once those costs begin to outweigh benefits, then attitudes towards tourism and tourists will become increasingly negative.

Importantly, the social exchange, or tourist-host encounter, must be reciprocal. *Reciprocity suggests that the resources exchanged should be roughly equivalent* (Ap 1992) and, therefore, neither party should feel they are being exploited. Once either the host or the tourist recognises a lack of reciprocity, for example, when a tourist feels that he or she is being 'ripped off' by the prices being charged for a souvenir or when hosts believe that they are being taken advantage of, such as when tourists intrude on their privacy by taking photographs, then the exchange becomes unbalanced. In this situation, the host is more likely to adopt a more negative attitude towards encounters than tourists because what is 'business as usual' for local people is a once-off experience for tourists. If the conditions of rationality, the satisficing of benefits and reciprocity are fulfilled, then the exchange will be perceived as fair and equitable; if the host and the tourist both feel that they have achieved a fair and satisfactory outcome, then each will have a positive perception of the encounter. For example, Belisle and Hoy (1980) found that the residents of Santa Marta, a resort on the coast of Colombia, South America, had a generally positive attitude towards tourism and tourists. Despite higher seasonal food prices and a greater incidence of robberies, drug smuggling and prostitution, tourism was seen as having led to improved local transport infrastructure and higher employment, benefits which, on balance, outweighed the costs. Similarly, the study of resident perceptions towards tourism development in Cyprus revealed an overall positive attitude amongst local people (Akis *et al* 1996).

Paradoxically, the need satisfaction that initiates the social exchange situation in the context of tourism can also frequently lead to unbalanced tourist-host encounters. Tourism is normally supported and promoted by host communities for the expected benefits of employment opportunities, higher income and social improvement but, as tourism in any resort develops, and as the local community becomes relatively more dependent on tourism as a source of income, then a subtle shift occurs in what may be described as the balance of power in tourist-host relationships. Either the social impacts begin to outweigh the benefits to the local community (see Chapter Ten) or local people find themselves in the situation of needing tourists more than tourists need them. In both cases, local people's attitudes and perceptions of tourists will begin to alter and become increasingly negative as individually or as a society they become increasingly dependent on tourists. In short, tourism development is dynamic and the context for tourist-host encounters can also change, influencing the nature of those encounters. *Encounters between tourists and the local inhabitants must be differentiated according to the stage of tourism development in which they occur* (de Kadt 1979: 50) and it is important to consider the tourist-host relationship itself as a dynamic process and one which may change in response to other factors.

The tourist resort life-cycle

Most of the studies into host perceptions of tourism and tourists tend to be undertaken at a particular point in time. That is, research is carried out at certain stage in the development of tourist destinations, at a particular point in what may be described as the life cycle of a resort, although one exception is Pi-Sunyer's (1989) longitudinal analysis of resident perceptions of tourists in a Catalan resort. Whilst such studies undoubtedly provide a valuable insight into the factors and variables which determine the nature of tourist-host encounters, it is also important to consider how host perceptions change over time, in particular how the nature of the relationship is influenced by the developmental stage of the destination. In a widely quoted study linked to product life cycle theory in marketing, Butler (1980) suggests that tourist destinations evolve through a six or seven stage process:

(i) **The exploration stage**
The first stage in the development of a tourist destination is characterised by relatively small visitor numbers. It is the stage when a resort or destination is 'discovered' by independent travellers or other explorer-type tourists and, as such, they will be accepted by local residents more as guests than as paying customers. Thus, commercial development of tourism is minimal,

contact with local residents is balanced and frequent and little or no marketing or promotion of the resort is occurring.

(ii) The involvement stage
As the number of visitors begins to increase, local people begin to provide facilities and accommodation. The potential for tourism development is recognised and, although still low key, some marketing is undertaken which further increases the number of visitors. As a result, the approach to tourism becomes more commercial although the relationship between tourists and local people remains harmonious.

(iii) The development stage
As tourist destinations progress into the third, development, stage they become transformed from relatively unknown, quiet destinations (what a travel writer would describe as 'undiscovered') into fully fledged resorts. Initially a wide range of locally owned businesses are set up to provide for the needs of tourists, but control of tourism rapidly passes to external organisations such as large hotel groups and international tour operators. The explorer or niche-market visitors have been replaced by mass, institutionalised tourists and the tourist-host relationship suffers as it becomes based on commercial transactions. Indeed, local residents become increasingly marginalised as tourism becomes dominated by external interests.

(iv) The consolidation stage
The consolidation stage is marked by a slow down in the rate of increase of visitors. Rather than new businesses opening up the existing hotels, restaurants and other facilities are more concerned with controlling costs. The destination has lost its exclusivity and 'unique selling points' and it has joined the ranks of many other similar destinations. During the season the resident population is vastly outnumbered by tourists, most of whom stay in an identifiable and distinct tourist zone within the resort. Thus, only local people involved in the tourism industry have any direct

contact with tourists, usually on a transitory, business related basis.

(v) The stagnation stage

Eventually the destination reaches a stage where its capacity has been reached or even, at times, exceeded. No new tourists are attracted to the resort which has become dependent on repeat business. The decline in growth has resulted in a lack of investment and so less attention is paid to the upkeep of buildings and infrastructure. Environmental, social and economic problems begin to emerge and the destination, in terms of both visitors and prices, moves downmarket.

(vi) The decline stage

Finally, the destination enters the stage of decline. Visitor numbers begin to fall as newer, more attractive resorts are developed (or, as in the case of British seaside resorts, overseas holidays become increasingly affordable and popular). The larger tourist businesses begin to pull out of the destination and new uses have to found for tourist accommodation and other facilities. Hotels may be converted into retirement flats or nursing homes and tourism activity falls to a low, but perhaps regular, level with minimal contact between visitors and members of the local community.

(vii) The rejuvenation stage

Rather than allowing the destination to completely decline, the signs are recognised and new uses, new markets and new sources of investment are sought. Attractions are updated and efforts are made to re-market the destination with a new, modern image. For example, the resort may begin to market itself as a business and conference centre, the season may be extended with new products, such as summer walking holidays being promoted at winter skiing destinations, or accommodation and facilities are improved and updated to keep in line with developments in other resorts.

A number of attempts have been made to link Butler's model to the 'life cycle' of actual tourist destinations, yet there are conflicting opinions as to its applicability. For example, Ioannides (1992) compares the growth and development of tourism in Cyprus with Butler's exploration, involvement and development stages, concluding that the high level of local involvement combined with increasing dependence on overseas tour operators and a mass, charter market indicates that the development stage has been reached.

More recent experience would indicate that Cyprus has, in fact, moved into a period of consolidation and potential stagnation (Sharpley 1998b). Similarly, the tourism history of British seaside resorts is another example of how destinations can progress through Butler's hypothetical process; some, such as Brighton and Torquay, have undergone rejuvenation, whereas as others are clearly in a state of decline (see Agarwal 1997). Conversely, Getz (1992), in a study of tourism development at the Niagara Falls, concludes that Butler's stages of consolidation, stagnation, decline and rejuvenation are not separate and identifiable but a perpetual process. That is, tourism planners and managers respond continually to shifts in demand and other problems which tourism destinations face and, rather than sinking into inevitable decline, destinations enter a stage of maturity: *for old destinations like Niagara Falls, and for most urban tourism areas, 'maturity' will likely be a permanent condition* (Getz 1992).

The important point to consider is how the developmental process of tourist destinations relates to the tourist-host relationship and, in particular, the perceptions of local people of tourism and tourists. Some links are identifiable through the degree and type of contact that local people have with tourists as Butler's model develops but, in another widely cited study, Doxey (1975), proposes a four stage process whereby the attitudes of local people change as tourism develops.

At the exploration stage, when there are relatively few visitors and contact between tourists and local people is likely to be frequent and balanced, the attitude of the host population is one of *euphoria*. Visitors are welcome, both as a form of new contact with 'the outside world' and as a new source of income which, in many cases, is an important

265

supplement to household earnings. However, as the level of tourism begins to grow, fewer members of the local population come into contact with tourists. Nor are tourists a rare sight; they begin to be taken for granted and the tourist-host encounter is motivated less by mutual personal interest than by commercial gain on the part of locals. Thus, the attitude of the majority of residents, in particular those who have limited or no contact with tourists, is one of *apathy*.

The third stage in Doxey's model is one of *annoyance*. Large numbers of tourists mean that the day-to-day life of residents becomes disrupted; there are queues in shops, traffic jams, local shops turn to the more profitable business of selling souvenirs and, generally, local residents are marginalised in their own town. The perceived benefits of tourism to the host community are beginning to be outweighed by the disruption that tourism is causing, a situation that leads, finally, to *antagonism* towards tourists. Local people have become dependent on tourism; they are no longer in control of the situation, the standard of living in the resort is declining as the quality of tourism facilities and the type of tourist becomes down market. The tourists and their money, once so openly welcomed, are now blamed for the changes that have taken place in the destination. In short, Doxey suggests that the growth and development of tourism can be mirrored by an increasingly negative attitude towards tourists amongst local people.

Similarly, Ap and Crompton (1993) identify four different strategies that local residents adopt in response to the level of tourism development. That is, they describe the actions taken by local people that result from their attitudes towards tourists. At the euphoric stage, local people *embrace* tourism; they make positive efforts to meet and develop long term relationships with visitors, many of whom may return on a regular basis. As the number of tourists grows and encounters become more formal, local apathy is marked by *tolerance* towards tourists. Despite some of the problems that tourism brings, the general feeling is that the local economy benefits from the income from tourists and local residents, therefore, tolerate the occasional disruption to their lives caused by tourists. However, as local residents become irritated by the presence of tourist they *adjust* their behaviour: activities, such as shopping, may be rescheduled to avoid crowds or they will go to places which they know will be quieter. Such a strategy is not always possible, in particular when tourism has reached the stage of consolidation, when tourism dominates their lives and local people have become antagonistic towards tourists. In this situation, if they are able to do so, residents may *withdraw*; they either move away temporarily, perhaps during the main season, or they may permanently move away from the area. For example, following the rapid development of Agia Napa, a mass tourism resort in Cyprus, the entire original village relocated a few kilometres away to avoid the problems and social impacts of tourism.

The implication of these studies is that not only will local people's attitudes and perceptions vary according to the level and type of tourism development, but that they will also adapt their behaviour accordingly. Much depends on the extent to which an individual is involved in the local tourism industry; it is likely that a person who earns a living from tourism will remain at the apathy/tolerance stage until business begins to decline, whereas residents who are not directly involved and who, therefore, suffer from the negative impacts without enjoying any apparent benefit, may quickly become antagonistic towards tourists. In either case, the end result is a tourist-host relationship that is unequal and unbalanced, a situation which may be related to the nature of tourism and tourism development itself.

Tourist host encounters and dependency

Much of the literature on the tourist-host relationship adopts what may be described as a micro perspective. That is, it considers the nature of the relationship from the point of view of individuals or localised groups of tourists and locals. In order to fully understand the ways in which the tourist-host relationship develops, we must consider the broader forces and influences that come into play, in particular the relationship between tourist generating countries or regions and tourist destinations. For example, it would be logical to assume that the local community in a destination that is fully in control of its tourism development would be more favourably disposed towards tourists than, say, local people who feel that, in some way or another, tourism has been imposed upon them or that they have become dependent on tourism and, by implication, tourists. For the latter community, tourism may be considered to be a form of imperialism or neo-colonialism and, from a sociological point of view, the resultant tourist-host relationship may be one based upon conflict.

The relationship between tourism and dependency in general has already been explored in Chapter Eight. However, the concept of neo-colonialism is of particular relevance to the present discussion and warrants further consideration. Imperialism or colonialism is essentially the expansion of a particular country's economic, political or military interests abroad and, in a sense, international tourism may be viewed as a new, modern form of colonialism. The basis of this argument is that, as we have seen, the great majority of tourists originate in the modern, developed countries of the Western world. At the same time, the tourism industry that facilitates the movement of tourists and the development of tourist facilities is itself based largely in the major tourism generating countries. Thus, being the suppliers of large numbers of tourists and, frequently, owning or managing facilities and attractions in destination areas as well as providing the necessary financial investment, the metropolitan centres of Europe and North America are able to exercise some degree of power and control over the development of tourism. This is particularly marked in developing countries but even Mediterranean destinations, such as Spain and Greece, have, in a sense, become colonised by their northern European neighbours. In the case of ex-colonies in the developing world which have gained their political independence from Western powers, this new dependence on the West for both the financial support to develop tourism and tourists themselves is, therefore, seen to be a return to the old days of colonialism, or neo-colonialism.

For example, The Gambia is a small, west African state which gained its independence from Britain in 1965. At that time the country was virtually unknown as a tourist destination; indeed, only three hundred tourist arrivals were recorded for the 1965-66 winter season (Dieke 1993). Since then, mainly as a result of its popularity as a winter sun destination, there has been a steady growth in the number of tourists travelling to The *good to say that hosts ~~are~~ are dependent from guests*

Gambia and currently about one hundred thousand tourists visit the country each year. Tourism contributes some ten per cent to the country's Gross Domestic Product (GDP), earning about £16.5 million annually, and The Gambia's Ministry of Information and Tourism hopes to increase tourism's contribution to GDP to 25 per cent. Whilst such figures indicate a reasonably healthy growth in tourism, they hide a number of important facts which demonstrate a less than healthy dependence on overseas finance and organisations. For example, around 60 per cent of visitors to The Gambia come from Britain with about 40 per cent of all visitors using Thomson's, a situation which puts tour operators in a powerful position when negotiating room rates. Also, many of The Gambia's hotels are either owned or managed by overseas organisations and a high percentage of its income from tourism is spent on importing goods to satisfy tourists' needs, whilst the collapse of the national airline in 1993 further increased the country's dependence on international sources of finance. Interestingly, attempts are being made to also develop a summer tourist season in The Gambia. By having to compete with other destinations closer to the main tourism generating countries in northern Europe, holidays in The Gambia are becoming increasingly cheaper and the country is correspondingly gaining less benefit from tourism (see Sharpley and Sharpley 1996 for more detail).

Mathieson and Wall (1982) identify three conditions, some or all of which may be linked to the concept of neo-colonialism and all of which are evident in the example of tourism development in The Gambia, which indicate a country's dependence on an overseas-controlled tourism industry. Firstly, many developing countries have become dependent on tourism as a source of foreign exchange. Thus, although the original policy of developing and promoting tourism may have been to develop and diversify the local economy, thereby enabling a greater degree of self-sufficiency, many countries have been unable to do so. For example, Cyprus turned to tourism to stimulate economic growth and diversification following both independence from Britain in 1960 and the Turkish occupation of northern Cyprus in 1974. Tourism is now the dominant industry on the island, accounting for over forty per cent of all exports and around twenty per cent of GDP, with the result that the Cypriot economy is largely dependent on tourism and, as with The

Gambia, disproportionately dependent on tourism from Britain (see Sharpley 1998b). Secondly, a large proportion of the earnings from tourism flow directly back to the tourism generating countries, both as profits from investments and as payments for imports to satisfy the needs of tourists. In some countries, such 'leakages' can be as high as seventy per cent of the earnings from tourism. Thirdly, tourism, as a form of neo-colonialism, is evidenced by foreign nationals holding management and other senior positions within the tourism industry, which is also another way in which the profits from tourism leak out of the country.

Often described as the economic costs of tourism development, these characteristics of neo-colonialism are by no means universal. Many destinations in both the developing and developed world have built up valuable and thriving tourism businesses based on policies which ensure local ownership and the retention of profits. For example, in Thailand foreign ownership of any business is limited to forty-nine per cent whilst in India no foreign national is permitted to work in the tourism industry. It is, therefore, over-generalistic to claim, as does Nash (1989: 39), that it is the influence of tourism generating countries *over touristic and related developments abroad that makes a metropolitan centre imperialistic and tourism a form of imperialism.* Also, many countries have undertaken tourism development programmes voluntarily and willingly and, by retaining their political, if not economic, independence, are able to dictate their own future. Bhutan, which both limits the number of tourists arriving each year and controls their activities so as not to disrupt and commercialise local culture, is an extreme but good example of how the promise of rapid economic growth has been rejected in favour of retaining independence and cultural and political integrity. But, in the context of tourist-host relationships, the development of tourism almost inevitably leads to some degree of economic dependence on the part of host communities and, therefore, the concept of tourism as a form of neo-colonialism provides a useful, broad basis for considering the longer-term direction and evolution of inter-action between tourists and local communities in all destination areas.

For example, the sense of economic dependence felt by destination communities may serve to undermine the potential for meaningful,

270

balanced tourist-host relationships, especially if an historical, colonial link exists. Thus, local people in India may well perceive that the attitude of British visitors has changed little since the days of the Raj and may feel resentful towards them, whilst in The Gambia, a country once at the centre of the slave trade, local people who work in the poorly paid, foreign dominated tourism industry may feel that little has changed. Similarly, local communities may have generalised attitudes towards visitors which are, again, amplified by their actual or perceived economic dependence upon them. For example, Pi-Sunyer (1989: 195) describes how the development of mass tourism in a Catalan resort led to stereotypical descriptions being applied to different nationalities of visitors. In the eyes of local people, Germans, French and Italian visitors lost their individuality and became identified by particular negative attributes, a process resulting from *the pressures and sheer magnitude of mass tourism...and...the sense of loss of control that such an influx implied.*

Nor is economic dependence and the resulting attitude towards tourists limited to international tourism. Local communities in a rural area in England, such as a national park, may be as equally dependent on domestic tourism from towns and cities as is a developing country on international tourists from a modern, Western country. The purchase of large numbers of local houses or apartments by tourists as second, holiday homes, leading to local people being unable to afford to buy their own homes, then becomes little more than a localised form of colonialism. The important point is that the economic dependence which comes hand in hand with virtually all levels of tourism development beyond the exploratory stage implies a lack of absolute control on the part of host communities and, hence, some degree of inequality in the resulting relationship between local people and tourists is inevitable.

Tourist-host relationships: harmony or conflict?

As pointed out earlier, encounters between tourists and local people in destination areas are frequently described as host-guest relationships, a term which implies a sense of willingness, equality and harmony. In

271

other words, it implies that tourists are invited as welcome (but paying) guests and that local people are happy and willing hosts. Thus, host-guest relationships within a destination society may be viewed as a form of structural consensus, as long as tourism is seen to be mutually beneficial and that the transactions or social exchanges between visitors and local people is fair, balanced and equitable. However, the analysis of the nature of contacts between tourists and members of local communities leads to a contradictory conclusion. That is, such encounters, when considered within the dynamic context of tourism development and the life cycle of tourist destinations, become identifiable with the gradual erosion of equality and balance in the relationship and the growing domination of the needs of tourism and tourists. In particular, the nature and economic rationale of tourism development indicates that, for the most part, encounters between tourists and local people bear more relation to conflict theory than harmonious inter-action, the exception being contacts in non-tourist areas or where visitors make a conscious effort to meet local, 'backstage' people.

The main point to emerge is that meaningful and balanced encounters between tourists and local people can only occur in situations of mutual dependence and where the local community has retained control over the development of tourism. As residents become more dependent on tourists as a source of income and as control falls into the hands of national or international organisations, the balance of power within the tourist-host relationship falls firmly in favour of the tourist. *Whenever tourism activity is concentrated in time and space, builds rapidly, dominates a local economy, disrupts community life, endangers the environment, and ignores community input, the seeds of discontent are sown* (Haywood 1988). If harmony is to be maintained and, by implication, the benefits to both tourists and local people optimised on a continual basis, the solution would appear to lie in maintaining the involvement and control of the community as a whole in the development of tourism, or in what has been called a community approach to tourism development (see Murphy 1983; 1985; and 1988).

The community approach to tourism development in its original form was, in effect, the precursor of what has become sustainable tourism development. Fundamental to the approach is the recognition that a thriving and healthy tourism industry depends upon an equally healthy and thriving local community. It is the local community that benefits from tourism but, at the same time, it is the local community that bears the costs of tourism and has to pick up the pieces once the tourists have gone. In other words, tourism is a resource industry, and local communities are as much a resource, or part of the tourism product, as are tourist facilities and attractions

The basic requirement for the community approach to tourism development is that all members of communities in tourist destination areas, rather than just those directly involved in the tourism industry, should be involved in the management and planning of tourism. The purpose of this approach is to ensure that the objectives of tourism development coincide with the community's wider social and economic goals and that the tourism industry *gives back to the community while extracting a living from it...*[and]*...that both the industry and its community base can benefit mutually from a long-term partnership* (Murphy 1983).

The concept of community involvement has been incorporated in a number of tourism planning and development projects, in particular the partnership or Tourism Development Action Programme (TDAP) approach. Primarily intended to develop partnerships between the public and private sectors as a more effective means of planning and financing tourism developments, TDAPs also have the purpose of achieving more widespread support and involvement amongst local communities (see Yale 1992: 23). The extent to which this has been achieved is debatable. Involvement tends to be limited to those who have a direct, usually financial interest, whilst decisions may frequently be based upon personal as opposed to community-wide concerns. It is widely recognised that harmonious tourist-host relationships are dependent, at least in part, on the involvement of local people in tourism planning at a community level. Pearce (1994: 117) also includes the education of both local people and communities, community ownership of tourist facilities, the facilitation of local residents' way of life and the undertaking of constant monitoring and research as equally essential ingredients of community based tourism development.

In reality, such involvement is unlikely (Taylor 1995). Tourism is an economic activity which involves tourists who are willing to spend money in return for certain goods and services, and organisations and businesses which will provide those goods and services at a profit. Under such circumstances, balanced and harmonious tourist-host relationships will only occur when the tourism product is small scale, locally owned and controlled, and not the major source of income and employment for the local community. As soon as the hosts become dependent, either on tourists themselves or on outside organisations, they become, in effect, a commodity. The profits of tour operators and other organisations represent a form of exploitation and the tourists, along with the tourism industry, are the exploiters. The tourist-host relationship becomes based upon conflict and, as considered in Chapter Ten, the local community begins to suffer from the social and cultural impacts of tourism.

Ten

Tourism: Socio-Cultural Consequences

Introduction

The growth and development of tourism during the latter half of the twentieth century has been remarkable. Between 1950 and 1990 the annual number of international tourist arrivals rose from 25 million to 458 million, whilst foreign exchange receipts grew from US$2.1 billion to US$266.2 billion. The rate of growth has not been constant; events of global significance, such as the OPEC oil crisis in the 1970s, the Chernobyl disaster in 1986 and the Gulf conflict in 1991, have had repercussions throughout the tourism industry causing a temporary slow-down in the growth of arrivals. But, the figures have continued to rise. By 1997, international arrivals amounted to 613 million, generating almost US$444 billion. If the worldwide earnings from domestic tourism are added to this, the value of tourism is even more staggering. In Britain alone it is calculated that tourism contributes some £30 billion to the economy each year whilst the World Travel and Tourism Council (WTTC) estimates that tourism has become the world's single largest industry, generating more than US$3.4 trillion (WTTC 1994).

In short, there is no doubting the economic value of tourism. As discussed in Chapter Eight, in addition to being a significant generator of foreign exchange, tourism can act as a catalyst for economic regeneration and diversification whilst, as a relatively labour intensive industry, it is an important source of employment in both developed and developing countries; around ten per cent of the world's workforce is employed in tourism. Thus, as tourism continues to grow both in scale and scope, it is not surprising that many countries have leapt onto the tourism

275

bandwagon, developing and exploiting their natural resources in an attempt to gain their share of the multi-billion dollar tourism market.

From a social and cultural perspective, this rapid expansion of tourism is important in two respects. Firstly, within individual destination areas or countries, the development of tourism as a vehicle for economic modernisation and diversification almost invariably leads to changes and developments in the structure of society. The *raison d'être* of tourism is to promote economic and social development and, therefore, some of these changes may be welcome. For example, general, society-wide improvements in income, education, health care, employment opportunities and local infrastructure and services are all elements of social development. Conversely, other changes may be less welcome. Traditional social or family values may be challenged, new economically powerful groups may emerge, or cultural practices may be adapted in order to suit the needs of tourists. In other words, destination societies may both benefit from and suffer the less desirable consequences of tourism as an economic development strategy.

Secondly, *tourism is unique as an export industry in that consumers themselves travel to collect the goods* (Crick 1989). The tourism product is 'exported' to tourists who travel to the destination, carrying with them the values, beliefs and behavioural modes of their own, home society as a form of cultural baggage. Thus, as the volume of international tourism has increased, so too has the contact between different societies and cultures. To some observers, this interaction between tourists and local communities threatens to dilute or even, potentially, destroy traditional cultures and societies: *tourists seem to be the incarnation of the materialism, philistinism and cultural homogenisation that is sweeping all before it in a converging world* (Macnaught 1982). To others, it represents an opportunity for sharing, for peace, understanding and greater knowledge amongst different societies and nations.

Whether considering the effects on a destination society brought about by the consequences of tourism development, the influence of ever-increasing numbers of tourists coming into contact with alien cultures, or a combination of both, it is inevitable that tourism, as a fundamentally social activity, will have an impact on those societies and cultures involved in tourism.

The rapid growth in tourism since the 1960s has been mirrored by increasing concern about the impacts of tourism on host destinations and there exists a large body of literature concerned with both an analysis of the physical, social, political or cultural impacts of tourism development and with potential solutions to the perceived problems (see, for example, Budowski 1976; de Kadt 1979; Britton 1982; Mathieson and Wall 1982; Holden 1984; Murphy 1985; Butler 1991; ETB 1991; Smith and Eadington 1992; Croall 1995; Wahab and Pigram 1997; Middleton 1998).

Much of the academic literature, reports in the media and what Mathieson and Wall (1982: 134) describe as *colourful stories,* adopt a negative stance, highlighting those aspects of tourism which are seen to be destructive or disadvantageous to tourist destinations (see Travis 1982). Much of the concern for the consequences of tourism development appears to be framed by a *powerfully entrenched, doom-laden apocalyptic view* (Middleton 1998), one which considers mass tourism in particular to be inevitably destructive. Also, the analysis and criticism of the social and cultural impacts is frequently based on a number of assumptions which, potentially, distort the overall picture. For example, it is often assumed that the social and cultural impact of tourism is a one-way process, that the flood of (usually Western) tourists visiting countries in the developing world almost invariably results in the Westernisation of traditional cultures. This chapter examines both the positive and negative social and cultural impacts of tourism and considers the extent to which the qualitative assessment of socio-cultural impacts can be measured against broader social and cultural change and the tangible, quantitative impacts of tourism development.

Tourism, Society and Culture

Murphy (1985: 117) describes tourism as a *socio-cultural event for the traveller and the host.* It is a social process which, in the context of both domestic and international tourism, brings together people from different

277

regions and different countries in a form of social interaction (see Chapter Nine). The resulting tourist-host relationship may frequently impact upon both the local community and on visitors. Tourism is also, from the point of view of destination areas, a means of improving and modernising the economic and social condition of the host community (that is, encouraging development) and, therefore, tourism may be described as an agent of socio-cultural change.

It is difficult to distinguish between changes or impacts that are specifically social and those which are cultural. The condition and structure of a society and its cultural characteristics are interlinked and changes in one almost inevitably lead to changes in the other. For the purposes of this chapter, the social impacts of tourism may be described as those which have a more immediate effect on both tourists and host communities and their quality of life, whereas cultural impacts are those which lead to a longer-term, gradual change in a society's values, beliefs and cultural practices (Murphy 1985: 117). In other words, social impacts are those concerned with issues such as health, moral behaviour, the structure of the family, gender roles, crime and religion whilst cultural impacts may determine behavioural and attitudinal changes, such as dress, food and social relationships, as well as changes in the production of cultural practices and artefacts. Before describing the specific social and cultural impacts of tourism, it is important to consider, firstly, the factors which determine the degree of socio-cultural impact and, secondly, the extent to which it is tourism and tourists, as opposed to other factors, that lead to social and cultural change.

(i)   Factors influencing socio-cultural change

Although it is possible to make general observations about the potential socio-cultural impacts of tourism, the degree to which these impacts influence or are experienced by host communities and tourists depends on a number of factors. Generally, the greater the gulf between the tourism generating country and the destination in terms of culture and economic development, the more significant are the social and cultural impacts likely to be (WTO 1981). Other, more specific factors may also be identified:

278

(a) Types/numbers of tourists

Both the volume and the type of tourist are significant factors in determining the potential socio-cultural impacts of tourism. As a general rule, explorer-type independent travellers who are relatively few in number and are more willing to seek out, experience and understand local culture are likely to have less impact than large numbers of mass tourists who demand facilities and amenities to which they are accustomed in their home society. Smith (1989: 12) links tourist types to potential impacts on host societies, following a continuum from low numbers/low impact to high volume charter tourists/high impact, whilst there are also connections between tourist types and behavioural characteristics and the way in which tourists interact with local communities (see Chapter Four). In some circumstances, an independent traveller may have more impact on an isolated community that has not been exposed to tourism than a large number of tourists in an established destination. Conversely, mass tourism in a self-contained club resort may have relatively little impact on the socio-cultural character of the country in which it is located although, as is often the case, such resorts may cause resentment amongst local people who feel that they are unable to benefit economically from tourists.

(b) Importance of the tourism industry

The primary purpose of tourism development is, as we have seen, socio-economic growth and development. In those destinations where tourism is part of, or leads to, a mixed economy, the socio-cultural impacts of tourism are likely to be weaker or less widespread than in a country where tourism is the major industry. Where local communities become entirely dependent on tourism, the socio-cultural impacts of tourism are likely to be most keenly felt. Furthermore, diverse economies are more likely to be able to support and supply the local tourism industry, reducing the need for imports and spreading the socially beneficial impacts of employment and income generation.

(c) Size and development of the tourism industry

In a similar vein to the degree of dependence on tourism, both the size of the tourism industry and its stage of development are important factors. A relatively large number of tourists in small communities will have greater impacts on local residents, whereas larger communities are likely to remain relatively unaffected by tourists. It is for this reason that a number of tourist destinations, such as the Seychelles, are adopting the policy of promoting themselves as up-market destinations, hoping to attract a smaller number of higher spending tourists. The purpose of this is to reduce the potential negative impacts of tourism whilst maintaining the economic benefits to the destination. It must also be remembered that the stage of tourism development in a destination will determine the degree of socio-cultural impact; established resorts will experience less continuing change than a newer destination.

(d) The pace of tourism development

Many tourist destinations have experienced the rapid and relatively uncontrolled development of tourism. In such cases, the socio-cultural impacts of tourism are likely to be greater than in countries or destinations which undertake a slow and controlled tourism development programme. In effect, local communities should be allowed to gradually adapt to the needs and benefits of tourism and tourists rather than having to undergo a process of rapid upheaval and change.

All tourism destinations are different and the influence of these factors in determining the degree to which the socio-cultural impacts of tourism are experienced is also variable. Nor are such impacts restricted to developing countries or international tourism in general, although much of the literature concentrates on these areas. For example, the local communities in many rural, coastal and urban tourism destinations in Britain are affected to some degree by domestic tourists. Overall, the level of impact in a tourism destination will result from the *interaction between the nature of the change agent and the inherent strength and ability of the host culture to withstand, and absorb, the change generators whilst retaining its own integrity* (Ryan 1991: 148). The implication is that the study of the socio-cultural impacts of tourism must be approached with some caution. It is inevitable that some change will occur as a result of tourism but such is the variety of factors influencing socio-cultural change that each case must be considered individually. For example, it would be logical to expect that the changes resulting from the development and growth of tourism in the Greek Cyclades islands would be relatively uniform but a study by Tsartas (1992) indicates otherwise. The islands of Ios and Serifos are similar in size, population and original socio-economic conditions but it was found that, owing to different types of tourism development (mass-charter tourism on Ios, moderate and controlled tourism on Serifos) different socio-cultural impacts were experienced on each island. The speed with which tourism had been developed, the length of time over which development had occurred and a variety of economic and political factors also played a role in determining the perceived socio-cultural impacts on each island.

(ii) Tourism as an agent of socio-cultural change

When visible and identifiable social and cultural changes occur in regions or countries which have adopted a policy of tourism development, it is frequently tourism, as opposed to other factors, that is seen to be the cause of such change. Also, the socio-cultural consequences of tourism are generally perceived to be negative, in particular in the context of tourism development in LDCs which are, potentially, more susceptible to Western influences. Yet, whilst there is little doubt that tourism can bring about changes which may both benefit host communities and be viewed as a 'cost', it is important to point out that, in most cases, tourism *contributes* to social and cultural change rather than being the *cause* of such change.

All societies and cultures are changing and, as a global, homogeneous culture emerges (see Chapter Three), no society is immune from outside influence. For example, there are very few communities which do not have access to a television and, hence, images of other countries and cultures. The activities of multinational corporations, internationalising Western culture (for example, McDonald's in Moscow, Kentucky Fried Chicken in Beijing), are catalysts of social change, whilst many countries are undergoing a process of industrialisation, urbanisation and rapid population growth which, potentially, have a far greater impact than tourism on social and cultural structures and values. As Smith (1989: 9) points out, *culture change, in the form of modernisation, has made impressive inroads into the backward areas and the poverty pockets of the globe, and the process is both ongoing and accelerating.* She goes on to conclude, in her study of Eskimo tourism in Alaska (Smith 1989: 75), that it is the effort of the government to improve housing, education, medical care and infrastructure, rather the growth of tourism, that has been the key element in bringing about modernisation and cultural change.

Frequently, little effort is made to distinguish the effects of tourism from other cultural changes occurring globally and it would seem that, owing to the highly visible nature of tourism and tourists, the development of tourism has become a scapegoat for socio-cultural change (Crick 1989). It is important, therefore, to recognise the dynamic character of all societies and cultures and to consider the potential socio-cultural impacts of tourism against this background. It is also important to set the parameters within which the impacts of tourism are assessed. In other words, impact studies often display what Wood (1980) describes as a *western ethnocentrism and romanticism*, a bias which, linked with the concept of postmodernity (see Chapter Three), assumes that it is better to preserve cultures which are traditional or pre-modern rather than allowing them to develop or modernise. Thus, tourism developments which, from the Western point of view, 'threaten' the social and cultural characteristics of many destinations are perceived as negative impacts although it is quite possible that local communities support such changes. Within the study of the socio-cultural impacts of tourism, it is necessary *to go beyond evaluations based on Western romantic ideals of cultural preservation to analyse the precise components of cultural change* (Wood 1980) and to assess the extent to which tourism is one of these components.

The Social Impacts of Tourism

Although the social and cultural effects of tourism are linked and distinctions may be difficult to identify (Lea 1988:62), for convenience they are divided here under separate headings. The social impacts of tourism, those which have a more immediate and visible effect on destination communities and, to an extent, on tourists themselves, may also be sub-divided into impacts resulting from the development of a tourism industry and the impacts of tourist-host interaction.

(i) Social Consequences of Tourism Development

Tourism is normally planned and developed as a source of income and foreign exchange, thereby providing the resources for social and economic development within destination communities. The actual economic costs and benefits of tourism development, such as the generation of income and the multiplier effect, are widely discussed in the literature (for example, see Bull 1995); here we are concerned with the social consequences of these costs and benefits. Generally, *tourism creates new opportunities in the formal and informal sectors of the economy, new criteria of social status, and contributes to changes in such basic social institutions as the family* (Harrison 1992: 22). A number of more specific positive and negative effects are identifiable:

(a) Improvements in the quality of life

In many instances, the development of tourism results, directly and indirectly, in improvements in the quality of life of local communities in destination areas. In less developed areas, basic infrastructural improvements required by tourism, such as roads and transport links, communication and information links, the supply of power, clean water, sewerage disposal systems and so on may all be of benefit to local communities, whilst facilities and amenities provided for tourists in both new and established resorts also represent general social improvements. For example, the income from tourism frequently supports a wider range of shops, restaurants, theatres and other facilities which are of equal benefit to local communities.

The development of tourism can also lead to an improvement of the physical environment, supporting the conservation and renovation of traditional buildings or environmental improvement programmes. More generally, tourism should, at least in theory, lead to greater investment in education, health and other social services to benefit the community as a whole, although this is not always the case.

Frequently, the growth of tourism is not matched by social improvements for local communities. It is generally accepted that jobs in tourism, other than management positions, tend to be low paid, low status and, frequently, seasonal. This is certainly the case in many beach resorts; for example, locals employed as waiters, bar tenders and other similar jobs in hotels in The Gambia earn barely enough to cover their travelling expenses and the work is seasonal.

It is also interesting to consider the employment situation in a city such as Glasgow where tourism is being promoted as one of the primary ways of transforming the city from a manufacturing to a service based economy. Many of the city's unemployed people used to work in shipbuilding or heavy engineering and it is difficult to consider jobs in tourism as suitable alternative employment (see Damer 1990). Tourism can also result in inflated land and house prices, extensive second-home ownership (see Coppock 1977), inflation and loss of services as, for example, local shops convert to more profitable souvenir outlets.

(b) Changes in the role of women

In many traditional societies, the role of women, particularly younger women, has been strictly governed and defined by social, religious and economic constraints. Indeed, the apparent male domination of many societies is plainly evident to tourists visiting many countries in the developing world. Nevertheless, the employment opportunities offered by tourism have gone a long way to reducing women's economic dependency on the family, representing a new freedom which, although putting strains on the traditional family structure and challenging broader social values, has improved the social condition for many women (see, more generally, Kinnaird and Hall 1994; Sinclair 1997). For example, Reynoso y Valle and de Regt (1979: 130) found that the development of tourism opened up a range of job opportunities for women outside the home, challenging the traditional position and machismo of the Mexican male. In other cases, the improved status of women need not necessarily lead to family or social stress. In Cyprus, where the rapid growth of tourism since independence in 1960 has created a large number of new jobs (tourism currently accounts for 25 per cent of all employment in Cyprus), *the improved financial status of females did not create conflicts between parents and children and husbands or wives, nor did it challenge the authority of the parents or husbands* (Andronikou 1979: 249). It has to be added that, under the Cypriot constitution, women enjoy equal rights and many senior positions, including the Director General of Cyprus Tourism Organisation, are currently held by women.

Tourism has also opened up opportunities for women in what may be described as the informal employment sector. In most tourist destinations, particularly in the developing world, the growth of tourism is accompanied by an increase in the number of people who work in unofficial jobs, such as fruit sellers, beach hawkers, garment manufacturers and, perhaps the most emotive subject of all, as prostitutes in the flourishing 'sex tourism' destinations, such as Thailand and the Philippines. This issue is considered in greater detail later in this chapter but there is no doubt that tourism, in both the formal and informal employment sectors, is largely dependent on women. The extent to which this has improved the social status of women varies from society to society; for example, in Bali, *women are central to the culture, and are indispensable to tourism. Without them the industry would collapse* (Osborne 1993) whereas, in many other countries around the world, the status of women in the industry is still subordinate to that of their male colleagues.

(c) Changes in community structure

The development of tourism can result in a number of changes in the structure and cohesion of local communities in destination areas with, again, developing countries being most susceptible. The lure or attraction of working in the tourism industry, offering not only employment but the opportunity to meet foreign visitors, draws many younger people to tourist development areas. This has resulted in increased rural-urban migration, a phenomenon which, although not directly caused but nevertheless exacerbated by tourism, leaves many rural areas with a disproportionately aged population and a lack of younger people to continue working in traditional agricultural businesses. Within resort areas it tends to be the younger generations who desire the upward social mobility offered by involvement in tourism and studies have shown that tourism tends to accentuate class differences, polarising local populations and creating a new younger, more prosperous group, perhaps with a broader, less traditional approach than the older generations.

(i) The Social Impacts of Tourist-Host Interaction

It is inevitable that the physical presence of tourists and their behaviour in tourist resorts and destinations will have some form of impact on local communities. Some of these impacts may be immediate, such as inappropriate behaviour, displays of conspicuous consumption or simply the inconvenience and nuisance caused by large numbers of holiday makers who may have little or no intention of meeting with or getting to know members of the local population (see Chapter Nine). Other effects may be more gradual, such as the local community adopting the behaviour, attitudes or moral codes of visitors through a process of acculturation. Most of the literature on the social impacts of tourism concentrates on the impacts of tourists on host populations but, socially and culturally, tourism is a two-way process. That is, although the physical flows of tourism are largely typified by the annual mass migration from northern Europe to the Mediterranean or, more generally, from the modern, developed nations to lesser developed or developing countries, it does not necessarily imply that the social effects of tourism also flow in one direction.

Relatively few attempts have been made to explore how local cultures and people may impact on visitors; within the tourism literature there is a noticeable lack of research into tourist-host encounters from the point of view of tourists. In one sense, crimes against tourists, such as pick-pocketing or mugging, fall into the category of impacts on tourists, although this is normally considered a result of tourism development in the destination. Tourists are also sometimes the target of politically-motivated activities. Since the advent of modern, mass travel, particularly to more remote destinations, there have been a number of well-publicised incidents where tourists have been attacked, kidnapped or murdered by terrorists or other groups for political ends. More recent examples of this include the massacre at Luxor in Egypt in 1998, the kidnap and subsequent death of tourists in The Yemen, also in 1998, and the murder of eight tourists in Uganda in March 1999. The link between tourism and politics is explored in the literature (Richter 1983; Matthews and Richter 1991), as is the more specific relationship between tourism and terrorism (Richter and Waugh 1986; Ryan 1991b; Pizam and Mansfeld 1996). It is also not uncommon for tourists to contract minor, usually stomach, ailments whilst abroad and, as greater numbers of tourists travel to more distant, exotic locations, the incidence of more serious illnesses is on the increase. Interestingly, it has also been reported that a number of 'old' diseases, such as diphtheria, which have virtually eradicated in Western societies, are now spreading as a result of tourism to previously inaccessible areas (see Clift and Grabowski 1997). Both crime and health problems are common 'reverse impacts' of tourism although, more typically, they are considered to be two of the risks of participating in tourism. Nevertheless, it is possible to identify a number of other ways in which local communities impact on visitors in a socio-cultural sense.

It is highly likely that fashions and tastes have become internationalised partly, if not solely, as a result of tourism. The multi-ethnic character of many populations and the influence of the media also play a significant role, but there is little doubt that overseas travel goes some way to reducing what may be described as cultural xenophobia in tourism generating countries.

For example, international cuisine, clothing styles and music are now more widely accepted in Britain than some years ago. Local, host communities may also impact on tourists in terms of adapting, for better or for worse, the attitudes and perceptions of visitors towards host societies and cultures. For example, in a study of young, British tourists visiting Greece and Morocco, Pearce (1982: 89) found that the tourists saw the Greeks as more religious and less affluent than expected and Moroccans were poorer and more greedy and mercenary than expected. In both cases, the study revealed that tourists returned home with a more positive attitude towards their own country, a finding which implies that an exploration of possible changes in tourists' perceptions of their own society and culture as a result of overseas travel would be a fruitful research topic.

It is important to note that the impact of local people on tourists is dependent on the nature of the encounter. In a study of Greek tourists visiting Turkey, Anastasopoulas (1992) concluded that the negative attitude of the Greeks towards their hosts derived largely from the organised, packaged nature of the tour and the role of the tour guides. This study, along with those by Milman, Reichel and Pizam (1990) and Pizam, Milman and Jafari (1991) also found that there is little empirical evidence to support the view that tourism can lead to greater understanding and harmony and that, in certain circumstances, host communities have a negative impact on visitor perceptions.

A further aspect of socio-cultural impacts on tourists is the way in which tourists adapt their behaviour as a result of encounters with local people. It would be logical to propose that the more contact a tourist has with local people, the less institutionalised the setting and the stronger the local culture, the more likely is the tourist to become acclimatised or 'acculturated'. For example, it is accepted that longer-term independent travellers undergo a period of culture shock when first travelling but that they gradually adapt to their new environment, often to the extent that they find it difficult to re-adjust to their own home culture and society when they return. In some cases, cultural characteristics of the destination society, such as the religion, might be adopted on a permanent basis by the tourist. Again, research is required to explore the two-way nature of the socio-cultural effects of tourism but, generally, it is still local communities which 'suffer' social impacts of tourism to a greater extent. These impacts are manifested in a variety of ways:

(a) The demonstration effect
One of the most visible and common social impacts of tourism, in particular in the context of tourism to less developed or poorer countries, is the introduction of alien values and ways of life into relatively traditional or isolated societies. As a result, local communities begin to adapt and change their own values and modes of behaviour, often in an attempt to emulate those of tourists, in a process known as the demonstration effect.

Up to a point, such a process is inevitable. Whilst on holiday, tourists demonstrate levels of affluence that are usually beyond the reach of local people, affluence which may be apparent simply because tourists can afford to travel in the first place. Frequently, they also display their relative wealth by their styles of dress, the camera or video equipment they carry with them or by indulging in conspicuous consumption. Such displays of wealth may often lead to resentment amongst local communities, particularly if they believe that they will be unable to achieve a similar level of affluence themselves. This resentment might be increased by the symbols of tourist development, such as expensive hotels or tourist zones, beaches or clubs which are 'off limits' to local people, and by the behaviour of tourists who do not respect local morals and customs. For example, the development of tourism on the island of

Phuket in Thailand has caused considerable local resentment, especially with respect to the 'privatisation' of public beaches, and has led to the formation of the Phuket Environmental Protection Group to fight for the preservation of the remaining undeveloped beaches (Rattachumpoth 1992). It is also likely that local people, in particular the younger generations, will begin to question and challenge local custom and tradition and will begin to strive for the material and financial affluence so openly displayed by tourists.

At a basic level, this demonstration effect may be manifested by local people adopting Western styles of dress and indulging in types of behaviour that lead to increasing polarisation between the older and younger generations. With the advance and spread of information and communication technology and the influence of mass, international media, such a process is, perhaps, inevitable and is merely accelerated by tourism. But, the regular displays of wealth may entice people to work in the tourism or other service industries or, of greater consequence to host societies, migrating to the tourism generating countries. One way of achieving this is by befriending tourists in the hope of achieving an invitation to visit, offers of financial support or, in the extreme, permanent relationships. For example, in the early days of its tourism development, The Gambia was particularly popular amongst single, middle-aged Scandinavian women. In some cases, relationships between female tourists and local men became more permanent, occasionally resulting in marriage, and a number of couples returned to Scandinavia. Similarly, in other countries, such as Thailand and the Philippines, it is recognised that younger females often view Western male tourists as potential tickets to a better life and become involved in relationships as a means of migrating abroad.

Thus, the demonstration effect can lead to a number of social impacts in destination communities. On a positive note it may result in economic and social development within the community by encouraging people to work for things they lack but, more commonly, it can amplify the financial and moral gap between generations. It can encourage behaviour that undermines or challenges traditional values whilst advancing the spread of Western, cultural homogenisation, and it may disrupt the social structure of local communities as younger people move to urban centres,

289

tourism development areas or abroad to tourism generating countries. More generally, it can also lead to local communities developing inaccurate, stereo-typical attitudes towards tourists based upon their observations of behaviour which itself is usually untypical, freed as tourists are from the social constraints and rules of everyday life.

(b) Crime

The association between travel and tourism and crime is not a new phenomenon; throughout the centuries travellers had to endure not only slow and uncomfortable travelling conditions but also the regular attention of people anxious to divest them of their belongings. Crime has also been an accepted feature of tourism in some countries for many years, such as in Italy where people on motorbikes snatch handbags from unsuspecting pedestrians. More recently, there has been increasing publicity about tourism-linked crime, in particular following the murder of a number of tourists in Florida in 1993 and 1994.

Although there is little evidence to directly link an increase in crime with the development of tourism, there is no doubt that where there are tourists in any significant numbers there will also be people attempting to benefit illegally from the presence of those tourists (see Pizam and Mansfeld 1996 for a broad treatment of tourism and crime issues). One early study found a positive connection between tourism and the level of crime in Florida, noting that the incidence of crime rose during the main tourist season (McPheters and Stronge 1974), whilst Mathieson and Wall (1982: 151), in a review of existing literature, concluded that there is a positive correlation between crime and tourism. It would be logical to suggest that this link exists because, to local members of the criminal fraternity, tourists represent easy pickings. Not only are they in unfamiliar surroundings, but also they will often be carrying large amounts of money or travellers cheques and expensive camera or video equipment. Also, in some countries, British or other passports are a valuable commodity on the black market. Thus, the potential gain for thieves may be high and, as Mathieson and Wall (1982: 151) point out, the risk of detection is often low.

In addition to criminal activities which are directed against individual tourists, other illegal activities may also thrive as a result of tourism. For example, in those countries where the official exchange rate overvalues the local currency, it is not unusual for black markets in currency exchange to exist, offering tourists far higher rates than available legally. In China, foreign tourists are required to exchange their cash or travellers cheques for what are known as Foreign Exchange Certificates, a currency which should also be used for all goods and services purchased in China. By maintaining an artificially low exchange rate, the authorities hope to maximise earnings of foreign exchange, but tourists are able to virtually double their money by dealing on the black market and obtaining local currency. Other illegal activities may include gambling, trading in counterfeit goods and so on. For local societies in destination areas, the impacts of tourism related crime are increased expenditure on law enforcement during the tourist season, financial loss as a result of fraud and black market dealings and, potentially, a fall in the number of tourist arrivals should a resort gain an unfavourable reputation for criminal activities, such as theft or mugging.

It should be noted that it is not always tourists who are the victims of crime (Ryan 1991: 159); often, it may be tourists themselves who commit crimes or become involved in illegal activities. This might be simply violent or drunken behaviour, resulting in a fine or a short term in prison, but tourists also engage in more serious crimes, such as drug smuggling, which, as evidenced by the experience of Western travellers in Thailand, can result in long jail sentences.

(c) Language

In most tourist-host encounters, language is the primary means of communication. More generally, language is also a significant cultural characteristic of any society and tourism can have both immediate and longer term impacts on host communities. This is most likely to occur in larger, more established tourist destinations which attract mass tourists. In this situation local people are, in effect, obliged to learn and use the language of the dominant nationality of visitors in order to be able to deal and communicate with visitors on either a commercial or personal basis. Thus, most local people in Spanish tourist resorts who regularly come into contact with tourists speak English and in the Turkish resort of Alanya, German is widely spoken.

It is not only through commercial necessity that foreign languages may be adopted or, in the case of some more isolated areas, that local dialects or languages begin to die out. The demonstration effect may result in local people wanting to learn the language of tourists and, either intentionally or unintentionally, adopting their mannerisms. Similarly, visitors may learn foreign languages or adopt local accents. For example, longer-stay British visitors in the United States frequently develop an American 'twang' in their speech. In more remote areas where the traditional, indigenous language is not widely spoken or only popular amongst the older generations, tourism may represent a threat to the very existence of that language. Thus, Brougham and Butler (1981) found that many local people on the Isle of Skye in Scotland felt that tourism was a major factor in the diminishing use of Gaelic, mainly as a result of increasing second-home ownership and the influx of seasonal workers from the mainland. Conversely, the impact of tourism on language may represent a benefit to local people, resulting in more job opportunities for those who learn a second language or become multi-lingual.

(d) Religion

Traditionally, religion was a major motivating factor of travel and tourism (see Chapter Two) and even nowadays a significant proportion of domestic and international tourism is for religious or spiritual purposes. Since the advent of modern mass tourism, the relationship between tourism and religion has undergone a fundamental transformation, as the majority of tourist visits to religious shrines, holy cities, temples, cathedrals, churches and other symbols or centres of religion are no longer for purely spiritual purposes. In other words, religion has become a commodity, a tourism product, and religious festivals or buildings have become spectacles to be gazed upon and collected along with other sights and attractions. As a result, in many destinations there has been increasing conflict between local communities, devout visitors and tourists. For example, simply the physical presence of large and often noisy groups of tourists who, frequently, take photographs of religious festivals or people worshipping with little consideration for the participants is a common and widespread problem. Visits to monasteries, religious retreats and centres of learning may also disrupt the lives of the inhabitants; even in Bhutan, where the number of tourists is strictly controlled, the authorities were compelled to prohibit tourists from visiting certain Buddhist monasteries as they were disturbing the monks.

Another situation where conflict may arise is where the traditional importance or meaning of religious rites or practices are not recognised, understood or respected by tourists. For example, in India, tourists frequently attempt to take photographs of the 'burning ghats', places alongside the River Ganges in Varanasi where deceased Hindus are cremated, thereby causing great offence to local people. In the extreme, disrespect for local religious custom may have severe consequences, such as tourists being physically attacked for taking photographs in temples or churches where it is forbidden.

Whilst it is easy to blame tourists for impacting upon local religious custom and practice, they themselves are often exploited by religious institutions, usually as a source of revenue. In some churches or cathedrals, collection boxes are often strategically placed near entrances and it is not uncommon to find book shops, souvenir stalls or even tea shops and restaurants located in religious buildings. In other cases, religious buildings have adopted a clearly definable dual purpose, separating their traditional function as a place of worship from their attraction to tourists and, hence, their earning potential. For example, entrance to a side chapel at St. Paul's Cathedral in London is free for worshippers, whereas entrance charges are levied on tourists visiting other parts of the building, including the crypt and the Whispering Gallery. Similarly, charges have been introduced for tourists wishing to visit Westminster Abbey. It may be argued that tourists are being taken advantage of and that the fundamental meaning and purpose of the building is being abused, but tourism represents a significant source of income for essential repair and maintenance work. In this sense, the relationship between tourism and religion is positive in as much as tourism is contributing towards the preservation of a building which is of religious, architectural and national importance (see Bates 1994 for a consideration of the problems facing Westminster Abbey as both place of worship and a major tourist attraction in London).

(e) Prostitution

One of the most emotive and publicised social impacts of tourism on destination countries, especially in the developing world, is the alleged effect it has on moral behaviour in general, and prostitution in particular. Cities such as Bangkok in Thailand and Manila in the Philippines have gained reputations for being the 'sex capitals' of the world, an image that has undoubtedly been reinforced by media attention and the availability of 'sex tours' that are openly advertised in some tourist generating countries, such as Japan. There is also no doubt that it is this image that draws many male Western tourists to these destinations.

Prostitution as a tourist 'attraction' is not limited to south east Asian countries. Amsterdam's red light district has long been a tourist sight, London's Soho is famous for its sex shows and, as Ryan (1991: 163) points out, the legalised brothels of Nevada are widely advertised in tourist centres such as Las Vegas. Indeed, virtually every major town and city around the world, whether or not a tourist destination, has a red light area. It is difficult to assess the extent to which tourism has led directly to an increase in prostitution and, frequently, the role of tourism in this context is overstated. On the one hand, the development of tourism creates the conditions under which prostitution may thrive; tourists have temporarily left the restrictions of their own society and may be willing to indulge in activities which they would not normally consider at home (see Chapter Five). Also, they are assured of anonymity, they may be willing to spend freely and, more generally, sex (the fourth 'S' after Sun, Sea and Sand) has been both an implicit and explicit part of tourism advertising for many years. For example, the Seychelles were once promoted as islands of love (See Turner and Ash 1975) and at one stage suffered from one of the highest rates of venereal disease in the world.

On the other hand, prostitution as a social impact of tourism must be considered in a broader context. For example, Thailand has a reputation as a 'sex tourism' destination (see Seabrook 1996) The clubs and bars of the Patpong area of Bangkok are frequented by tourists and in popular beach resorts, such as Phuket and Koh Samui, it is easy for Western visitors to find a Thai 'girlfriend' who will remain with them for the duration of their stay. Although the clubs of Bangkok undoubtedly depend on tourism for their business, and prostitution in beach resorts has certainly increased because of tourism, it has been estimated that, overall, there are up to one million Thai women who are involved in prostitution

(Harrison 1992: 25). Of these, it has been alleged that only about seven per cent depend on overseas visitors, indicating that tourism has become the scapegoat for a wider social problem. The real cause of prostitution in Thailand possibly lies in the country's role as a rest and recreation centre for American soldiers during the Vietnam war, cultural norms and practices and, as is the case for most women who turn to prostitution, poverty. In countries without social welfare and with a social and cultural tradition which rejects unmarried mothers, prostitution may offer the only hope of survival. In this sense, and putting the wider moral issues to one side, tourism related prostitution may actually be viewed as a benefit to those concerned.

The conclusion must be that, generally, tourism does not actually cause prostitution but contributes to it, although there are extreme cases, such as young boys in Sri Lanka being forced into male prostitution, where the link is more direct. Nevertheless, the social impact may be devastating, particularly with the spread of AIDS and other sexually transmitted diseases. It may be hoped that the publicity surrounding sex tourism and prostitution, especially in developing countries, will highlight the wider social problems in those countries and lead to greater controls but, at the same time, sex tourism represents the darker side of tourism-induced exploitation of people and their culture.

The Cultural Impacts of Tourism

Many of the impacts of tourism on host destinations and societies are relatively immediate, affecting family and social structures, gender roles, moral behaviour and so on. Over time, the culture of host societies may also change and adapt either directly or indirectly as a result of tourism. Much of the literature concentrates on the way in which cultural forms, such as arts and crafts or animate expressions of culture, such as carnivals, festivals, religious events and historical re-enactments change as a result of tourism-related commoditisation (see Chapter Seven). For example, traditional art forms and techniques may be trivialised and become mass produced for the tourist market, whilst tourism may be responsible for the transformation of cultural events into commercialised, staged spectacles which are devoid of all cultural meaning to the

295

participants. Equally, tourism can provide both the impetus and the financial support for the preservation or revitalisation of traditional cultural practices. One of the principles of sustainable tourism development is that tourism should contribute to the conservation of local culture by, for example, designing and constructing buildings in the vernacular style using traditional materials and methods.

Artefacts, music, festivals and other practices are only symbols and expressions of culture, or cultural products. That is, the true culture of a society refers to its values and norms, its actual identity. It indicates the meanings people attach to different social institutions, such as education, religion, work and leisure, and, in effect, a society's culture is its way of life. All cultures and societies, unless totally isolated from the outside world, are constantly changing and developing, both as a result of changes within society and from outside influences. Internal economic, social and environmental developments within a society may be reflected in broader, cultural change, whilst international communication and information systems, advances in transport technology and a whole host of other factors have contributed to a sharing and dissemination of national cultures around the world. This has been manifested, in particular, in the spread of Western culture, or what has been referred to as the 'coca-colonisation' of the world.

One such factor which has contributed to cultural change is international tourism, especially tourism to countries which, culturally, are significantly different from the tourism generating country. It is difficult to separate the influence of tourism from other factors which induce cultural change and, as a high profile industry, it is frequently blamed for changes that are almost inevitable with or without the development of tourism. But, it is generally accepted that tourism accelerates cultural change through the process of acculturation.

(i)   Tourism and acculturation

The theory of acculturation is that, when two different cultures come into contact, over time they will become more like each other though a process of borrowing (Nuñez 1989). That is, each society, to a greater or lesser extent, will adopt the values and attitudes of the other. By implication, if one culture is stronger or more dominant than the other, then it is more likely that the borrowing process will be one way. The extent to which this will occur is also dependent on a variety of other factors, such as relative social and economic characteristics, the nature of the meeting, and the numbers of people involved. Thus, tourism, as an economic activity based upon inter-action between different societies and cultures, inevitably results in some form of acculturation.

In many instances, tourism induced acculturation may be slight and impossible to differentiate from broader cultural change. Thus, tourism between Europe and North America has little cultural impact when compared with the influence of television and the steady drift of American culture across the Atlantic. In other situations, tourism may be the dominant factor in cultural change, particularly in relatively isolated, developing countries. For example, since the early 1960s, when it became a popular destination for travellers on the Europe to India overland trail, Nepal has become a mainstream tourist destination on the subcontinent (although the area in Kathmandu where the 1960s 'hippies' found lodgings is still known as 'Freak Street'!). From just six thousand arrivals in 1962, about a quarter of a million tourists now visit the country each year (Shackley 1994), only about fourteen per cent of whom go on treks in the mountains. Much of the visible Westernisation of Kathmandu has, therefore, resulted directly from tourism.

The degree of acculturation experienced by a destination society depends on a variety of factors. Different types of tourists have different expectations, demands and motivations and, generally, acculturation is directly linked with the nature of tourist-host encounters (see Chapter Nine). When such encounters are minimal or non-existent, such as when local populations are shielded from tourist resorts, then acculturation will also be limited. For example, most of the tourism development at Monastir on the Tunisian coast is in the *Zone Touristique*; there is little contact between tourists and nearby villages with the result that, in comparison with the tourist towns of Monastir and Sousse, there is little evidence of western culture. Moreover, where tourism is predominantly organised and institutionalised, the level, type and duration of contact

ists and local people and, hence, the potential for
n, is often in the hands of culture brokers. These may be tour
, tour guides, translators or local representatives of holiday
ies, all of whom act as mediators between tourists and local
e. As Mathieson and Wall (1982: 163) explain, by controlling
tourist-host encounters they may also play a positive role in minimising
the social and cultural impacts of tourism.

(ii)   Tourism and Cultural Dependency

In the extreme, the cultural impact of tourism may result in the situation
where the destination society becomes culturally dependent on the
tourism generating country (see Erisman 1983), the difference between
this and acculturation being the degree of control exercised by the local
community. In other words, the implication of acculturation is that the
cultural transformation of a society may be conscious or subconscious
but it is, nevertheless, voluntary. Conversely, cultural dependency is an
involuntary condition, where the culture of a host society is *so
conditioned by and so reflects the expansion of an external culture that
there is a dominant/subordinate relationship between the cultural
centre... and the cultural periphery* (Erisman 1983). It results from
economic and political dependency, a situation that has emerged in some
developing countries which have come to be increasingly reliant on
tourism, and represents foreign control over the cultural development of
society. In a sense, cultural dependency signifies the final stage in the
process of tourism-related neo-colonialism, the final abdication of the
control of a tourism destination's economic, social and cultural future
into the hands of a foreign country. Though not widespread, some
destinations in the West Indies have, according to Erisman, become
culturally dependent on the United States.

Measuring the socio-cultural impacts of tourism

As tourism is developed in more and more countries around the world,
increasing attention is being paid to the impacts of tourism on the society
and culture of host populations. Academics, researchers, pressure groups

and the tourism industry itself are becoming increasingly concerned about the negative effects of tourism and new, alternative forms of tourism are being suggested to minimise these impacts. Sustainable tourism development has become the buzz word of the 1990s, tourism development that respects the environment, optimises benefits to tourists and to local communities and which minimises harmful effects on the tourism environment (for example, see Eber 1992).

It is difficult to argue against the logic of sustainable tourism development although, as suggested in Chapter Eight, it is unlikely to provide in practice any long term solutions to the problems of mass tourism development. There is much controversy about the effectiveness and practical worth of sustainable, alternative tourism in a world that appears to be becoming increasingly polarised between the tourism industry on the one hand and pressure groups on the other, although organisations, such as Green Flag International, work as mediators between the industry and environmental lobbies. But, tourism development has been responsible for a variety of negative impacts around the world, some of which threaten entire eco-systems. The important point is, whilst it is relatively easy to measure or define physical or environmental impacts, applying concepts such as physical or ecological carrying capacity as the limits to development (see O'Reilly 1986), the same cannot be said for socio-cultural impacts. In other words, what are the yardsticks by which social and cultural change are measured, and what are the limits beyond which such change should be halted?

In one respect, any form of tourism which impacts upon the life of local communities beyond an agreeable or acceptable limit (from the point of view of the residents) can be said to have exceeded the destination's social carrying capacity. That is, the scale and type of tourism should, in theory, be restricted to that which optimises economic and social benefits to the local community without causing undue problems. When considering social and cultural change, however, impacts are too often judged according to the values of modern Western societies rather than against the actual needs of the communities in destination areas. Too often, a Western cultural arrogance dictates what is right or wrong for other societies and cultures, societies which should be allowed to benefit from tourism, to modernise, to enjoy the standards of health, education, transport and housing that are taken for granted in the developed world. Similarly, with respect to domestic tourism, it is frequently the residents of towns and cities who try to impose their values on the residents of rural areas with little understanding for the needs of rural communities.

Tourism is a contradictory phenomenon (Crick 1989). It depends upon an attractive environment, yet threatens to destroy it; it trivialises and commoditises cultural production, but can also preserve culture (see Grahn 1991); it brings economic benefits to communities, yet it undermines traditional family and social structure; it provides opportunities for younger people, yet it polarises generations; it can lead to international understanding, yet it reinforces prejudices and international differences. By its very nature, tourism is a source of conflict and the imposition of the values of tourists, in defining the social and cultural limits for tourism development, does little to reduce that conflict. Tourism does have socio-cultural consequences which may be viewed as either positive or negative but the responsibility for assessing those impacts, for setting the limits of change, lies not with tourists or the tourism industry, but with host communities themselves.

Postscript

Tourism and society: towards the future

Predicting the future of any sphere of social or economic activity is fraught with difficulties. At best, a reasonable picture can be built up from the analysis of past trends, historical evidence, relevant current information and educated guesswork; at worst, it can amount to little more than crystal-ball gazing. Attempting to forecast future trends in tourism is no exception. Statistics which detail the historical growth in tourism arrivals, tourism flows and other information can be combined with relevant factors, such as demographic trends and changes in the supply of tourism, to provide a reasonably accurate idea of the shorter term future. But, accurate predictions require accurate information and it is generally accepted that, on a worldwide basis, tourism statistics tend to be of variable quality.

Also, tourism is a notoriously fickle business; it can be affected by exchange rate fluctuations, economic recessions in tourism generating countries, adverse political conditions in destination regions, wars, changes in taste or fashion, and a host of other factors. Nevertheless, since the 1960s, international tourism has grown at a steady, if not spectacular, rate and, in the longer term, has proved to be relatively immune to short term political and economic upheavals. Since 1980, the number of international tourism arrivals has grown at between four and five per cent annually, a rate of growth which is forecast to continue well into the next century.

The World Tourism Organisation has identified two sets of variables which will influence the way in which tourism develops into the future. These are market forces, or factors which include changes in the demand

301

for and supply of tourism products and services, and exogenous variables, factors which although not directly connected with tourism can still have impact upon it. The latter group includes political, economic, legislative, technological and social trends. From a sociological perspective there are factors identifiable in both sets of variables which will combine to influence the future direction and growth of tourism in both a domestic and an international context.

The demand for tourism in the major generating countries will be influenced by a variety of factors. Demographic and social trends, such as ageing populations, increasing numbers of single or childless households, couples having children later in life, the early retired and populations which enjoy greater levels of both free time and disposable income, will result in both the absolute numbers of tourists increasing and an increase in the number of holidays taken by individuals. Importantly, the present middle-aged and younger generations are those which have grown up with tourism. They are used to tourism, they do not see it as a luxury but as an essential feature of modern, social life, and many are experienced tourists. This may result in a two-tier demand structure for tourism, namely, those who are content with the traditional, institutionalised type of package holiday, and those who demand a greater variety of destination and type of holiday. The latter may also become identified as the new type of environmentally-aware tourists, 'good' tourists who demand sustainable tourism products although, as discussed in earlier chapters, this is more likely to result from the cultural (postmodern) values in tourism generating countries than from a genuine concern for the environment.

New tourism-generating countries will also appear on the world tourism map, both as a result of the industrialisation of some developing countries and the spread of democracy. The countries of eastern Europe and the former Soviet Union are regarded as valuable potential source of tourists although political unrest and economic instability will limit growth in the early years. The emergent economic powers in the Far East, such as Korea and Taiwan, will join Japan as major tourism generators, although much of the international travel generated will be inter-regional. These new tourism generators will also become tourist destinations in their own right; the East Asia and Pacific (EAP) region accounted for the largest growth in international arrivals between 1980 and 1990, achieving growth of about ten per cent per annum compared with less than four per cent annual growth in Europe. Such growth is expected to continue: the WTO has forecast that the EAP will become the second largest receiving region in the world by 2010. The European region will continue to be the world's largest generator and receiver of tourism, although its overall share of international arrivals is likely to continue to decline from roughly 59 per cent in 1996 to about 45 per cent in 2010. The growth in tourism will be facilitated by increasing efficiency within the tourism industry, in particular within the context of air transport where technological advances in both aircraft and information/management systems will ensure that, subject to energy costs, prices will remain at a low level. As a result, international tourism is likely to be characterised by ever increasing long-haul, as opposed to intra-regional, travel.

There is optimism that tourism, as an *economic* activity, will maintain and strengthen its reputed position as the world's largest industry. That optimism must be tempered by the recognition that tourism, perhaps more importantly, is a *social* activity. Some societies generate tourism, others receive and depend on tourism; the international travel and tourism industry depends on the continuing desire of individuals to travel. Thus, developments and changes in the structures and values of societies may influence future developments in tourism both positively and negatively. For example, globalisation is a double-edged sword; firstly, it may lead to greater homogenisation, integration and universalisation amongst the world's nations which, as discussed in Chapter Three, may result in either an increase or a decrease in tourism. Secondly, it may lead to a resurgence in nationalism and, perhaps, an eventual reaction against the inherently imperialistic nature of international tourism. Similarly, much of the tourism to destinations outside the developed, western world depends upon and is motivated by the 'otherness', the distinct social and cultural characteristics, of those destinations. Maintaining those characteristics in order to remain attractive to tourists, those destinations may, in the extreme, become little more than 'living museums' satisfying the thirst of tourists for 'authentic' experiences. In short, international tourism may, in the longer term, achieve the opposite of its primary purpose of economic, technological and social modernisation and development in destination countries.

At the same time, tourism will remain a fickle industry, susceptible to a variety of internal and external influences. As more distant, exotic destinations become popular, for example, the use of tourism and tourists for political ends may become more widespread; it is a sad fact but, perhaps, no coincidence that a feature of international tourism in the late 1990s was an increasing incidence of terrorist attacks on tourists. Societal change in tourism generating countries may also influence the future development of tourism. For example, less than one hundred years ago it was unfashionable to have a suntan. If fashions were to change once again, or concern about the cancer risks of sunbathing were to increase, the impact on the traditional sun, sea and sand summer package business could be catastrophic. Changes in work practices and more flexible approaches to education, such as a change in the traditional three term and long summer holiday system of schooling, would be of benefit to tourists, the industry and destinations alike as the constraints of seasonality are removed. In a more general sense, the quality of life in modern, Western countries may improve to the extent that, as Krippendorf (1987) hopes, people will no longer feel the need to escape. Equally, the development of technology, such as virtual reality, or the spread and acceptance of attractions such as the Center Parc concept, may prove to be a more enjoyable and relaxing experience than the 'actual reality' of tourism which is becoming increasingly characterised by crowds, delays, pollution, traffic jams, mass production, and so on. Whatever the future holds for tourism, however, it is essential that knowledge about the interdependence between tourism and the societies that motivate, generate and receive tourists is increased and used to guide its future development to the benefit of all.

References

Abercrombie, N., Warde, A. *et al* (1988) *Contemporary British Society: A New Introduction to Sociology*, Cambridge: Polity Press.

Abram, S., Waldren, J. and Macleod, D. (ed.) (1997) *Tourists and Tourism: Identifying with People and Places*, Oxford: Berg.

Adams, W. (1990) *Green Development: Environment and Sustainability in the Third World*, London: Routledge.

Adler, J. (1989) Origins of Sightseeing, *Annals of Tourism Research* 16 (1): 7-29.

Agarwal, S. (1997) The Resort Cycle and Seaside Tourism: An Assessment of its Applicability and Viability, *Tourism Management* 18 (2): 65-73.

Akis, S., Peristianis, N. and Warner, J. (1996) Resident Attitudes to Tourism Development: The Case of Cyprus, *Tourism Management* 17 (7): 481-494.

Anastasopoulos, P. (1992) Tourism and Attitude Change: Greek Tourists Visiting Turkey, *Annals of Tourism Research* 19 (4): 629-642.

Andronikou, A. (1979) 'Tourism in Cyprus', in E. de Kadt (ed.), *Tourism:Passport to Development?*, New York: Oxford University Press: 237-264.

Ap, J. (1992) Residents' Perceptions on Tourism Impacts, *Annals of Tourism Research* 19 (4): 665-690.

Ap, J. and Crompton, J. (1993) Residents' Strategies for Responding to Tourism Impacts, *Journal of Travel Research* 32 (1): 47-50.

Apostolopoulos, Y., Leivadi, S. and Yiannakis, A. (ed.) (1996) *The Sociology of Tourism: Theoretical and Empirical Investigations*, London: Routledge.

REFERENCES

Ariel de Vidas, A. (1995) Textiles, Memory and the Souvenir Industry in the Andes, in M. Lanfant, J. Allcock and E. Bruner (ed.) *International Tourism: Identity and Change*, London: Sage Publications: 67-83.

Arnould, E. and Price, L. (1993) River Magic: Extraordinary Experience and Extended Service Encounter, *Journal of Consumer Research* 20 (June): 24-45.

Atkins, D. (1994) Britannia Waives the Legroom, *Daily Telegraph*, April 16th

Baran, P. (1963) On the Political Economy of Backwardness, in A. Agarwala and S. Singh (ed.) *The Economics of Underdevelopment*, Oxford: Oxford University Press: 75-92.

Baran, P. (1973) *The Political Economy of Growth*, Harmondsworth, Penguin.

Barthes, R. (1967) *Elements of Sociology*, New York: Hill and Wang.

Bastin, R. (1984) Small Island Tourism: Development or Dependency?, *Development Policy Review* 2 (1): 79-90.

Bates, P. (1994) Pilgrims or Tourists?, *In Focus*, Tourism Concern 11: 14-15.

Baudrillard, J. (1988) *Selected Writings*, Cambridge: Polity Press.

Beioley, S. (1995) Green Tourism - Soft or Sustainable?, *ETB Insights, Vol 6*, London: English Tourist Board: B79-89.

Belisle, F. and Hoy, D. (1980) The Perceived Impact of Tourism by Residents: A Case Study in Santa Marta, Colombia, *Annals of Tourism Research* 7 (1): 83-101.

Belk, R., Wallendorf, M. and Sherry, J. (1989) The Sacred and the Profane in Consumer Behaviour: Theodicy on the Odyssey, *Journal of Consumer Research* 16 (June): 1-38.

Bhattacharyya, D. (1997) Mediating India: An Analysis of a Guidebook, *Annals of Tourism Research* 24 (2): 371-389.

Bilton, T., Bonnett, K., Jones, P., Stanworth, M., Sheard, K. and Webster, A. (1996) *Introductory Sociology, 3rd Edition*, Basingstoke: Macmillan.

Bocock, R. (1993) *Consumption*, London: Routledge.

Boniface, P. and Fowler, P. (1993) *Heritage and Tourism in the Global Village*, London: Routledge.

Boorstin, D. (1964) *The Image: A Guide to Pseudo-Events in America*, New York: Harper & Row.

Boote, A. (1981) Market Segmentation by Personal Values and Salient Product Attributes, *Journal of Advertising Research* 21: 29-35.

Boulding, K. (1992) The Economics of the Coming of Spaceship Earth, in A. Markyanda and J. Richardson (ed.) *The Earthscan Reader in Environmental Economics*, London: Earthscan: 27-35.

Bourdieu, P. (1986) *Distinction: A Social Critique of the Judgement of Taste*, London: Routledge.

Brendon, P. (1991) *Thomas Cook: 150 Years of Popular Tourism*, London: Secker & Warburg.

Britton, R. (1979) The Image of the Third World in Tourism Marketing, *Annals of Tourism Research* 6 (3): 318-329.

Britton, S. (1982) The Political Economy of Tourism in the Third World, *Annals of Tourism Research* 9 (3): 331-358.

Britton, S. (1987) Tourism in Small Developing Countries: Development Issues and Research Needs, in S. Britton and W. Clarke (ed.) *Ambiguous Alternative: Tourism in Small Developing Countries*, Suva: University of the South Pacific: 167-186.

REFERENCES

Britton, S. (1991) Tourism, Capital and Place: Towards a Critical Geography of Tourism, *Environment and Planning D: Society and Space* 9(4): 451-478.

Brohman, J. (1996) New Directions in Tourism for Third World Development, *Annals of Tourism Research* 23(1): 48-70.

Brougham, J. and Butler, R. (1981) A Segmentation Analysis of Resident Attitudes to the Social Impact of Tourism, *Annals of Tourism Research* 8 (4): 569-590.

Browne, K. (1992) *An Introduction to Sociology*, Cambridge: Polity Press.

Buck, R. (1977) The Ubiquitous Tourist Brochure: Explorations of its Intended and Unintended Use, *Annals of Tourism Research* 4 (4): 195-207.

Buck, R. (1978) Towards a Synthesis in Tourism Theory, *Annals of Tourism Research* 5 (1): 110-111.

Budowski, G. (1976) Tourism and Conservation: Conflict, Co-existence or Symbiosis?, *Environmental Conservation* 3 (1): 27-31.

Bull, A. (1995) *The Economics of Travel and Tourism, 2nd Edition*, Melbourne: Longman.

Burkhart, A. and Medlik, S. (1981) *Tourism: Past Present and Future, 2nd Edition*, Oxford: Butterworth Heinemann.

Burns, P. and Holden, A. (1995) *Tourism: A New Perspective*, Hemel Hempstead: Prentice Hall International.

Butler, R. (1980) The Concept of a Tourism Area Cycle of Evolution, *Canadian Geographer* 24: 5-12.

Butler, R. (1980) Alternative Tourism: Pious Hope or Trojan Horse? *Journal of Travel Research* 28 (3): 40-45.

Butler, R. (1991) Tourism, Environment, and Sustainable Development, *Environmental Conservation* 18 (3): 201-209.

Butler, R. (1992) Alternative Tourism: The Thin End of the Wedge, in V. Smith and W. Eadington (ed.) *Tourism Alternatives: Potentials and Problems in the Development of Tourism*, Philadelphia: University of Pennsylvania Press: 31-46.

Buzard, J. (1993) *The Beaten Track*, Oxford: Oxford University Press.

Casson, L. (1974) *Travels in the Ancient World*, London: George Allen and Unwin.

Campbell, C. (1987) *The Romantic Ethic and the Spirit of Modern Consumerism*, Oxford: Blackwell.

Cater, E. (1993) Ecotourism in the Third World: Problems for Sustainable Tourism Development, *Tourism Management* 14 (2): 85-90.

Cavaco, C. (1995) Rural Tourism: The Creation of New Tourist Spaces, in A. Montanari and A. Williams (ed.) *European Tourism: Regions, Spaces and Restructuring*, Chichester: John Wiley & Sons: 129-149.

Cha, S., McCleary, K. and Uysal, M. (1995) Travel Motivations of Japenese Overseas Tourists: A Factor-Cluster Segmentation Approach, *Journal of Travel Research* 34 (1): 33-39.

Chambers, E. (1997) *Tourism and Culture: an Applied Perspective*, Albany: State University of New York Press.

Clarke, J. and Critcher, C. (1985) *The Devil Makes Work: Leisure in Capitalist Britain*, Basingstoke: Macmillan.

Cleverdon, R. (1982) *The Economic and Social Impact of International Tourism in Developing Countries*, London: EIU.

Clift, S. and Grabowski, C.P. (1997) *Tourism and Health*, London: Cassell.

Cohen, E. (1972) Towards a Sociology of International Tourism, *Social Research* 39 (1): 64-82.

REFERENCES

Cohen, E. (1973) Nomads from Affluence: Notes on the Phenomenon of Drifter Tourism, *International Journal of Comparative Sociology* 14 (1-2): 89-103.

Cohen, E. (1974) Who is a Tourist? A Conceptual Clarification, *Sociological Review* 22 (4): 527-555.

Cohen, E. (1979a) Rethinking the Sociology of Tourism, *Annals of Tourism Research* 6 (1): 18-35.

Cohen, E. (1979b) A Phenomenology of Tourist Experiences, *Sociology* 13: 179-201.

Cohen, E. (1984) The Sociology of Tourism: Approaches, Issues and Findings, *Annual Review of Sociology* 10: 373-392.

Cohen, E. (1988a) Authenticity and Commoditisation in Tourism, *Annals of Tourism Research* 15 (3): 371-386.

Cohen, E. (1988b) Traditions in the Qualitative Sociology of Tourism, *Annals of Tourism Research* 15 (1): 29-46.

Cohen, S. and Taylor, L. (1976) *Escape Attempts: The Theory and Practice of Resistance in Everyday Life*, Harmondsworth: Penguin.

Cooper, C. (ed.) (1991) *Progress in Tourism, Recreation and Hospitality Management Vol III*, London: Bellhaven Press.

Cooper, C,. Fletcher, J., Gilbert, D. and Wanhill, S. (1993) *Tourism: Principles & Practice*, London: Pitman.

Coppock, J. (1977) *Second Homes:Curse or Blessing*, Oxford: Pergamon Press.

Craig-Smith, S. (1996) Economic Impact of Tourism in the Pacific, in C.M. Hall and S. Page (ed.) *Tourism in the Pacific: Issues and Cases*, London: International Thomson Business Press: 36-48.

Crick, M. (1989). Representations of International Tourism in the Social Sciences, *Annual Review of Anthropology* 18: 307-344.

Croall, J. (1995) *Preserve or Destroy: Tourism and the Environment*, London: Calouste Gulbenkian Foundation.

Crompton, J. (1979) Motivations for Pleasure Vacation, *Annals of Tourism Research* 6 (4): 408-424.

Cronin, L. (1990) A Strategy for Tourism and Sustainable Developments, *World Leisure and Recreation* 32 (3): 12-18.

Culler, J. (1981) Semiotics of Tourism, *American Journal of Semiotics* 1 (1-2): 127-140.

Curry, S. (1992) Economic Adjustment Policies and the Hotel Sector in Jamaica, in P. Johnson and B. Thomas (ed.) *Perspectives on Tourism Policy*, London: Mansell: 193-213.

D'Amore, L. (1988) Tourism - A Vital Force for Peace, *Annals of Tourism Research* 15 (2): 269-271.

Dalen, E. (1989) Research into Values and Consumer Trends in Norway, *Tourism Management* 10 (3): 183-186.

Damer, S. (1990) *Glasgow: Going for a Song*, London: Lawrence and Wishart.

Dann, G. (1977) Anomie, Ego-Enhancement and Tourism, *Annals of Tourism Research* 4 (4): 184-194.

Dann, G. (1981) Tourist Motivation: An Appraisal, *Annals of Tourism Research* 8 (2): 187-219.

Dann, G. (1989) The Tourist as Child: Some Reflections, *Cahiers de Tourisme*, Série C: 135, Aix-en-Provence: CHET.

REFERENCES

Dann, G. (1994) Tourism: The Nostalgia Industry of the Future, in W. Theobald (ed.) *Global Tourism: The Next Decade*, Oxford: Butterworth Heinemann: 55-67.

Dann, G. (1996) *The Language of Tourism: A Socio-Linguistic Perspective*, Wallingford: CAB International.

Dann, G. (1999) Writing Out the Tourist in Space and Time, *Annals of Tourism Research* 26 (1): 159-187).

Dann, G. and Cohen, E. (1991) Sociology and Tourism, *Annals of Tourism Research* 18 (1): 155-169.

Dann, G., Nash, D. and Pearce, P. (1988) Methodology in Tourism Research, *Annals of Tourism Research* 15 (1): 1-28.

Davidson, R. (1998) *Travel and Tourism in Europe, 2nd Edition*, Harlow: Longman.

Davidson, T. (1994) What are Travel and Tourism: Are They Really an Industry?, in W. Theobald (ed.) *Global Tourism: The Next Decade*, Oxford: Butterworth Heinemann: 20-26.

Davis, F. (1979) *Yearning for Yesterday: A Sociology of Nostalgia*, New York: Free Press.

de Kadt, E (1979) *Tourism: Passport to Development?*, New York: Oxford University Press.

Deitch, L. (1989) The Impact of Tourism on the Arts and Crafts of the Indians of the Southwestern United States, in V. Smith (ed.) *Hosts and Guests:The Anthropology of Tourism, 2nd Edition*, Philadelphia: University of Pennsylvania Press: 223-236.

Department of the Environment (1999) *Transport and the Regions* (www.detr.gov.uk)

Dernoi, L. (1981) Alternative Tourism: Towards a New Style in North-South Relations, *International Journal of Tourism Management* 2 (4): 253-264.

Diamond, J. (1997) Tourism's Role in Economic Development: The Case Re-Examined, *Economic Development and Cultural Change* 25 (3): 539-553.

Dieke, P. (1993) Tourism and Development Policy in The Gambia, *Annals of Tourism Research* 20 (4): 423-449.

Dieke, P. (1995) Tourism and Structural Adjustment Policies in the African Economy, *Tourism Economics* 1 (1): 71-93.

Dilley, R. (1986) Tourist Brochures and Tourist Images, *Canadian Geographer* 30 (1): 59-65.

Dimanche, F. and Havitz, M. (1994) Consumer Behaviour and Tourism: Review and Extension of Four Study Areas, *Journal of Travel and Tourism Marketing* 3 (4): 37-57.

Dos Santos, T. (1970) The Structure of Dependency, *American Economic Review* 60 (2): 231-236.

Dowling, R. (1992) Tourism and Environmental Integration: The Journey from Idealism to Realism, in C. Cooper and A. Lockwood (ed.) *Progress in Tourism, Recreation and Hospitality Management Vol IV*, London: Bellhaven Press: 33-46.

Doxey, G. (1975) A Causatiuon Theory of Visitor-Resident Irritants: Methodology, and Research Inferences, *The Impact of Tourism*, Sixth Annual Conference Proceedings of the Travel Research Association, San Diego, 195-198.

Dunning, J. and McQueen, M. (1982) Multinational Corporations in the Hotel Industry, *Annals of Tourism Research* 9 (1): 69-90.

Eber, S. (ed.) (1992) *Beyond the Green Horizon: Principles for Sustainable Tourism*, Godalming: WWF/Tourism Concern.

313

REFERENCES

EC (1993) *Taking Account of Environment in Tourism Development*, DG XXIII Tourism Unit, Luxembourg: Commission of the European Communities.

Eco, U. (1995) Travels in Hyperreality, in *Faith in Fakes*, London: Minerva: 1-58.

Eagles, P.(1992) The Travel Motivations of Canadian Ecotourists, *Journal of Travel Research* 31 (2): 2-13.

Eagles, P. and Cascagnette, J. (1995) Canadian Ecotourists: Who Are They?, *Tourism Recreation Research* 20 (1): 22-28.

Edwards, A. (1987) *Choosing Holiday Destinations: The Impact of Exchange Rates and Inflation*, Special Report No.1109, London:, Economic Intelligence Unit.

Edwards, E. (1993) The Tourist Icon in Tourism, *In Focus*, Tourism Concern, 6: 4-5.

EIU (1992) Cyprus, *International Tourism Reports No.2*, London: Economic Intelligence Unit.

Emery, F. (1981) Alternative Futures in Tourism, *International Journal of Tourism Management* 2 (1): 241-255.

Erisman, M. (1983) Tourism and Cultural Dependency in the West Indies, *Annals of Tourism Research* 10 (3): 337-361.

ETB (1991) *Tourism and the Environment: Maintaining the Balance*, London: English Tourist Board.

ETB (1993) Holiday Tourism by the British, ETB *Insights, Vol IV* : F-6, London: English Tourist Board.

Explore (1997) *Brochure 1997/98*, Aldershot: Explore Worldwide Ltd.

Feather, N. (1976) *Values in Education and Society*, New York: Free Press.

Featherstone, M. (1990) Perspectives on Consumer Culture, Sociology 24 (1): 5-22.

Featherstone, M. (1991) *Consumer Culture and Postmodernism*, London: Sage Publications.

Feifer, M. (1985) *Going Places*, London: Macmillan.

Fitzgerald, F. 91983) Sociologies of Development, in P. Limqueco and B. McFarlane (ed.) *Neo-Marxist Theories of Development*, Beckenham: Croom Helm: 12-28.

Forster, J. (1964) The Sociological Consequences of Tourism, *International Journal of Comparative Sociology* 5 (2): 217-227.

Frank, A. (1969) The Development of Underdevelopment, *Monthly Review* 18 (4): 17-31.

Galtung, J. (1986) Towards a New Economics: On the Theory and Practice of Self-Reliance, in P. Ekins (ed.) *The Living Economy: A New Economy in the Making*, London: Routledge: 97-109.

Gerakis, A. (1965) The Effects of Exchange Rate Devaluation and Revaluation on Receipts from Tourism, *IMF Papers* 12 (1).

Getz, D. (1991) *Festivals, Special Events and Tourism*, New York: Van Nostrand Reinhold.

Getz, D. (1992) Tourism Planning and Destination Life Cycle, *Annals of Tourism Research* 19 (4): 752-780.

Gilbert, D. (1990) Conceptual Issues in the Meaning of Tourism, in C. Cooper (ed.) *Progress in Tourism, Recreation and Hospitality Management, Volume II*, London: Bellhaven Press: 4-27.

Gilbert, D. (1991) An Examination of the Consumer Behaviour Process Related to Tourism, in C. Cooper (ed.) *Progress in Tourism, Recreation and Hospitality Management, Volume III*, London: Bellhaven Press: 78-105.

REFERENCES

Gilbert, D. and Houghton, P. (1991) An Exploratory Investigation of Format, Design, and Use of UK Tour Operators Brochures, *Journal of Travel Research* 30 (2): 20-25.

Godfrey, K. (1996) Towards Sustainability? Tourism in the Republic of Cyprus, in L. Harrison and W. Husbands (ed.) *Practising Responsible Tourism: International Case Studies in Tourism Planning, Policy and Development*, Chichester: John Wiley & Sons: 58-79.

Goffman, I. (1959) *The Presentation of Self in Everyday Life*, Harmondsworth: Penguin.

Gold, J. and Ward, S. (ed.) (1994) *Place Promotion: The Use of Publicity and Marketing to Sell Towns and Regions*, Chichester: John Wiley & Sons.

Goodall, B. (1991) Understanding Holiday Choice, in C. Cooper (ed.) *Progress in Tourism, Recreation and Hospitality Management, Volume III*, London: Bellhaven Press: 58-77.

Goodland, R. (1992) The Case That The World has Reached Its Limits, in R. Goodland *et al* (ed.) *Environmentally Sustainable Economic Development: Building on Brundtland*, Paris: UNESCO: 15-27.

Gottlieb, A. (1982) Americans' Vacations, *Annals of Tourism Research* 9 (2): 165-187.

Goulet, D. (1968) On the Goals of Development, *Cross Currents* 18: 387-405.

Goulet, D. (1992) Development: Creator and Destroyer of Values, *World Development* 20 (3): 467-475.

Grabler, K., Maier, G., Mazanec, J. and Wöber, K. (1997) *International City Tourism: Analysis and Strategy*, London: Pinter.

Graburn, N. (1976) *Ethnic and Tourist Arts: Cultural Expressions from the Fourth World*, Berkeley: University of California Press.

Graburn, N. (1983) The Anthropology of Tourism, *Annals of Tourism Research* 10(1): 9-33.

Graburn, N. (1989) Tourism: The Sacred Journey, in V. Smith (ed.) *Hosts and Guests: The Anthropology of Tourism, 2nd Edition*, Philadelphia: University of Pennsylvania Press: 21-36.

Grahn, P. (1991) Using Tourism to Protect Existing Culture: A Project in Swedish Lapland, *Leisure Studies* 10 (1): 33-47.

Grant, D. and Mason, S. (1998) *Holiday Law, 2nd Edition*, London: Sweet and Maxwell.

Gray, H. (1970) *International Travel-International Trade*, Lexington: DC Heath.

Gray, H. (1982) The Contributions of Economics to Tourism, *Annals of Tourism Research* 9 (1): 105-125.

Gray, T. (1884) *Journal in the Lakes*, London: Macmillan.

Greenwood, D. (1989) Culture by the Pound: An Anthropological Perspective on Tourism as Cultural Commoditisation, in V. Smith (ed.) *Hosts and Guests: The Anthropology of Tourism 2nd Edition*, Philadelphia: University of Pennsylvania Press: 171-185.

Hall, D. (1993) Tourism in Eastern Europe, in W. Pompl and P. Lavery (ed.) *Tourism in Europe: Structures and Develoipments*, Wallingford: CAB International: 341-358.

Hall, S., Held, D. and McLennan, G. (1992a) Introduction, in S. Hall, D. Held and T. McGrew (ed.) *Modernity and its Futures*, Cambridge: Polity Press: 1-11.

Hall, S., Held, D. and McGrew, T. (ed.) (1992b) *Modernity and its Futures*, Cambridge: Polity Press.

Harkin, M. (1995) Modernist Anthropology and Tourism of the Authentic, *Annals of Tourism Research* 22 (3): 650-670.

REFERENCES

Harrigan, J. and Mosley, P. (1991) Evaluating the Impact of World Bank Structural Adjustment Lending, *Journal of Development Studies* 27(3): 63-94.

Harrison, C. (1991) *Countryside Recreation in a Changing Society*, London: TMS Partnership.

Harrison, D. (1988) *The Sociology of Modernisation and Development*, London: Routledge.

Harrison, D. (ed.) (1992a) *Tourism and the Less Developed Countries*, London: Bellhaven Press.

Harrison, D. (1992b) Tourism to Less Developed Countries: The Social Consequences, in D. Harrison (ed.) *Tourism and the Less Developed Countries*. London: Bellhaven Press: 19-34.

Harrison, L. and Husbands, W. (ed.) *Practising Responsible Tourism: International Case Studies in Tourism Planning, Policy and Development*, Chichester: John Wiley & Sons.

Harvey, D. (1990) *The Condition of Postmodernity*, Oxford: Blackwell.

Haywood, M. (1988) Responsible and Responsive Tourism Planning in the Community, *Tourism Management* 9 (2): 105-118.

Herbert, D. (ed.) (1995) *Heritage, Tourism and Society*, London: Pinter.

Hewison, R. (1987) *The Heritage Industry: Britain in a Climate of Decline*, London: Methuen.

Hewison, R. (1993) Field of Dreams, *The Sunday Times*, January 3rd.

Hoggart, K., Buller, H. and Black, R. (1995) *Rural Europe: Identity and Change*, London: Arnold.

Høivik, T. and Heiberg, T. (1980) Centre-Periphery Tourism and Self-Reliance, *International Social Science Journal* 32 (1): 69-98.

Holbrook, M. and Hirschman, E. (1982) The Experiential Aspects of Consumption: Consumer Fantasies, Feelings and Fun, *Journal of Consumer Research* 9: 132-140.

Holden, P. (ed) (1984) *Alternative Tourism with a Focus on Asia*, Bangkok: ECTWT.

Hollinshead, K. (1993) *The Truth About Texas: a Naturalistic Study of the Construction of Heritage*, Unpublished PhD Thesis, Austin: Texas A&M University.

Holloway, J. C. (1998) *The Business of Tourism, 5th Edition*, Harlow: Longman.

Holloway, J. C. and Plant, R. (1992) *Marketing for Tourism*, London: Pitman Publishing.

Holt, D. (1995) How Consumers Consume: A Typology of Consumption Practices, *Journal of Consumer Research* 22 (June): 1-16.

Hughes, G. (1995) Authenticity in Tourism, *Annals of Tourism Research* 22 (4): 781-803.

Hunter, C. (1995) On the Need to Re-Conceptualise Sustainable Tourism Development, *Journal of Sustainable Tourism* 3 (3): 155-165.

Hvengaard, G. (1994) Ecotourism: A Status Report and Conceptual Framework, *Journal of Tourism Studies* 5 (2): 24-35.

Inskeep, I. and Kallenberger, M. (1992) *An Integrated Approach to Resort Development, Six Case Studies*, Madrid: World Tourism Organisation.

Ioannides, D. (1992) Tourism Development Agents: The Cypriot Resort Cycle, *Annals of Tourism Research* 19 (4): 711-731.

Iso-Ahola, S. (1982) Toward a Social Psychological Theory of Tourism Motivation: A Rejoinder, *Annals of Tourism Research* 9 (2): 256-262.

REFERENCES

IUCN (1991) *Caring for the Earth: A Strategy for Sustainable Living,* Gland, Switzerland: World Conservation Union.

Jafari, J. (1977) Editors Page, *Annals of Tourism Research* 5 (1): 8.

Jafari, J. (1989) Sociocultural Dimensions of Tourism: An English Language Literature Review, in J. Bystrzanowski (ed.) *Tourism as a Factor of Change: A Sociocultural Study,* Vienna: Vienna Centre: 17-60.

Jameson, F. (1984) Postmodernism, or the Cultural Logic of Late Capitalism, *New Left Review,* 146: 53-92.

Jary, D. and Jary, J. (1991) *Collins Dictionary of Sociology,* London: Harper Collins.

Jebb, M. (1986) *Walkers,* London: Constable.

Jenkins, C. (1980) Tourism Policies in Developing Countries: A Critique, *International Journal of Tourism Management* 1 (1): 22-29.

Jenkins, C. (1990) Tourism: Is Future Demand Changing? in M. Quest (ed.), *The Horwath Book of Tourism,* London: Macmillan: 46-55.

Jenkins, C. (1991) Tourism Development Strategies, in L. Likorish (ed.), *Developing Tourism Destinations,* Harlow: Longman: 61-77.

Jenner, P. and Smith, C. (1992) *The Tourism Industry and the Environment,* Special Report No.2453, London: Economic Intelligence Unit.

Johnson, P. and Thomas, B. (ed.) (1992) *Choice and Demand in Tourism,* London: Mansell Publishing.

Kahle, L., Beatty, S. and Homer, P. (1986) Alternative Measurement Approaches to Consumer Values: The List of Values (LOV) and Values and Lifestyles (VALS), *Journal of Consumer Research* 13: 405-409.

Kamakura, W. and Mazzon, J. (1991) Value Segmentation: A Model for the Measurement of Values and Value Systems, *Journal of Consumer Research* 18: 208-218.

Kariel, H. (1989) Tourism and Development: Perplexity or Panacea?, *Journal of Travel Research* 28 (1): 2-6.

Kinnaird, V. and Hall, D. (ed.) *Tourism: A Gender Analysis*, Chichester: John Wiley & Sons.

Klemm, M. (1992) Sustainable Tourism Development: Languedoc-Roussillon Thirty Years On, *Tourism Management* 13 (2): 169-180.

Krippendorf, J. (1986) Tourism in the System of Industrial Society, *Annals of Tourism Research* 13 (4): 517-532.

Krippendorf, J. (1987) *The Holiday Makers*, Oxford: Heinemann.

Lash, S. (1990) *Sociology of Postmodernism*, London: Routledge;

Lash, S. and Urry, J. (1987) *The End of Organised Capitalism*, Cambridge: Polity.

Lea, J. (1988) *Tourism and Development in the Third World*, London: Routledge.

Lee, G. (1987) Tourism as a Factor in Development Co-Operation, *Tourism Management* 8 (1): 2-19.

Lélé, S. (1991) Sustainable Development: A Critical Review, *World Development* 19 (6): 607-621.

Lett, J. (1983) Ludic and Liminoid Aspects of Charter Yacht Tourism in the Caribbean, *Annals of Tourism Research* 10 (1): 35-56.

Lett, J. (1989) Epilogue to Touristic Studies in Anthropological Perspective, in V. Smith (ed.) *Hosts and Guests: The Anthropology of Tourism, 2nd Edition*, Philadelphia: University of Pennsylvania Press: 275-279.

Lickorish, L. (1990) Tourism Facing Change, in M. Quest (ed.) *The Horwath Book of Tourism*, London: Macmillan: 108-127.

REFERENCES

Lillywhite, M. and Lillywhite, L. (1991) Low Impact Tourism, in D. Hawkins and J. Brent Ritchie (ed.) *World Travel and Tourism Review: Indicators, Trends and Forecasts*, Wallingford: CAB International: 162-169.

Loker-Murphy, L. and Pearce, P. (1995) Young Budget Travellers: Backpackers in Australia, *Annals of Tourism Research* 22 (4): 819-843.

Lowenthal, D. (1990) *The Past is a Foreign Country*, Cambridge: Cambridge University Press.

Lowyck, E., Van Langenhove, L. and Bollaert, L. (1992) Typologies of Tourist Roles, in P. Johnson and B. Thomas (ed.)*Choice and Demand in Tourism*, London: Mansell Publishing: 13-32.

Ludwig, D., Hilborn, R. and Walters, C. (1993) Uncertainty, Resource Exploitation, and Conservation: Lessons from History, *Science* 269, No 5104: 17 & 36.

Luk, S., de Leon, C., Leong, F. and Li, E. (1993) Value Segmentation of Tourists' Expectations of Service Quality, *Journal of Travel and Tourism Marketing* 2 (4): 23-38.

Lumley, R. (ed.) (1988) *The Museum Time-Machine*, London: Routledge.

Lury, C. (1996) *Consumer Culture*, Cambridge: Polity Press.

Lyotard, J. (1984) *The Postmodern Condition: A Report on Knowledge*, Manchester: Manchester University Press.

Mabogunje, A. (1980) *The Development Process: A Spatial Perspective*, London: Hutchinson.

MacCannell, D. (1973) Staged Authenticity: Arrangements of Social Space in Tourist Settings, *American Journal of Sociology* 79: 589-603.

MacCannell, D. (1976) *The Tourist: A New Theory of the Leisure Class*, New York: Shocken Books.

MacCannell, D. (1989) *The Tourist: A New Theory of the Leisure Class, 2nd Edition*, New York: Shocken Books.

Macnaughten, P. and Urry, J. (1998) *Contested Natures*, London: Sage Publications.

Macnaught, T. (1982) Mass Tourism and the Dilemmas of Modernisation in Pacific Island Communities, *Annals of Tourism Research* 9 (3): 359-381.

Madrigal, R. and Kahle, L. (1994) Predicting Vacation Activity Preferences on the Basis of Value-System Segmentation, *Journal of Travel Research* 32 (3): 22-28.

Mannell, R. and Iso-Ahola, S. (1987) Psychological Nature of Leisure and Tourism Experience, *Annals of Tourism Research* 14 (3): 314-331.

Mansfeld, Y. (1992) From Motivation to Actual Travel, *Annals of Tourism Research* 19 (3): 399-419.

Maslow, A. (1943) A Theory of Human Motivation, *Psychological Review* 50: 370-396.

Matthews, H. and Richter, L. (1991) Political Science and Tourism, *Annals of Tourism Research* 18(1): 120-135.

Mathieson, A. and Wall, G. (1982) *Tourism: Economic, Physical and Social Impacts*, Harlow: Longman.

Mayo, E. (1975) Tourism and National Parks: A Psychographic and Attitudinal Study, *Journal of Travel Research* 14(1): 14-17.

McCarthy, T. (1994) Booking Trends, *Travel Weekly Plus* 2, March, p.35.

McCracken, G. (1986) Culture and Consumption: A Theoretical Account of the Structure and Movement of the Cultural Meaning of Consumer Goods, *Journal of Consumer Research* 13: 71-84.

McGrew, A. (1992) A Global Society?, in S. Hall, D. Held, and T. McGrew (ed.) *Modernity and its Futures,* Cambridge: Polity Press: 61-116.

323

REFERENCES

McIntosh, R. and Goeldner, C. (1990) *Tourism:Principles,Practices and Philosophies*, New York: Wiley.

McKean, P. (1989) Towards a Theoretical Analysis of Tourism: Economic Dualism and Cultural Involution in Bali, in V. Smith (ed.) *Hosts and Guests:The Anthropology of Tourism, 2nd Edition*, Philadelphia: University of Pennsylvania Press: 119-138.

McKercher, B. (1993) Some Fundamental Truths About Tourism, *Journal of Sustainable Tourism* 1 (1): 6-16.

McLennan, G. (1992) The Enlightenment Project Revisited, in S. Hall, D. Held and T. McGrew (ed.) *Modernity and its Futures,*Cambridge: Polity Press: 327-377.

McPheters, L. and Stronge, W. (1974) Crime as an Environmental Externality of Tourism, *Land Economics* 50: 359-381.

McQueen, M. (1983) Appropriate Policies Towards Multinational Hotel Corporations in Developing Countries, *World Development* 11 (2): 141-152.

Middleton, V. (1988) *Marketing in Travel and Tourism*, Oxford: Heinemann.

Middleton, V. (1998) *Sustainable Tourism: A Marketing Approach,* Oxford: Butterworth Heinemann.

Mill, R. and Morrison, A. (1985) *The Tourism System*, New Jersey: Prentice Hall International.

Miller, D. (1987) *Material Culture and Mass Consumption*, Oxford: Blackwell.

Millman, R.. (1989) Pleasure Seeking vs the 'Greening' of World Tourism, *Tourism Management* 10 (4): 275-278.

Milman, A., Reichal, A. and Pizam, A. (1990) The Impact of Tourism on Ethnic Attitudes: The Israeli-Egyptian Case, *Journal of Travel Research* 29 (2): 45-49.

Mintel (1994) *The Green Consumer I: The Green Conscience,* London: Mintel International.

Mishan, E. (1969) *The Costs of Economic Growth,* Harmondsworth: Penguin.

Mosley, P. and Toye, J. (1988) The Design of Structural Adjustment Programmes, *Development Policy Review* 6 (4): 395-413.

Moutinho, L. (1987) Consumer Behaviour in Tourism, *European Journal of Marketing* 21 (10): 5-44.

Mowforth, M. and Munt, I. (1998) *Tourism and Sustainability: New Tourism in the Third World,* London: Routledge.

Müller, T. (1991) Using Personal Values to Define Segments in an International Tourism Market, *International Marketing Review* 8 (1): 57-70.

Munt, I. (1994) The 'Other' Postmodern Tourism: Culture, Travel and the New Middle Classes, *Theory, Culture and Society* 11 (3): 101-123.

Murphy, P. (1983) Tourism as a Community Industry, *Tourism Management* 4 (3): 180-193.

Murphy, P. (1985) *Tourism: A Community Approach,* London: Routledge.

Murphy, P. (1988) Community Driven Tourism Planning, *Tourism Management* 9 (2): 96-104.

Murray, R. (1989) Fordism and Post-Fordism, in S. Hall and M. Jacques (ed.) *New Times,* London: Lawrence & Wishart.

Nash, D. (1981) Tourism as an Anthropological Subject, *Current Anthropology* 22 (5): 461-481.

Nash, D. (1989) Tourism as a Form of Imperialism, in V. Smith (ed.) *Hosts and Guests:The Anthropology of Tourism, 2nd Edition,* Philadelphia: University of Pennsylvania Press: 37-52.

REFERENCES

Nash, D. (1996) *Anthropology of Tourism*, Oxford: Pergamon Press.

Nash, D. and Smith, V. (1991) Anthropology and Tourism, *Annals of Tourism Research* 18 (1): 12-25.

Novak, T. and MacEvoy, B. (1990) On Comparing Alternative Segmentation Schemes: The List of Values (LOV) and Values and Lifestyles (VALS), *Journal of Consumer Research* 17: 105-109.

Nuñez, T. (1963) Tourism, Tradition and Acculturation: Weekendismo in a Mexican Village, *Ethnology* 2 (3): 347-352.

Nuñez, T. (1989) Touristic Studies in Anthropological Perspective, in V. Smith (ed.) *Hosts and Guests: The Anthropology of Tourism, 2nd Edition*, Philadelphia: University of Pennsylvania Press: 265-274.

Opperman, M. (1993) Tourism Space in Developing Countries, *Annals of Tourism Research* 20 (4): 535-556.

Opperman, M. and Chon, K. (1997) *Tourism in Developing Countries*, London: International Thomson Business Press.

O'Reilly, A. (1986) Tourism Carrying Capacity: Concept and Issues, *Tourism Management* 7 (4): 254-258.

Osborne, C. (1993) Making the Most out of Tourism, *In Focus*, Tourism Concern, 10: 10-11.

Ousby, I. (1990) *The Englishman's England: Taste, Travel and the Rise of Tourism*, Cambridge: Cambridge University Press.

Owen, R. (1991) *A New View of Society and Other Writings*, Harmondsworth: Penguin.

Page, S. and Getz, D. (ed.) (1997) *The Business of Rural Tourism: International Perspectives*, London: International Thomson Business Press.

Palma, G. (1995) Underdevelopment and Marxism: from Marx to the Theories of Imperilaism and Dependency, in R. Ayers (ed.) *Development*

Studies: An Introduction through Selected Readings, Dartford: Greenwich University Press: 161-210.

Parker, S. (1983) *Leisure and Work*, London: Allen and Unwin.

Parrinello, G. (1993) Motivation and Anticipation in Post-Industrial Tourism, *Annals of Tourism Research* 20 (2): 233-249.

Passariello, P. (1983) Never on Sunday? Mexican Tourists at the Beach, *Annals of Tourism Research*, 10 (1): 109-122.

Pastor, M. (1987) The Effects of IMF Programs in the Third World: Debate and Experience from Latin America, *World Development* 15 (2): 249-262.

Pearce, D. and Butler, R. (ed.). (1992) *Tourism Research: Critiques and Challenges*, London: Routledge.

Pearce, P. (1982) *The Social Psychology of Tourist Behaviour*, Oxford: Pergamon Press.

Pearce, P. (1988) *The Ulysses Factor*, New York: Springer-Verlag.

Pearce, P. (1992) Fundamentals of Tourist Motivation, in D. Pearce and R. Butler (ed.) *Tourism Research: Critiques and Challenges*, London: Routledge: 113-134.

Pearce, P. (1994) Tourist-Resident Impacts: Examples, Explanations and Emerging Solutions, in W. Theobald (ed.) *Global Tourism: The Next Decade*, Oxford: Butterworth Heinemann: 103-123.

Pearce, P. and Caltabianao, M. (1983) Inferring Travel Motivation from Travellers Experiences, *Journal of Travel Research* 22: 16-20.

Pearce, P. and Moscardo, G. (1986) The Concept of Authenticity in Tourist Settings, *Australian and New Zealand Journal of Sociology* 22 (1): 121-132.

Perdue, R., Long, P. and Allen, L. (1987) Rural Resident Tourism Perceptions and Attitudes, *Annals of Tourism Research* 14 (3): 420-429.

REFERENCES

Perlmutter, H. (1991) On the Rocky Road to the First Global Civilisation, *Human Relations* 44 (9): 897-1010.

Pfaffenberger, B. (1983) Serious Pilgrims and Frivolous Tourists, *Annals of Tourism Research* 10 (1): 57-74.

Picard, M. (1995) Cultural Heritage and Tourist Capital: Cultural Tourism in Bali, in M. Lanfant, J. Allcock and E. Bruner (ed.) *International Tourism: Identity and Change*, London: Sage Publications: 44-66.

Pimlott, J. (1947) *The Englishman's Holiday*, London: Faber & Faber.

Pitts, R. and Woodside, A. (1986) Personal Values and Travel Decisions, *Journal of Travel Research* 25 (1): 20-25.

Pi-Sunyer, O. (1989) Changing Perceptions of Tourism and Tourists in a Catalan Resort Town, in V. Smith (ed.) *Hosts and Guests: The Anthropology of Tourism, 2nd Edition*, Philadelphia: University of Pennsylvania Press: 187-199.

Pizam, A. (1978) Tourism's Impacts: The Social Cost to the Destination Community as Perceived by its Residents, *Journal of Travel Research* 16 (1): 8-12.

Pizam, A. and Calantone, R. (1987) Beyond Psychographics - Values as Determinants of Tourist Behaviour, *International Journal of Hospitality Management* 6 (3): 177-181.

Pizam, A. and Mansfeld, Y (ed.) (1996) *Tourism, Crime and International Security Issues*, Chichester: John Wiley & Sons.

Pizam, A., Milman, A. and Jafari, J. (1991) Influence of Tourism on Attitudes: US Students Visiting USSR, *Tourism Management* 12 (1): 47-54.

Plog, S. (1977) Why Destination Areas Rise and Fall in Popularity, in E. Kelly (ed.) *Domestic and International Tourism*, Wellesley, Mass.: Institute of Certified Travel Agents.

Pompl, W. and Lavery, P. (1993) *Tourism in Europe: Structures and Developments*, Wallingford: CAB International.

Poon, A. (1993) *Tourism, Technology and Competitive Strategies*, Wallingford: CAB International.

Porritt, J. (1984) *Seeing Green*, Oxford: Blackwell.

Pretes, M. (1995) Postmodern Tourism: The Santa Claus Industry, *Annals of Tourism Research* 22 (1): 1-15.

Pritchard, A. and Morgan, N. (1995) Evaluating Vacation Destination Brochure Images: the Case of Local Authorities in Wales, *Journal of Vacation Marketing* 2 (1): 23-38.

Rattachumpoth, R. (1992) Phuket: Holiday Paradise Where Locals Are Banned, *Contours* 5 (8): 13-15.

Redclift, M. (1987) *Sustainable Development: Exploring the Contradictions*, London: Routledge.

Reid, D. (1995) *Sustainable Development: An Introductory Guide*, London: Earthscan.

Reynoso y Valle, A. and de Regt, J. (1979) Growing Pains: Planned Development in Ixtapa-Zihuatanejo, in E. de Kadt (ed.) *Tourism: Passport to Development?*, New York: Oxford University Press: 111-134.

Richter, L. (1983) Tourism Politics and Political Science: A Case of Not So Benign Neglect, *Annals of Tourism Research* 10 (3): 313-335.

Richter, L. and Waugh, W. (1986) Terrorism and Tourism as Logical Companions, *Tourism Management* 7 (4): 230-238.

Riley, P. (1988) Road Culture of International Long-Term Budget Travellers, *Annals of Tourism Research* 15 (3): 313-328.

Ritzer, G. (1996) *The McDonaldisation of Society, Revised Edition*, Thousand Oaks, California: Pine Forge Press.

REFERENCES

Robinson, M. and Boniface, P. (1999) *Tourism and Cultural Conflicts*, Wallingford: CAB International.

Roche, M. (1992) Mega-Events and Micro-Modernisation: On the Sociology of New Urban Tourism, *British Journal of Sociology* 43 (3): 563-600.

Rojek, C. (1993) *Ways of Escape*, Basingstoke: Macmillan.

Rojek, C. and Urry, J. (ed.) (1998) *Touring Cultures*, London: Routledge.

Rokeach, M. (1973) *The Nature of Human Values*, New York: The Free Press.

Rosenow, J. and Pulsipher, G. (1979) *Tourism: The Good, The Bad and The Ugly*, Lincoln: Three Centuries Press.

Ross, G. (1994) *The Psychology of Tourism*, Melbourne: Hospitality Press.

Rostow, W. (1960) *The Stages of Economic Growth: A Non-Communist Manifesto*, Cambridge: Cambridge University Press.

Rothman, R. (1978) Residents and Transients: Community Reaction to Seasonal Visitors, *Journal of Travel Research* 16: 8-13

Ryan, C. (1991) *Recreational Tourism: A Social Science Perspective*, London: Routledge.

Ryan, C. (1991b) Tourism, Terrorism and Violence: The Risks of Wider World Travel, *Conflict Studies 244*, London: Research Institute for the Study of Conflict and Terrorism.

Ryan, C. (1997) The Chase of a Dream, the End of a Play, in C. Ryan (ed.) *The Tourist Experience: A New Introduction*, London: Cassell: 1-24.

Schmoll, G. (1977) *Tourism Promotion,* London: Tourism International Press.

Schumacher, E. (1974) *Small is Beautiful: A Study of Economics as if People Mattered*, London: Abacus.

Seabrook, J. (1996) *Travels in the Skin Trade: Tourism and the Sex Industry*, London: Pluto Press.

Seers, D. (1969)The Meaning of Development, *International Development Review* 11 (4): 2-6.

Seers, D. (1977) The New Meaning of Development, *International Development Review* 19 (3): 2-7.

Selwyn, T. (1992) Tourism, Society and Development, *Community Development Journal* 27 (4): 353-36.

Selwyn, T. (ed.) (1996) *The Tourist Image: Myths and Myth Making in Tourism*, Chichester: John Wiley & Sons.

Shackley, M. (1994) The Land of Lo, Nepal/Tibet: The First Eight Months of Tourism, *Tourism Management* 15 (1): 17-26.

Sharpley, R. (1996a) Tourism and Consumer Culture in Postmodern Society, in M. Robinson *et al* (ed.) *Tourism and Cultural Change*, Sunderland: Business Education Publishers: 203-216.

Sharpley, R. (1996b) *Tourism and Leisure in the Countryside, 2nd Edition*, Huntingdon: Elm Publications.

Sharpley, R. (1998) *Tourism and Sustainable Development: A Theoretical and Empirical Analysis*, Unpublished PhD thesis, Lancaster University.

Sharpley, R. (1998b) *Island Tourism Development: The Case of Cyprus*, Newcastle: Centre for Travel and Tourism.

Sharpley, R. and Sharpley, J. (1996) Tourism in West Africa: The Gambian Experience, in A. Badger *et al* (ed.) *Trading Places: Tourism as Trade*, Wimbledon: Tourism Concern: 27-33.

Shaw, G. and Williams, A. (1994) *Critical Issues in Tourism: A Geographical Perspective*, Oxford: Blackwell.

REFERENCES

Shaw, G. and Williams, A. (1997) *The Rise and Fall of British Coastal Resorts: Cultural and Economic Perspectives*, London: Mansell Publishing.

Sheldon, P. and Var, T. (1984) Resident Attitudes Towards Tourism in North Wales, *Tourism Management* 5 (1): 40-48.

Shields, R. (1991) *Places on the Margin: Alternative Geographies of Modernity*, London: Routledge.

Shih, D. (1986) VALS as a Tool of Tourism Market Research: The Pennsylvania Approach, *Journal of Travel Research* 24 (4): 2-11.

Short, J.(1991) *Imagined Country: Society, Culture and Environment*, London: Routledge.

Sigaux, G. (1966) *History of Tourism*, London: Leisure Arts Ltd.

Silver, I. (1993) Marketing Authenticity in Third World Countries, *Annals of Tourism Research* 20 (2): 302-318.

Silverberg, K., Backman, S. and Backman, K, (1996) A Preliminary Investigation into the Psychographics of Nature-Based Travellers to the South-Eastern United States, *Journal of Travel Research* 35 (2): 19-28.

Simpson, B. (1993) Tourism and Tradition: From Healing to Heritage, *Annals of Tourism Research* 20 (2): 164-181.

Sinclair, M. T. (1997) *Gender, Work and Tourism*, London: Routledge.

Smith, V. (ed.) (1977) *Hosts and Guests: the Anthropology of Tourism, 1st Edition*, Philadelphia: University of Pennsylvania Press.

Smith, S. (1990) A test of Plog's Allocentric/Psychcentric Model: Evidence from Seven Nations, *Journal of Travel Research* 28 (4): 40-43.

Smith, V. (ed.) (1989) *Hosts and Guests: the Anthropology of Tourism, 2nd Edition*, Philadelphia: University of Pennsylvania Press.

Smith, V. (1989) Eskimo Tourism: Micro-Models and Marginal Men, in V. Smith (ed.) *Hosts and Guests: the Anthropology of Tourism, 2nd Edition*, Philadelphia: University of Pennsylvania Press: 55-82.

Smith, V. and Eadington, W. (ed.) (1992) *Tourism Alternatives: Potentials and Problems in the Development of Tourism*, Philadelphia: University of Pennsylvania Press.

Solomon, M. (1994) *Consumer Behaviour: Buying, Having and Being,* 2nd Edition, Needham Heights, Mass.: Allyn and Bacon.

Stanton, M. (1989) The Polynesian Cultural Centre: A Multi-Ethnic Model of Seven Pacific Cultures, in V. Smith (ed.) *Hosts and Guests: the Anthropology of Tourism, 2nd Edition*, Philadelphia: University of Pennsylvania Press: 247-262.

Steele, P. (1995) Ecotourism: An Economic Analysis, *Journal of Sustainable Tourism* 3 (1): 29-44.

Streeten, P. (1977) The Basic Features of a Basic Needs Approach to Development, *International Development Review* 3: 8-16.

Sutton, W. (1967) Travel and Understanding: Notes on the Social Structure of Touring, *International Journal of Comparative Sociology* 8: 217-233.

Swingewood, A. (1991) *A Short History of Sociological Thought*, Basingstoke: Macmillan.

Taylor, George. (1995) The Community Approach: Does It Really Work?, *Tourism Management* 16 (7): 487-489.

Taylor, Gordon. (1994) Styles of Travel, in W. Theobald (ed.) *Global Tourism: The Next Decade*, Oxford: Butterworth Heinemann: 188-198.

Theobald, W. (1994) The Context, Meaning and Scope of Tourism, in W. Theobald (ed.) *Global Tourism: The Next Decade*, Oxford: Butterworth Heinemann: 3-19.

333

REFERENCES

Thompsons (1994) Winter Sun Brochure, London: Thomson Holidays.

Thompson, K. (1992) Social Pluralism and Post-Modernity, in S. Hall, D. Held and T. McGrew (ed.) *Modernity and its Futures*, Cambridge: Polity Press: 221-271.

Thrane, C. (1997) Values as Segmentation Criteria in Tourism Research: The Norwegian Monitor Approach, *Tourism Management* 18 (2): 111-113.

Thurot, J. and Thurot, G. (1983) The Ideology of Class and Tourism: Confronting the Discourse of Advertising, *Annals of Tourism Research*, 10 (1): 173-189.

Todaro, M. (1994) *Economic Development in the Third World, 5th Edition*, Harlow: Longman.

Towner, J. (1984) The Grand Tour: Sources and a Methodology for an Historical Study of Tourism, *Tourism Management* 5 (3): 215-222.

Towner, J. (1985) The Grand Tour: A Key Phase in the History of Tourism, *Annals of Tourism Research* 12 (3): 297-333.

Towner, J. (1988) Approaches to Tourism History, *Annals of Tourism Research* 15 (1): 47-62.

Towner, J. (1995) What is Tourism's History?, *Tourism Management* 16 (5): 339-343.

Towner, J. (1996) *An Historical Geography of Recreation and Tourism in the Western World 1540-1940*, Chichester: John Wiley & Sons.

Travis, A. (1982) Physical Impacts: Trends Affecting Tourism. Managing the Environmental and Cultural Impacts of Tourism and Leisure Development, *Tourism Management* 3 (4): 256-262.

Trilling, L. (1974) *Sincerity and Authenticity*, Oxford Paperbacks, London: Oxford University Press.

Tsartas, P. (1992) Socioeconomic Impacts of Tourism on Two Greek Isles, *Annals of Tourism Research* 19 (3): 516-53.

Tunbridge, J. and Ashworth, G. (1996) *Dissonant Heritage: the Management of the Past as a Resource in Conflict*, Chichester: John Wiley & Sons.

Turner, L. and Ash, J. (1975) *The Golden Hordes: International Tourism and the Pleasure Periphery*, London: Constable.

Turner, V. (1973) The Centre out There: the Pilgrim's Goal, *History of Religions* 10: 191-230.

Turner, V. and Turner, E. (1978) *Image and Pilgrimage in Christian Culture*, New York: Columbia University Press.

UNDP (1990) *Human Development Report*, New York: Oxford University Press.

UNESCO (1976) The Effects of Tourism on Socio-Cultural Values, *Annals of Tourism Research* 4 (1): 74-105.

Urry, J. (1988) Cultural Change and Contemporary Holiday-Making, *Theory, Culture and Society* 5: 35-55.

Urry, J. (1990a) *The Tourist Gaze*, London: Sage Publications.

Urry, J. (1990b) The Consumption of Tourism, *Sociology* 24 (1): 23-35.

Urry, J. (1992) The Tourist Gaze and the Environment, *Theory, Culture and Society* 9: 1-26.

Urry, J. (1994) Cultural Change and Contemporary Tourism, *Leisure Studies* 13(4): 233-238.

Urry, J. (1995) *Consuming Places*, London: Routledge.

Uzell, D. (1984) An Alternative Structuralist Approach to the Psychology of Tourism Marketing, *Annals of Tourism Research* 11(1): 79-99.

van Raaij, W. and Francken, D. (1984) Vaction Decisions, Activities and Satisfactions, *Annals of Tourism Research* 11 (1): 101-112.

Vellas, F. and Bécherel, L. (1995) *International Tourism: An Economic Perspective*, Basingstoke: Macmillan.

Voase, R. (1995) *Tourism: The Human Perspective*, London: Hodder & Stoughton.

Vogt, J. (1978) Wandering: Youth and Travel Behaviour, *Studies in Third World Societies* 5: 19-40.

Vukonic, B. (1996) *Tourism and Religion*, Oxford: Pergamon.

Wahab, S. (1975) *Tourism Management*, London: Tourism International Press.

Wahab, S. and Pigram, J. (1997) *Tourism, Development and Growth: the Challenge of Sustainability*, London: Routledge.

Wall, G. (1997) Sustainable Tourism: Unsustainable Development, in S. Wahab and J. Pigram (ed.) *Tourism, Development and Growth: The Challenge of Sustainability*, London: Routledge: 33-49.

Walsh, K. (1992) *The Representation of the Past: Museums and Heritage in the Post-Modern World*, London: Routledge.

Walter, J. (1982) Social Limits to Tourism, *Leisure Studies* 1: 295-304.

Walton, J. (1983) *The English Seaside Resort: A Social History,1750-1914*, Leicester: Leicester University Press.

Walvin, J. (1978) *Beside the Seaside*, London: Allen Lane.

Ward, C. and Hardy, D. (1986) *Goodnight Campers! The History of the British Holiday Camp*, London: Mansell Publishing.

Warde, A. (1992) Notes on the Relationship between production and Consumption, inR. Burrows and C. Marsh (ed.), *Consumption and Class*, Basingstoke: Macmillan: 15-31.

WCED (1987) *Our Common Future*, World Commission on Environment and Development, Oxford: Oxford University Press.

Weaver, D. (1994) Ecotourism in the Caribbean Basin, in E. Cater and G. Lowman (ed.) *Ecotourism: A Sustainable Option?*, Chichester: John Wiley & Sons: 159-176.

Webster, A. (1990) *Introduction to the Sociology of Development, 2nd Edition*, Basingstoke: Macmillan.

Welch, R. 91984) The Meaning of Development: Traditional View and More Recent Ideas, *New Zealand Journal of Geography* 76: 2-4.

Wheeler, M. (1992) Applying Ethics to the Tourism Industry, *Business Ethics* 1(4): 227-235.

Wheeller, B. (1991) Tourism's Troubled Times, *Tourism Management* 12 (3): 91-96.

Wheeller, B. (1992a) Eco or Ego Tourism: New Wave Tourism, *ETB Insights, Vol III*, London: English Tourist Board: D41-44.

Wheeller, B. (1992b) Alternative Tourism: A Deceptive Ploy, in C. Cooper and A. Lockwood (ed.) *Progress in Tourism, Recreation and Hospitality Management Vol IV*, London: Bellhaven Press: 140-145.

Whelan, T. (ed.) *Nature Tourism: Managing for the Environment*, Washington DC: Island Press.

Wight, P. (1996) North American Ecotourism Markets: Motivations, Preferences and Destinations, *Journal of Travel Research* 35 (1): 3-10.

Wilkinson, P. (1989) Strategies for Tourism in Island Microstates, *Annals of Tourism Research* 16 (2): 153-177.

REFERENCES

Williams, A. and Shaw, G. (1991) Tourism and Development: Introduction, in A. Williams and G. Shaw (ed.) *Tourism and Economic Development: Western European Experiences*, London: Bellhaven Press: 1-12.

Wilson, A. (1992) *The Culture of Nature: North American Landscape from Disney to Exxon Valdez*, Cambridge, Mass: Blackwell.

Witherspoon, S. (1994) The Greening of Britain: Romance and Rationality, in R. Jowell *et al* (ed.) *British Social Attitudes: the 11th Report*, Aldershot: Dartmouth: 107-139.

Witt, C. and Wright, P. (1992) Tourist Motivation: Life after Maslow, in P. Johnson and B. Thomas (ed.) *Choice and Demand in Tourism*, London: Mansell Publishing: 33-55.

Witt, S., Brooke, M. and Buckley, P. (1991) *The Management of International Tourism*, London: Unwin Hyman.

Witt, S. and Moutinho, L. (ed.) *Tourism Marketing and Management Handbook*, Hemel Hempstead: Prentice Hall International.

Wood, K. and House, S. (1991) *The Good Tourist: A Worldwide Guide for the Green Traveller*, London: Mandarin.

Wood, R. (1980) International Tourism and Cultural Change in South East Asia, *Economic Development and Cultural Change* 28: 561-581.

Woodside, A. and Pitts, R. (1976) Effects of Consumer Lifestyles, Demographics and Travel Activities on Foreign and Domestic Travel Behaviour, *Journal of Travel Research* 14 (3): 15.

WTO (1980) *Manila Declaration on World Tourism*, Madrid: World Tourism Organisation.

WTO (1981) *The Social and Cultural Dimension of Tourism*, Madrid: World Tourism Organisation.

WTO (1992) *Tourism Trends to the Year 2000 and Beyond*, Madrid: World Tourism Organisation.

WTO (1993) *Sustainable Tourism Development: A Guide for Local Planners*, Madrid: World Tourism Organisation.

WTO (1998a) *Tourism: 2020 Vision: Influences, Directional Flows and Key Trends*, Madrid: World Tourism Organisation.

WTO (1998b) *Tourism Highlights 1997*, Madrid: World Tourism Organisation.

WTO/WTTC (1996) *Agenda 21 for the Travel & Tourism Industry: Towards Environmentally Sustainable Development*, World Tourism Organisation / World Travel and Tourism Council.

Wright, P. (1985) *On Living in an Old Country*, London: Verso.

WTTC (1991) *Travel and Tourism in the World Economy*, Brussels: World Travel and Tourism Council.

WTTC (1994) *Travel & Tourism: Progress and Priorities*, Brussels: World travel and Tourism Council.

Yale, P. (1992) *Tourism in the UK*, London: Elm Publications.

Yale, P. (1995) *The Business of Tour Operations*, Harlow: Longman.

Yearley, S. (1991) *The Green Case: A Sociology of Environmental Issues, Arguments and Politics*, London: Routledge.

Young, G. (1973) *Tourism: Blessing or Blight?* Harmondsworth: Penguin.

Zukin, S. (1990) Socio-Spatial Prototypes of a New Organisation of Consumption: The Role of Real Cultural Capital, *Sociology* 24 (1): 37-55.

Zuzanek, J. and Mannell, R. (1983) Work Leisure Relationships from a Sociological and Social Psychological Perspective, *Leisure Studies* 2: 327.

Index

Entries in *italics* refer to authors listed in the References section on pages 305-339.

FROM TOURIST ATTRACTIONS TO HERITAGE TOURISM
SECOND EDITION - Pat Yale

Expanded and updated edition, including the U.K. in detail, the U.S.A. and the rest of the world. From museums to stately homes, castles, palaces and gardens, religious buildings, archaeological sites and ancient monuments, including industrial and transport heritage. A standard reference work for tutors as well as a good, advanced level class text. Level PG Diploma, degree, etc. Book, 368pp, 1 85450 189 5, £14.95

EUROPEAN LEISURE BUSINESSES:
strategies for the future, Brian Eaton

Topical, well-researched organisation studies on major companies in the European Leisure Industry – Stakis, First Leisure,, Eurocamp, David Lloyd Leisure, Rank, Allied Leisure, Ladbrokes & VCI, & the history, strategy & competitive environment of European leisure. Illus., maps, charts/tables. Book 288 pp., 1 85450 230 1, £12.95

TRAVEL AND TOURISM, THIRD EDITION - Patrick Lavery

Introduction to the main sectors of the tourism industry, defining and outlining the development in the UK, Europe, USA. Enlarged and updated with a new chapter on sustainable tourism. Level HND+. GNVQ+ suitable, an adopted and recommended text in many colleges and universities. Book, 288pp, 1 85450 199 2, £9.95. Tutor's Manual, exercises/OHPs, 1 85450 024 4, £69.00

TRAVEL AND TOURISM: A NORTH-AMERICAN-EUROPEAN PERSPECTIVE
Patrick Lavery/Carl Van Doren

Overview of the industry and the role of private/public sectors in the UK, USA and Europe. Level introductory, beginners + on higher education courses. Book, 224pp, 1 85450 125 9, £11.95

MUSIC INDUSTRY MANAGEMENT AND PROMOTION - Chris Kemp

Music industry management & promotion, plus useful tips if you enter the business. Selecting a band; the agent; managing publicity; marketing; managing the venue; staffing, crew & security; the perfect promotion;finance & administration; managing the band/setting up a tour; music events outdoors; record companies; Studio production. Book 288pp + Single User Program PC disks, 1 85450 149 6, £15.95 Network Version on PC disk + Tutor's Manual, 1 85450 142 9, £104.25

TOURISM IN THE U.K. - Pat Yale
The business and management of tourism. With commentary on UK tourist attractions. Adopted by many colleges and schools as set text for those new to the business of tourism. Level BTEC Nat., A level+. Book - maps/charts/diagrams, 320 pp, 1 85450 017 1, £7.95
Tutor's Manual - exercises/notes/OHPs, 1 85450 094 5, £49.00

TOURISM LAW, SECOND EDITION - Jim Corke
Updated and revised edition of the first text specially written on the law relating to tourism and travel. New material on EC regulations. Level HND+.
Book, 480pp, 1 85450 028 7, £11.95 Tutor's Manual, 1 85450 140 2, £59.00

TOURISM, TOURISTS AND SOCIETY SECOND EDITION - Richard Sharpley
An in-depth study of the relationship between tourism and the societies that both generate and host tourism and tourists. Includes: the effects of social change on the pattern of tourism consumption; motivation for tourism; impact of tourism on host societies; and commoditisation and authenticity.
Book, 288pp, 1 85450 280 8 £14.95
Tutor's Manual - exercises/notes/OHPs, 1 85450 233 6 £69.00

WATER BASED RECREATION: managing resources for leisure
Fiona McCormack
Comprehensive treatment of the scope and development of water based resources for leisure. Aspects of management, marketing, environmental issues, conservation, conflicting uses, access and future trends. The first encapsulation and full coverage of this important and growing area of leisure management. The author is a qualified and experienced sailor and instructor. Book, 320pp, 1 85450 154 2, £14.95
Tutor's Manual, exercises/notes/OHPs, 1 85450 152 6, £59.00

Computer Software (pc disks + manual)

TRAVEL COMPANY BUSINESS - Ray Garnett
Interactive group exercise in business decisions for a Travel Company. Can be networked. Demo disk available. Level HND+.
Disk and Tutor's Manual, 1 85450 035 X, £82.19 inc. VAT